D0436821

A DESTINATIONS BOOK

· THE LAST ·
OLD PLACE

A Search Through Portugal

DATUS C. PROPER

INTRODUCTION BY JAN MORRIS

to Tony & Eleanor

SIMON & SCHUSTER

New York · London · Toronto · Sydney · Tokyo · Singapore

SIMON & SCHUSTER
Simon & Schuster Building
Rockefeller Center
1230 Avenue of the Americas
New York, New York 10020

Designed by Marc Strang
Manufactured in the United States of America

1   3   5   7   9   10   8   6   4   2

Library of Congress Cataloging-in-Publication Data
Proper, Datus C.
The last old place: a search through Portugal / Datus C. Proper:
introduction by Jan Morris.
p.   cm.
Includes bibliographical references and index.
1. Portugal—Description and travel—1981–   2. Portugal—Social
life and customs. 3.   Proper, Datus C.—Journeys—Portugal.
I. Title.
DP526.5.P76   1993
914.6904'44—dc20   92–22628   CIP

ISBN: 0-671-78226-6

To

Adriano the Fearless

CONTENTS

4 The World Beyond Fear 49

Adriano as hero-driver—Gypsies—A cure for sneezing—Field guide to the fauna of southern Portugal—A clash of pruderies—A Sacred Promontory—Fishermen as its guardians—Prince Henry the Navigator (and vestal)—The English connection—The discovery of science—Sailing off the end of the world—Finding India on purpose and America by mistake—Colonization by procreation—Conquests to shame Don Juan—The dream time—The exploring urge today

5 Migrants 67

A beach bereft of clothing—Dream boats—British, Danes, Dutchmen, and other English-speakers—Partridges, modesty, and wine of the country—Salazar as Hobbes and Reagan as Locke—A violent fruit—Human versus canine humor—Men are merriest when they are from home—St. James at the partridges!—The bravest of the Christians—Hedgehogs don't fly—Voyage through the alimentary canal—A snack of snipe—A Pleistocene fantasy—Fondling a bécasse—Shooting yourself—A man of the revolution in search of his violence

6 Walls 83

Giraldo the Fearless—Bars sunny and dark—The motorcycle as donkey and charger—Beja—The Battler conquers senility—A lamentable shortage of Moors—Being lazy in a clean house—Bread, peace, happiness, and love—The revolution of 1974—Communist steaks—Physicians without liability insurance—Soap operas—A coherent newspaper—Saved by Communists—Looking at meninas—Monsaraz—Nuno Álvares slept here—A good-smelling church—Évora—Giraldo shows how to cope with walls—The decay of sex—A human sacrifice

7 Sunlight 99

Chasing goddesses—Temple of Diana—The Cro-Magnon migration—Time when myths began—The invention of

INTRODUCTION

by Jan Morris

 Good travel books strike a subtle but often inexact balance between description and self-portraiture—some lean one way, some the other. The difficulty of the author's task is to make sure that whether the country described is predominant, or the author himself, the two unobtrusively unite. The join must be seamless, so that readers are left with the feeling that they have been exploring a single subject, an amalgam of the writer and the written-about.

The best travel books go one further, and make one feel that the two participants might have been specifically made for each other. I think of Bruce Chatwin and the Australian Outback, Paul Theroux and the Chinese railway system, Charles Doughty and the Arabian desert—and now Datus Proper and the Portuguese Republic. This book is as much memoir as reportage, self-revelation as often as geographical analysis, but the equilibrium amounts to a perfect partnership: between a highly individual, relatively little known European country, and a distinctly idiosyncratic, extremely worldly American author.

Mr. Proper indeed calls himself an innocent—to be a stranger in the world is, he says, "part of the American condition." But he is a very sophisticated innocent. A diplomat by trade, a linguist, a lover of literature and history, and above all perhaps a passionate fly fisherman, he is the absolute opposite of your package tourist. Not only do his talents, both intellectual and social, evidently make him a natural traveler but as he says "my fishing rod naturalizes me." He is that rare figure of the late twentieth century, the American gentleman, wandering the world with urbane grace and humor, and making friends.

On the other side of the balance, there Portugal awaits him. Datus Proper knows it well, but very few Americans do. Squeezed in the flank of Spain, overshadowed by the mighty Spanish genius, it is one of those countries that offer no very obvious image of themselves—no immediately recognizable icons, no universally familiar superstars. It is, however, a country of intense and piquant character, parts of it still primitive by American standards, which has been given a special quiet dignity by its heroic history. In this book it is represented not only by landscapes, by poetic quotation, and historic allusion but also by an almost allegorical traveling companion, Adriano, who accompanies the author throughout the journey, and who plays the part of a *genus loci*.

And such a part is very proper, for the book is full of playful allusion—sudden vivid cameos, snatches of myth, frequent digressions to go fishing, drink wine, discuss the comparative merits of languages, or contemplate Portuguese housewifery. It is not a gushing book. Mr. Proper pulls no punches about Portugal, and one feels that Portugal was perfectly frank with him. It is a collaboration between honest partners, not at all unlike one another: for when our author says of Portuguese people that they have "a view of what is good and a stubborn willingness to stay with it," that is just what one feels of him too, as he quotes another stanza of his beloved Camões, splits another bottle with Adriano, and puts his rod together for another go at the trout.

But then it is really hardly a travel book at all, in any conventional sense, but more the record of an easy friendship between a man and a nation—the man's emotions, the nation's presence, inextricably blended.

PREFACE

This book travels through Portugal from south to north—a trip that you can follow on flat pages without getting lost, assuming that you don't mind a few detours.

You have two guides. Adriano was born in Portugal, so for him it is home, a place to defend. For the other guide—me—it is non-home, a place to ask questions. How do people survive in remote villages without cars? Why does their food taste so good? A traveler asking such questions is, of course, always comparing one place to another. To opine that Portugal has good bread and bad roads is to suggest that my own country, on the contrary, has bad bread and good roads. I shall make the comparisons explicit. The Portuguese may find that this book says as much about my world as theirs. They may be right.

Some people travel to escape, and for them the road is an end in itself, a way of not being home. Adriano and I, on the other hand, are foragers. For us travel is a means to an end, a search for something we want. At times we travel off the road, with hiking boots and fishing rods. These devices get us into places where no one remembers seeing a foreigner. Adriano knows where to look for trout and heroes, mountains and caravels, natural history and the human kind.

What interests me most is this: In Portugal, the full cycle of humanity fits onto one small stage. Cro-Magnon humans enter at the beginning of time. Their descendants grow wheat when they run out of woolly mammoths. Ulysses founds the capital city. Romans create the Portuguese language. Moors foster irrigation, falconry, and walled cities. A perfect hero wins the battle for national independence. His country is one of the world's smallest—but it is the one whose sailors discover the world.

I aim to catch the whole show. It is, I suppose, spread over too many centuries to have dramatic unity, but at least it makes time travel convenient. Parts of rural Portugal are still in the Middle Ages. You think that you are moving on a north/south axis and find, instead, that you have been transported back through the centuries.

The trip is as orderly as I can make it, considering that this is a book with no plot. The only organizing principle is the country itself.

I saw Portugal stage-lit, once. I had climbed the castle of Monsaraz under clouds blown in from the sea. What passed below my tower was a random scene, not the logical countryside of a map. Farms in the foreground came to life only when spotlighted by moving columns of sun. The walls of four villages gleamed white and melted back into obscurity. Car windows in the east flashed like the armor of Spanish knights crossing the Guadiana River. Time was compressed, human works created and extinguished—all at the whim of cumuli scudding overhead. I looked up and saw clouds stacked in the same fanciful shapes as the walls below me. For a dizzy moment, everything in time and space was vapor, layers of castles starting in shadows below and reaching higher than imagination.

I tried to compose the scene, to fit the fragments into a whole.

FIGVRA·DE·LYSBOA

LOST SOULS

Nymphs of the Tagus, you have inspired in me a new and burning zeal. To your stream I have always paid glad tribute in my humble verse. Grant me now nobler, sublimer strains. . . . Give me the grand, resounding fury, not of rustic pipe or flute, but of the trumpet of war that fires men's breasts. . . . Give me a song equal to the deeds of your warlike people, a song destined to be known and sung throughout the world, if indeed a poet may achieve so much.

CAMÕES, *The Lusiads,*[1] Canto One

Lisbon played with travelers through all the centuries, teasing her waterline lower at the top of each swell, pulling lonely sailors up the masts for a look. That's how she ought to be seen. Red roofs should rise between broad brown Tagus River and broader blue Atlantic Ocean, then green spaces, roads, and harbor with sails fluttering. You are not permitted that kind of entrance today. You just fly in from the sea and there's Lisbon spread out over the hills. You aren't ready yet.

My world was an airplane. The seat in front of me held a young, skinny, brown-haired woman reading a magazine article titled "Shop Till You Drop." On her right was a blonde with hair fluffed to look like the cover girl on her *Glamour* magazine. The cover had a subtitle: *Men at 20, 30, 40.* Across the aisle were two Glamourous men. One had dark silky hair cascading to his shoulders in curls like d'Artagnan. The other was wearing a pair of knee-high leather boots and carrying a *faux* British cartridge bag. In his lap, where it wouldn't get squashed, was an Indiana Jones hat. The men were talking across the aisle to the women, and Indiana Jones, who had the nearest seat, seemed to have beat d'Artagnan to the blonde.

I imagined a Portuguese waiter (old black shoes freshly polished, hair neatly combed) encouraging these people to enter his restaurant. They would be trying to look casual about the dead fish in the window. He would help them to a table with a different view. He would offer to hang Indiana Jones's hat out of harm's way. He would recommend a lunch of lean pork—safer for English-speakers than, say, the squid. He would hold a fork and spoon in his right hand like tongs, serving from a platter with deft little flourishes. The foreigners would not notice him teasing the neckline of the blonde lower with deft little glances. The waiter would prefer to be a sailor discovering the world, like his ancestors, but given the current weak demand for explorers, he would be, at least, a good waiter.

This is the way to survive a flight from New World to Old. You achieve an out-of-body feeling, floating above the seats and looking down on your victims. You try to sleep through a film called *Back to the Future*. You see passengers who, in trying to achieve distinctive Looks, manage to be so similar that any Portuguese waiter will know what they are afraid to eat before they enter the restaurant. The only one who is really different is you.

Everybody on the plane was up there floating around and thinking the same thing: *This crowd is full of fakes but I'm the real item.* During out-of-body experiences you don't notice the traffic.

My luggage turned out to have missed the plane, but Adriano was at the airport waiting. I knew that he would be. Unlike some airlines, Adriano takes commitments seriously. He had offered to guide me around his country, starting with Lisbon. Our trip was to be my narrative spine.

Spine is Adriano's specialty. In courtly manners, gray hair, and avuncular smile, he resembles an old French actor named Maurice Chevalier. The spine is just below the smile and firmly attached to it. Adriano hears my notions, weighs them, and tells me where I have gone wrong or guessed right. He pretends that this is no burden, which must be a matter of training. He is a lawyer. When I lived in Lisbon a few years back, he accepted my case. I had made some comment that did not adequately capture the valor of Portuguese trout, and Adriano set me right. If his country's 10 million citizens were subjected to an Interpretive Aptitudes Test—an examination measuring courage, endurance, patience, and tact—then Adriano would score in the top percentile.

And for all that, I did not know him well. Considering his vigor at seventy-seven years of age, he must have been a hell-raiser in his youth, but he never talked about indiscretions. Fathers usually don't, and he is a generation older than me. Adriano is not what he used to be anyhow. He is what he has chosen to make himself. He is a product of will, of decisions imposed on circumstances. He is what he wants to be. He believes in it. He shows himself as he wishes to be known—wrapped in good wool and Portugal's myth.

If this sounds enigmatic, it is because Adriano is as much place as person. He and his ancestors have been part of the same land since before it had a name. Of course such a person does not rush to reveal himself like an American who has just climbed off one more airplane and is anxious to disclose what he is, if only he were sure. Adriano has already been defined by Portugal, which has in turn been defined by him. He has been digging into his landscape for so long that he has changed it more than nature.

Adriano's top stratum is a coat and tie and neat little green-felt hat. In the country he wears a coat of rougher tweed. There is also a fishing outfit, but I will save that for our travels, because Adriano is not a person with whom you should rush to be familiar. His clothing is chosen for the occasion rather than the weather. If called upon, he would shed wool, don steel, and do battle with his country's enemies. The dents would be neatly hammered out and the armor would be polished to shine like a mirror so that opposing knights might see their nemesis clearly. ("Better a good enemy than a bad friend," Adriano says.)

In the absence of other invaders, Adriano drove me to his house near the airport and showed me the room into which I would put my baggage, if the airline ever found it. Maria Tereza, his wife, agreed to be my advisor on cooking. (Adriano's knowledge of the process begins when good smells reach the table.) It is a large table, for reasons that I discovered as I greeted several of the couple's six children and more of their grandchildren. None of them—or perhaps just a few—actually lived in the place, but they liked to spend time there. Anybody would.

The house was a big cube, painted outside in that dull pink-on-concrete color which, for some reason, looks good under the sun of Mediterranean latitudes. It was not a poor man's home, but it used its terrain as economically as if it were. The front was separated from the street by little more than a fringe of geraniums on a low wall, saving as much land as possible for the *quintal*—literally, the small farm—behind the house. I walked back there, confident that the sunshine would cure my jet lag. An article in *The New York Times* had said so. (If I understood correctly, jet lag results when the soul of a traveler becomes detached from the rest of his person, remaining afloat over the Atlantic while the body wanders in Lisbon. The soul locates the body more easily out under the sun.)

As compared to a yard in suburban America, the *quintal* felt bigger without occupying more area. The secret was depth. Adriano had dug into the earth's strata, building two terraces that rose in broad steps behind the house, supported by retaining walls. He had also built high boundary walls around the whole of the *quintal*, as if it were a medieval city on a hillside. What happened was paradoxical: The walls seemed to expand what they confined. Human labor had cubed the square, adding a third dimension. Mere area had been turned into space, a one-family scale model of a nation.

The top terrace was remote and lonely. Wild things belonged there—birds on migration, perhaps, dropping in like Adriano's friends and family, having a feed from the same produce. I climbed up to make myself conspicuous to my detached soul. There was no grass underfoot. The earth (what little of it was not cultivated) was bare, red, and weed-free. The trees were so small as to be hardly distinguishable from the shrubs, and all produced something to eat. The largest were two mulberry trees. Their fruit was sweet, unlike the mulberries I knew in Iowa. Even the Portuguese variety was not, for me, quite good enough to justify the space it took up, but there was a story. The word for mulberry is *amora,* which comes close to *amor,* meaning love. The play on words was old even when Camões used it in sixteenth-century poetry. I imagined the young Adriano deciding, when he built the house for Maria Tereza, that there had to be room for *amoras.*

A lemon tree near the house produced blossoms at all seasons, drifting scent through open windows. The fruit was as big and juicy as an orange, good for marinating meats and making pies, barely recognizable as a relative of dry little supermarket lemons. The grapes were the kind you ate fresh, not the serious wine varieties, but they arched over a trellis to make a shady passage. The *quintal* also produced bananas, cherries, plums, apricots, peaches, and figs.

The figs were the best. They would grow heavy enough to droop on their stalks, and then for a couple of days I would want nothing else but some fresh cheese of ewe's milk. I would not be greedy: A dozen figs, barely overripe, would be enough, until dinner.

I have left for last the tall cabbages—a direct translation from the Portuguese. In America we have kale, which looks the same and tastes good, but different. Tall cabbage grows on a stalk higher than lilies and is the Portuguese national vegetable. Its leaves are picked as needed. It lasts for a year and is always, at all seasons, available in the *quintal* of every Portuguese house. If you fail to find tall cabbage within 20 feet of the door, you took the wrong airplane, like your baggage, and are not in Portugal.

The Portuguese word *quintal* must be used because English has no word for this space. In America, the land around a house is a yard. Its function is shade, which is provided by trees; and because we like longer views, there are no walls. The yard therefore becomes a display.

In Britain and Ireland, trees would channel the rain down one's neck. Instead, the houses have what is called—and often is—a garden. The theme is again decorative, a tapering-off of walls into nature. If old and new English-speaking worlds look different, it is because our natural conditions are different. We want the same things.

The Portuguese do not. The theme and function of their *quintais* is the same: husbandry, not ornament. They spend less, eat better, and have the smell of blossoms in their rooms.

While I was bending over to sniff the cabbage, there was a faint popping noise. It could have been the sound of jet-stiff back. I preferred to think of it as the sound of soul finding its lodging, which was probably in the same general region. Given a choice, I might have preferred to be joined by my luggage instead of my soul. There was, in one bag, a four-piece fishing rod calculated to save me from the Portugal of shops and museums and highways. The return of the psyche was a good beginning, though. With it in possession, I felt safe in entering my room and going to sleep.

The bed's linen had a Lisbon scent, a memory that had lost me. I must have caught the right plane.

"You smell good, Lisbon," goes a folk song, and so she does, once you get away from the fumes of the streets. I think I could pick line-dried Portuguese sheets from those anywhere else in the world. There is not the pine smell of Minnesota linen, the sun smell of Montana, or the wet-grass smell of Ireland. Instead there are lemon blossoms, eucalyptus that drifts in from somewhere, a hint of salt water, and herbs: wild lavender, if that is the right translation for *rosmaninho,* and others too diluted to maintain individual identity. Aromatic herbs thrive in the Mediterranean climate. Wet winters soak the deep roots and dry summers cure the leaves, suck out their fragrance, drift it to the clothesline. But the smell is impossible to describe. It is impossible even to remember, strictly speaking, until you catch it again. The brain can store sights like paintings in a museum, but the limbic system buries odors down near the emotions. You think that you have forgotten a scent and then, when you return to the right place, it finds you and courses through you in waves, washing you back through the years to another set of sheets with another person between them. You are never prepared. The trip through time is so unexpected that it comes with a quick little shiver.

I was ready for the blackbird's song at dawn, however. Its music found a place in my memory halfway between reason and emotion. And besides, I had seen the bird in the *quintal.* Adriano had built a vast cage, big enough to hold a small tree, and in its leaves hopped a wild thing, shiny as coal but for a bright yellow beak. The blackbird had not adjusted even to a captivity as spacious as this. His challenge of the first light was better than an alarm clock's but not what a blackbird's song ought to be. The phrases were aggressive and short, omitting the trills of a free bird.

Now, any good scientist will tell you, these days, that the singing of birds "functions as part of the great Darwinian struggle for reproductive success."[2] I believe this myself, in my scientific (as opposed to mythic) mode. A blackbird's songs are claims on territory, warnings to other males wearing Indiana Jones hats. I have emitted such songs myself, over the years. But I took pleasure in my song, apart from its function, and spent more time on my guitar than would have been rigorously necessary for reproductive purposes.

You may think that you have caught me at anthropomorphism, which is the attribution of human characteristics to non-human creatures. Please look again. I have not said that blackbirds are like me. I have said that I am like blackbirds.

If you know only American blackbirds, it will seem odd that I should mention the song at all, but the old-world blackbird is no kin. It is a kind of thrush, with a song like that of the American robin—which, by the way, has in common with the European robin only a red breast. This is the kind of confusion we create when we classify singers by their color instead of their music.

At breakfast, I opined that the caged blackbird needed a *mulher*. It means either mate or woman, and you will just have to believe me when I tell you that this is the word a Portuguese might use.

"He has had two *mulheres*," said Adriano. "Each of them started to build a nest. Then he killed them."

The murdered *mulheres* made me feel virtuous, as one always feels when learning of another's infamy. In this case, moreover, I had suspected the villain. Heard him singing like a city man instead of a country boy. Asked the right questions. Exposed murder most fowl. With more such detective work, I might yet discover a Portugal of broad public interest, grotesque as a soap opera.

· 2 ·

THE LAST OLD PLACE

*There will be no pursuit here of mere national aggrandizement,
no praising with false attributions, flights of fancy and feats of
the imagination, as is the Muse's wont in other lands. The deeds
I tell of are real. . . .*

CAMÕES, *The Lusiads*, Canto One

Until now I have assumed that readers know where we are. Lisbon is on the near side of Europe, and everybody has heard of that. It is the continent populated by Europeans, some of whom had enough get-up-and-go to get up and come to America at the beginning of history, while the rest stayed behind and fought with each other.

But Lisbon is not Portugal. Capitals in any country are made up of politicians, celebrities, shops, and tourists who fancy politicians, celebrities, and shops. Capitals are where the airplanes land. For Americans in Portugal, capitolism must be a terminal disease, because I did not meet another of my countrymen outside Lisbon during my entire trip through Adriano's countryside. Americans visit France (discovered food) and England (discovered Shakespeare), but not Portugal (discovered the world). I am therefore sneaking into this chapter enough of an image of Portugal to let you see where we are headed.

To picture the country, start by picturing California. Erase its inhabitants, because the Portuguese try to be as little like Californians as possible. What is similar is the land: a strip of it at the southwest corner of a continent. The strip runs from north to south and faces west toward salt water. The two biggest cities are on the sea—Lisbon in the south and Oporto in the north. Good food grows in the ocean and good ports provide shelter. I would not think of mentioning ports in describing California; but the Portuguese are people of ports, not only in the homeland but in all the little antique pieces of Portugal scattered around Brazil, Africa, India, Ceylon, Indonesia, Malaysia, and China. The discoverers did not pass by good harbors. When you see a thick-walled old fort above the best anchorage around, you can start looking for Portuguese artifacts.

Portugal is smaller than California, but then the European scale is smaller than the American. Portugal has no Death Valley deserts, no mountains high enough to hold snow in summer, and no rifts that would catch the eye of an astronaut. The Portuguese language, like the English of England, lacks even a satisfactory word for canyon. You can say *desfiladeiro,* but it lacks the scale and resonance of *cañon,* which we borrowed from Spaniards who had seen America. And yet northern Portugal is the steepest, most awkward place in which I have ever tried to scramble. We will get to the reasons for this prickly geology later. Meanwhile, if a Portuguese tells you that a place is *mau de andar,* hard-going, believe him. If you could stretch northern Portugal flat, it would be bigger than Texas, Heaven forbid. Texas does not seem like a mystery to me but northern Portugal still does.

The southern half of the country, like the equivalent piece of California, has warmth without the pestilential humidity of Florida. Such climates attract rich old folks and some young ones. In the dream time, however, California's natives were poor, and Portugal's natives still are. There has never in history been an abrupt break in the way land is used. I imagine that Viriato (a hero waiting in the wings) would still feel at home with the shepherds, or in the vineyards, or on the little terraced plots of grain and greens.

The language is always Portuguese. I learned it when my work took me to Angola, Brazil, and finally to Portugal itself. Villagers in the mountains must have wondered, when they watched me emerge from a river dripping, how they would get me pointed back to wherever it was that I came from. When it turned out that I could communicate, the Portuguese were appreciative. The language made me one of them, in a restricted sense, because no one else in Europe spoke it. For my part, I was paradoxically secure because the place was foreign. A language had to be good if it carried me over the Range of the Star to a fireside, a place to sleep, red wine from a pitcher, and a tripe-and-beans stew better than they serve *Chez François* back in Washington, D.C.

This is by way of confessing bias. I feel warm in Portugal even when the rain is cold. I intend, nevertheless, to paint a warts-and-all portrait, and then to beg forgiveness from Adriano. The problems with his Portugal could be cured by firing a few politicians. The problem with my Portugal starts outside its borders. All of western Europe is becoming a hypermarket. Little Portugal is busy constructing its wings of the mall.

The hardest part is understanding why one-seventh of the Iberian peninsula and one-fifth of its population took it on themselves to form an independent country in the first place. What's the rationale? How did they justify this venture to their bankers? In Wall Street terms, the country has only begun to make sense since it joined the European Community, and yet Portugal has been fighting off an unfriendly merger with Spain since the Middle Ages. The border is political, dividing countries with fewer physical differences than England and Scotland. Once in a while the line follows bends of a river, but then it loops off between farmers' fields. You look for partridges on the Portuguese side and call them *perdizes*. At a low stone wall that looks no more formal than the rest, you stop and talk to the Castilian with a hoe on the other side. He says *perdices*. The relationship with Spain is sibling rivalry: sharp resistance when one steps on the other's toes but an acknowledged commonality.

For all that, the border has stayed firmly in its place during the centuries when most others in Europe swayed back and forth. Portugal's boundaries have been unchanged for practical purposes since 1249, when the Moors were pushed from their last foothold in the Algarve. The line is there because the Portuguese want it there. They have wanted it badly enough to fall on it in battle after battle, year after year, century after century, and usually against the odds. The English wanted an independent Portugal too, and sometimes their help won what would otherwise have been lost. The Portuguese would have fought anyhow. They did most of the dying in most of the battles. They had no fundamental reasons beyond preferring to die Portuguese and poor rather than live Spanish and a little less poor. You can't help agreeing with the bankers, and the

Spanish, that this sort of thing is craziness. And then you walk the battlefield of Aljubarrota and yearn to be afflicted by such a lunacy.

Because enough of the battles were not lost, Portugal exists. Until recently it had no friendly neighbor. There was big Spain on one side, the bigger blue Atlantic on the other, and poverty in between. A good economic history of Portugal is available, but I do not recommend it unless you like depressing stories. The history would be called a long depression except that a depression must have higher spots on each side.

The Portuguese turned to the sea, which swallows sailors of all nationalities with perfect impartiality. At first there was inshore fishing. Even that was difficult, because the Atlantic here has no continental shelf and few sheltering islands. And then the sailors went farther, and farther, and discovered the world—a phrase that I do not use lightly. The world of the Middle Ages was a cramped and fearful place, by our lights. Its map was drawn by theologians on the basis of instructions in the Bible, in much the same way that today's creationists decide on the origin of species. There is this difference: Few people today think that the creationists have the last word on dinosaurs. In the Middle Ages, you believed the theologians or died. At the world's end was a waterfall, or something, over which mariners tumbled into eternity if they pushed their luck.

Prince Henry the Navigator pushed his luck a little further each year. In time the Portuguese reached India, monopolized the spice trade, and for a few improbable decades made Lisbon the richest city in Europe. The ships sailed on to China, even Japan. At the time Portugal had a population of not much more than a million people: far too few to follow up on the opportunities. The wonder is that such an unpromising candidate for discovery made the breakthrough. In this millennium, tiny Portugal has made more impact on the world than giant China. The trade monopoly did not last, could not. The wealth disappeared. The myth remained.

The myth is not credible. It happened, but it should not have. You must take it lightly, like the song about the ant that walked off with a rubber-tree plant. If you stare at the myth head-on, you see

a reflection of yourself, ant-sized. You shift your eyes with a giggle.
Heroism burns too bright for us cowards.

My ancestors settled America, conquered it, plowed it, and built a
model for the world. It is a good model by my lights. Even with the
wisdom of hindsight, it would be impossible to pick a better set of
forefathers. They came from the only country in the world that
knew how to make democracy work. If America were now blown
off the globe, I would still find it impossible to be anything but
American. My country is "a matter of mind and heart"[1] rather than
a coincidence of geography and person, like Portugal. But something important would have happened in America even if other
people had settled it. Something had to happen, given the world's
best blend of soil, water, and climate.

Nothing had to happen in Portugal. The country was fought
into life like Greece, sung into existence like Narnia. These are
places that we children crave, places where time is all jumbled
together, where heroes battle, and where little ships discover new
worlds at the edge of creation.

Such a country cannot be navigated in length and breadth. Even in
Lisbon, there is a third dimension, like the walls that cube the
square of Adriano's *quintal*. The dimension is time. Portugal is not
of a piece. It looks small and unified—may indeed be the only state
of the New Europe without minority problems—but in the third
dimension is vast and disparate, top-heavy with history, a tiny ship
with a great billowing sail.

Adriano and I will therefore jump back and forth from now (a
day in May with the blackbird complaining) to earlier times. We
will do this repeatedly throughout our journey, because there is no
other way to see the country. The flashbacks of a few years should
be easy to follow, but we will also visit the fifteenth century in
Sagres, the fourteenth in Aljubarrota, and the second century B.C.
in Viseu. In Castro Laboreiro we will look down, find our feet on
a Roman road, and wonder where we are.

Old roads are erased on most maps. They show worlds predis-
covered, two-dimensional. We Americans welcome such progress in

our own country but not elsewhere. We have, I think, a sort of national yearning for the history that our high school texts omit. We suspect that something may have happened between Adam and George Washington. We support industries that provide us with coats of arms. We search Ireland or West Africa for roots, which is to say for that portion of us to be found underground. When we get to the Old World, we expect houses antedating those in the Historic Preservation District of Bozeman, Montana. We want people dressed in clothes more venerable than those President Nixon designed for his White House guards. We demand antiques made before World War II. We fancy the real old stuff, and it is easier to find in Portugal than most places.

By this I do not mean that any part of Europe lacks antiquities. In Hampshire I stayed on the banks of the River Itchen in a cottage that was four hundred years older than mine, back home on the banks of Humility Creek. Life was the same, though. I could reach the dream time only by hopping back across the stream on isolated outcroppings of artifacts. In Portugal, time travel is easier because progress has not paved the countryside. The place feels older than any other large populated area in the West. Spain has insulated Lusitania, the ocean has sequestered it, history has kept it intact, and poverty has been the best of preservatives.

In the epigraphs, Luís de Camões will give you the Portuguese myth, having written much of it.

First, however, he wrote love poems to fine ladies including, perhaps, one of Her Royal Highnesses, and was equally indiscrete in his brawls with male courtiers. He was run out of Lisbon, sent on a seventeen-year exile to India and Macau. He was shipwrecked in the Mekong Delta, saving only his life and the manuscript of what was to be published as *The Lusiads*. His follies robbed him of the good life and gave him hungry immortality. If he had behaved himself, he might have galloped with the king and his falconers, gone to parties with the literary set, and set up housekeeping with the lady of his verses. Judging from his erotic poetry, however, he was not cut out for the platitudes of marriage:

Amor é fogo que arde sem se ver;
é ferida que dói e não se sente;
é um contentamento descontente;
é dor que desatina sem doer.

Love is a fire that burns unseen,
A wound that aches and is not felt
It is contentment malcontent,
A maddening pain without grief.

The stanza comes not from the *The Lusiads,* an epic, but from Camões's lyric poetry (my translation). It made the scales fall from my eyes. In Angola I had heard too much of Camões, seen too much of his portrait with one eye blinded by the Moors. He had been drafted to serve as a symbol for a Portuguese colonial policy gone blind in both eyes. I assumed that he was no better than the folk songs called *fados,* which were played interminably by the only radio station in the country. I was wrong: You could move his sonnets in with Shakespeare's and not feel cheated. The two poets had similar impacts on their language, too. If Portuguese today seems baroque to English-speakers, it may be because Camões purposely did not use the sparse language of sonnets for *The Lusiads.* He asked the nymphs of the River Tagus to grant him "a style at once grandiloquent and flowing," and they did.

Camões's national epic was first published in 1572. He had written it while sailing to Africa and India and China, surviving troubles bigger than jet lag. His topic was surely the greatest of any travel book ever: discovery of the world. His poetic fiction was based on historical facts that would have been sensational even if he had understated them. His public was proud of the national achievement. He had little competition. He should have become wealthy, but he died in poverty eight years later, thinking himself a failure. It was his first good career decision. Once buried, he started going through editions as quickly as Izaak Walton. In the nineteenth century alone there were at least 145 editions, including 11 in English and others in French, German, Italian, Spanish, Swedish, Hungarian, Danish, Polish, and Latin.[2]

Some of the editions are bound like altar Bibles. Their illustrations show caravels running before a storm, new peoples welcoming the truth faith, Nuno Álvares routing the Castilian invaders at Aljubarrota, Venus with a robe that won't stay up, and a man with crossbow finding, instead of game, nymphs bathing in a woodland pool. (He does not look disappointed.) Camões, as you see, caught humanity's myth, not just that of Portugal.

Like Camões, Adriano and I will start our trip in Lisbon. The poet did not keep his promise to avoid flights of fancy and perhaps we will slip too. This much you may believe: Camões's Portugal is Adriano's, chapter and verse. Adriano recites the epic to me in his husky old man's voice, quavering just a little, and the time machine works. I am in a land that is all heroes and no resources, a land with little stone houses where Merlin would feel at home, a land with the kind of food that my people, I fear, will not achieve even if we give the world new worlds on other planets.

• 3 •

LISBON

And now it was fair Lisbon's turn, princess of cities, built by Ulysses. . . .

CAMÕES, *The Lusiads*, Canto Three

A Mercedes taxi took me from Adriano's house to downtown Lisbon. The car looked like new, though its engine was noisy as a Model A Ford's. Diesel engines rattle from the beginning and this one, according to the driver, had hauled passengers more than 2 million kilometers. That's 1 million, 200,000 miles. Junkyard sprawl is not a problem in Portugal; the first car entered the country in 1895 and is still around somewhere.

The driver was able to maintain this mechanical conversation without slowing down enough to make me comfortable, so I tried something else. A girl carrying books sprinted across the street ahead of us, allowing me to observe that the girls seemed to be growing up faster than they used to, and that did it. The driver leaned back, held the wheel pensively with straight arms, and let the traffic stack up behind us.

"There are," he assured me, "no *mulheres* in the world like the Portuguese *mulher.*" He had studied the matter. For years he had worked in France. His own *mulher* was French, and a good one. He had no regrets. He had also worked in Israel, traveled throughout Europe and the Middle East, and made one foray into Canada. When he said that there was no woman like the *mulher portuguesa*, he was not speaking lightly. He offered none of the illustrative detail or acrobatic ribaldry that a Brazilian would achieve in the same Portuguese language. There was none of the stark physiology that might appeal to an American taxi driver. There was not even the lewd understructure of an Englishman. There was, on the other hand, none of the Irishman's lowered eyes and blushes. There was a sober analysis. My Lisbon driver had given thought to a matter that, after all, deserved consideration; and having come to a correct conclusion, he was prepared to stake his reputation on it.

If you are under the impression that my driver was talking about women, be advised that he also demonstrated the Portuguese approach to life in general and politics in particular. What the rest of the world treats lightly, he pondered. He thereby showed himself to be a serious person (a subject on which there is more later).

In this way, anyhow, I reached Commiseration without needing it. The *Largo da Misericórdia*—Wide Place of Commiseration, literally—was named after the Church of *Misericórdia*, which sat on the wide place. It was not very wide, just a burp in the street. I should have crossed the *Largo* and entered the church for a look but was not quite as fond of suffering as I should have been. Just wanted to buy some old books. The stores that sold them were clustered around the Commiseration, by coincidence. Perhaps real-estate prices were low enough here, after the Inquisition, that even booksellers could afford a place to shelve such of their wares as had not already been stacked around sinners and burnt in those holy bonfires called *autos da fé*. (A literal translation would be "solemn public acts of faith," but the Portuguese term entered the English language—one of the first to do so.)

The old-book shop that I needed was said to be in the *Travessa da Queimada*—literally the Crossing of the Burn. The Burn may have been one of those fires that afflicts Lisbon every couple of centuries, along with earthquakes. The *Travessa* had the width of an alley and was designed for pedestrians, or perhaps for donkeys, though cars were pushing through, beeping politely to warn the people who were about to be crushed.

The buildings that fronted the pavement were of stone or brick, in either case as dingy as the cobbles underfoot. The facades rose only four or five stories—quite high enough during earthquakes— but they formed a solid row. Inside, people must have been busy, because property in old Lisbon had grown too expensive for doing nothing. The trick was to guess what was going on. On the odds, a few buildings would have been divided into apartments with antique furniture and oriental rugs and fireplaces. Even their windows, however, would be left unpainted to disguise opulence from petty thieves and tax assessors. Other buildings would be jammed with poor folks who had been there forever, with rent controlled. And there would be some shops, all of which considered advertising to be in bad taste.

My bookstore was not given away even by a brass plate on the entrance of the building. I spotted the little sign on the next floor above, turned into a dark entrance, and climbed stairs decorated by tiles painted while Portugal was still a world power. I opened the door with hesitation and knew that this was the right place. It smelled of noble rot, yellowing paper, and cracked leather bindings. (Books, like songs, will either stand aging or they won't, and the way to be sure is to wait till the weaklings have dropped out.) A gentleman several years younger than the building greeted me. He knew the precise location of every book. There were rooms and rooms of them, rooms sometimes illumined by windows that looked over an abandoned courtyard. Many volumes had been bound by hand. Until a few years after the revolution of 1974, Lisbon bookbinders had been both good and inexpensive, so that books of any quality were routinely rebound after purchase. They still deserved good homes, but there were no other customers. Who would want old Portuguese books?

Two Americans did. They were climbing the stairs as I descended, and we talked. She had corn-silk hair, again. She was slim and leggy in high-heeled shoes that had not, so far, been broken by the cobblestones. Her husband and I both appreciated the effect. He was carrying her packages in plastic bags with the logotypes of several Lisbon stores. The couple had been travel shopping. They had bought lace, shoes, handbags, copper pans, china, cut glass, and linen. They had tried to buy handmade rugs, but the ones they liked could not be had without a long wait. They wanted books. They did not speak Portuguese, so I supposed that books were supposed to be decorative. I steered the couple to *The Lusiads*, illustrated.

You might wonder (if you do not spend much time overseas) how I recognized the Americans on the bookseller's stairs. It was easy: They looked like mallards that had shed their feathers and grown all new outfits in coordinated colors. Adult Portuguese molt only once, at mating time. After that, they buy new clothing as the old wears out, piece by piece.

And then there were the packages. The American vacation is a purchasing expedition. You can identify an American tourist by his burdens, gift-wrapped. We had a big country, once, but ran out of parking space a few years back and converted Europe to a mall.

During the four years when I lived in Lisbon, I ducked most of the shopping because my wife (being Irish) had not thought of using me as a caddy. Just once, when she had an injury that kept her out of the game, I ventured into the Cascais open-air market. It was a sensual place: chickens glancing, oysters exhaling, and fishwives whining. I don't remember what they said: something about the freshness of their offerings, no doubt. The tone was the message. It was the one used by Jewish comedians explaining how their mothers got them to take second helpings of chicken soup. Voices raised from quaver to shriek. I picked up the first sole, paid the asking price, and fled.

It was not a bad sole. It was a day or two old and half again more expensive than it should have been, but it tasted all right.

From then on I insisted that shopping was sex linked. No one, I argued, had ever seen a Portuguese fish-husband. The men went down to the sea in ships and the women went down to the market for suckers, of which I was one. My wife was not. She would pick up a victim, sniff its gills, poke its eye, hold it up to the light, sigh, demand a fresh one from under the counter, and buy it for less than I would pay for the merchandise that gave the market its pungency. One needed the right genes and I did not have them.

Downtown Lisbon smells of seafood because the windows of so many restaurants display lunch-in-the-raw. The sole and whitings and mullet are on ice. Lobsters and shrimp dance in still life around them. Sometimes there are big oysters, tiny clams, and barnacles. Snails do not deserve window space. The displays are miniature markets rather than decorations in the French style. The Portuguese are suspicious of show, I think, but I am too hungry to think very hard about it.

A wooden case of sardines in coarse salt reminded me of what I had been wanting for years, if only I'd known it. The waiter inside brought the usual Lisbon starters: a dish of olives and a little loaf of bread without butter—a roll, in American terms, but crisp-crusted instead of fluffy. He asked if I wanted fresh cheese, but I didn't; it might have interfered with the smell of sardines on the grill. I pulled off chunks of the bread, spilling bits of flaky crust on the white tablecloth, alternating with olives.

Fresh Portuguese sardines are not like those you buy in cans. They are big, 9 or 10 inches long. As soon as they are caught, they are packed in a wooden box with salt. For cooking, they are dusted off and grilled intact. To scale and gut a sardine would be as unthinkable as pitting an olive. I don't know the theory. Probably there is no theory: Someone a long time ago just discovered that the easiest method worked. The grilled sardine became the practical equivalent of an American hamburger, though with skin and bones and innards that demand more attention. The residents of Lisbon fire up their grills anywhere—including the sidewalk, if they live in apartments. Restaurants are shy about serving such common fare but do it because it is too good to ignore.

I went through half a dozen sardines and looked around for more, but there were no more, so I had a Nun's Belly. It quivered roundly and tasted of egg yolks. It would have been made by a confectioner somewhere nearby. If you wanted to make an angel food cake—which nobody in Portugal does—you could go to that confectioner and buy fresh egg whites by the liter, cheap. This summarizes the difference between Portuguese and American cooking. We discard the yolks and they discard the whites.

I hiked downhill toward Adriano's office, grateful to Nun's Belly. There was a little more work to be done.

The best book on the battle of Aljubarrota had to be bought new because the archaeology had just been completed. I knew that the battle had secured Portugal's independence from Spain in 1385, but the event seemed as unlikely as, say, the battle of Marathon. There was no technology then, no standoff weapons. A man in his right mind would not have fought on an open battlefield against five-to-one odds. The Portuguese did it and won. Their secret was leadership—that of Constable Nuno Álvares Pereira. He was as indispensable to their independence as George Washington to America's. Washington, however, could lose battle after battle and still win the war. Nuno Álvares had to win them all. Following him seemed like a better idea than trotting after a spouse with a credit card.

The salesgirl cut a piece of thin brown paper with a pair of scissors, put the paper on the counter, laid the book on it, made adjustments, and folded the wrapping with neat little corners. The fit was precise, with not a centimeter of material wasted. She fastened the paper with tiny bits of tape. All the while her head was bent over the project, dark hair smelling good. Her fingers flickered at her work. It was as if she had sat me in front of a fire and helped me out of my armor. I had forgotten that packages were treated this way in Portugal. I would have liked to buy some other book, any other, and watch the ceremony again, but was too shy.

What one is meant to watch, in Lisbon, is the singing of the *fado*, but I hiked by the *fado* houses without pause. They looked authentic because they were. The *fado* is folk music, grass-roots Portugal, found nowhere else. My wife liked it long before she learned what the words meant. The music went right to her emotions, she said. It made her want to cry and laugh and dance.

It made me want to plug my ears. I lack my wife's Celtic sensibilities and for me the *fado* had a quaver redolent of fishwife. The operative word is *saudade*, feebly translated as nostalgia. Portugal is full of *saudades* because times have seldom been good, but at least they used to be glorious. You might like the fado if you are devoted to American country music. The theme is being beaten by life: wife ran off, lost my job, and Daddy got cancer from his chaw. In America, these songs are sung in an accent (related to Scots-Irish) that is almost extinct outside Nashville. In Portugal, nobody knows how the fado started, but there were Celts here once, and maybe what they left behind was black-dressed women bemoaning.

I'd rather blame it on the Moors, though. They sing with a quaver too, don't they? Anyhow, Celtic music is fine in Ireland. One of these years my wife and I will go back there for the music. We'll live on brown bread and marmalade because the restaurants are worse than they are in America. Then we will go to Portugal and plump out. There is a division of labor among Celts: Irish sing; Portuguese cook.

One of my projects was to count the men on horseback in Lisbon. As best I could determine on my hike, there were two, precisely. This must be the lowest man-on-horseback ratio in the Western world. Half of every traffic circle in Washington is dominated by the front end of a horse, and the other half of every traffic circle in Washington is dominated by the back end of a horse. We are not the equestrian champions, either. All of Europe and Spanish America did horses.

The Portuguese are not so much modest as devoted to a different vehicle. When they gave "new worlds to the world" (Camões again), they did it from decks, not steeds. There is a discoverer monument peering out over the Tagus. It must have seemed all right when it was built, not very long ago, but it looks like Socialist Realism now. This has not been a good century for statuary.

Every morning from 1978 through 1982, I was obliged to watch the discoverers on my way to work, bodies in art deco, eyes on far horizons. When a chance came to get even, I seized it. President Carter was planning a visit. I assured my counterpart in the Portuguese Foreign Ministry that Mr. Carter loved poets. It may even have been true. In any case, the president did his duty with grace, laying his wreath on Camões's tomb instead of the monument. I hope that the precedent caught on. Poets deserve more flowers than they get, these days.

The above amounts to an underhand confession: During my first stay in Lisbon, I was assigned to the American Embassy. Before that, I served in Angola and Brazil, where the Portuguese language is also spoken. You need to know that my affair with Portugal and its language was prolonged. (By now too, you will have seen that diplomat's memoirs are not my genre.)

*   *   *

Adriano's law office, which I reached eventually, was on a narrow street that had survived the fires and earthquakes. It was in one of the oldest and most low-lying of Lisbon districts. Everything about the area was so cramped that I kept ducking my head, as if even the sky hung low. I dodged the street umbrellas and tables that constituted most of a restaurant, the rest being a closet holding three cooks and a stove. The buildings, had they been used for low-income housing in America, would have brought thrills of opprobrium to every decent journalist. The population of Lisbon flocked to those narrow streets, jostling happily. The scale must have been Portuguese in some fundamental way.

The office was one floor up. To get there, I walked through an entrance that must have been elegant once, as entrances go, but had been converted to a clothing store for chic young ladies. This was the neighborhood in which they wished to buy their clothes, and the merchants knew that there was no profit in arguing with chic young ladies. A man heading for the office must make for the back of the store—not a long walk, but with its obstacles—and then open a sliding curtain at the foot of the stairs. I said *bom dia*, loudly, to the woman running the store, and then made sure that I had the right curtain. The others opened on rooms in which the young ladies were trying on young clothes. I kept my eyes rigorously on the top of the stairs as I climbed, ignoring the sound of dressing-room curtains swishing shut.

Portuguese gentlemen do this sort of thing with aplomb. It gives me a red face. With practice, however, it would also give me excellent peripheral vision.

Adriano sat in a miniature museum, smaller than the desk of a partner in a New York law firm. Everything but the hand-painted tiles on the walls contributed to the fragrance: mahogany furniture covered in red leather, red tapestry curtains, and rows of law books bound in brown leather. The youngest part of the decor was Adriano, a perfect fit. There were no pictures of his family. (Maybe that's an American thing.) The only bright colors were in a small calendar with a picture of a trout stream in Spain.

Adriano left the office with me, headed for the subway. We

walked past a movie theater featuring naked ladies. This was un-
Portuguese, something that happened before anyone could decide
how to stop it. (There was no sex in Portugal before 1974. In that
year the revolution ended censorship and the ladies ripped off their
clothes, just like that.) Andriano pretended that the offending posters were not there. I mentioned them. "We don't make such films
here," he said. "They are German and French." It was his way of
sparing my feelings. The posters were advertising a Hollywood
production.

The subway to Adriano's home was old but clean, with no
graffiti. The worst smell was an excess of cologne. In the corridor
leading to the trains, two blind women sat quietly with cups. On the
train a beggar moved from car to car, playing a recognizable tune
on an instrument that looked like a rock. He got no money but, like
the begging women, he was inoffensive. The secret seemed to be
homogeneity: not of race, because there were faces on the train
from the old African and Indian colonies, but of culture. The language was the same for all with accents that were, at most, regional.
The leading inner-city problem was that everybody wanted to live
there and few could afford it. I did not see what I could write about
this place.

Help was on the way: A honking sound moved through the car
toward me. It was made by a young man twisted, bent, and carrying
a cup. This, now, was the stuff of which books are made. I would
have interviewed the beggar, extracted the essence of his deformity,
except that he had no more vocabulary than a whooping crane.
Worse yet, he was washed and combed. He must have had a mother
who wanted her boy to look nice at work.

Once, during my diplomatic days, I did see the grotesque in Lisbon.
It was at the famous Casino of Estoril, just west of the city. People
with money go there to rid themselves of that affliction without the
depressing, drawn-out business of investing in dry oil wells. The
casino is spectacularly profitable and therefore runs spectacular
advertisements showing persons of girlish face and womanly body,
all bending over roulette wheels or grasping the handles of slot

machines. The spectacular maidens are just entertainers. When not in casinos they travel on ocean liners. The clientele in both cases is older and richer than the entertainers by an average of sixty years and one million dollars. You can't fool me.

My wife could, though. She wanted to spend an evening at the casino. She had found two other curious couples who would go with us. She appealed to my interest in anthropology. She assured me that in Portugal it is possible to get a good dinner even in casinos. And she reported that the entertainers divest themselves of clothing even as the suckers divest themselves of dollars.

It was almost true. We watched the floor show through dinner and as much longer as I could stay awake, which was till after midnight (an endurance record). The entertainers were highly qualified for the striptease that they did not perform. Next day we learned that I had given up just ten minutes too soon. But that wasn't the sad part.

The sad part was the old woman. They must have had men, once; only men would have bought those ugly, floor-dragging fur coats. The old women kept them on as they wandered around the stuffy casino losing tokens and sometimes winning, without changing expression. They were mostly ex-beautiful maidens, I thought; their features had the ghosts of either looks or plastic surgery. Their hair was young, from the rear. And then they would turn around and look at me through sockets deep and hollow.

Those folks were real travelers. Each had tried to leave herself behind. To that purpose she had hopped on a jet plane and, before she knew it, found herself in one more casino, watching the wheel spin, hoping for a triumph before her soul caught up.

Some cities are all casino, hustling for a few hours and then empty, empty as the eyes of gamblers. Lisbon was not like that. Real people lived there. You hiked rough sidewalks beneath their windows, smelled salt cod boiling, heard women cackling over the telephone. They had not been squeezed into the suburbs, not all of them, not yet.

Lisbon was not a mall, either. I mean, it was not roofed over like

Minneapolis. And ambience: Even the new buildings hid behind old facades. A roofless climate and quaint storefronts do not add up to a mall—do they?

No, the problem with the town was just that it was not country. You know part of the story from the epigraph, but Camões did not finish the tale so I will help him out.

Ulysses[1] founded Lisbon, which is a corruption of his name, among other things. He did not foresee the complications. He ordered the building of a few houses, a wharf, and a wall for defense, then waved his sword and declared the thing done. A group of distinguished female first citizens pounded their forks on their plates and told him that they were hungry. He replied that he was not a detail man. They pounded louder. He convened a group of farmers from the Alentejo, just south of town, and recommended that they grow more wheat. As an incentive, he commandeered existing stocks. At this point the first citizens of Lisbon concurred that he had founded a place worth living in.

The urban and rural people did not live very differently, at first; town was just the place where country came to market. In time, however, the people inside the wall forgot how to be hunter-gatherers, and then they lost even the skills they had learned as farmers. Agriculture had become efficient enough to support the city in grand style. This was called civilization. Everybody who was anybody moved to Lisbon.

Over the next few thousand years, several things happened. They included diesel fumes, a strike of baggage handlers, the Inquisition, British tourists, the *fado*, the revolution, American tourists, X-rated films, casinos, and malls. Lisbon came to share "the blindness of the contemporary urban world to everything that is not itself, to nature most of all."[2] Certain people decided that there was a better place to be. Especially in springtime.

This was May. Adriano and I reversed the move from country to town—not to get away from ourselves but to get back. The blackbird could not escape its walls but we could leap ours. We could forage for a country lost in mountains and fields, a place in time rather than space.

Mind you, our nostalgia was of the kind available only to those who live in two worlds. Romanticism has its limits. Being naturally stingy, we found it easy to be frugal, but we ate from dishes that had been washed in hot water, and twentieth-century medicine was never far away. At night we welcomed fireplaces. And then, every day, we hunted for Portugal and gathered pieces of it.

When we compared our findings, we saw that we had discovered different countries. Adriano's had more imagination than mine.[3] I would gather facts; he would add the myths that made sense of them. I would catch a brace of trout; he would produce goblets of wild strawberries, add a little sugar, and teach me how to drink the last drops of juice with a dash of red wine.

We went by car and afoot. We traveled from Sagres in the south, where the last rocky piece of Europe drops off into the Atlantic, to Castro Laboreiro in the north against Spanish Galicia. Some of the places were new to me and some of my questions may have been new to Adriano.

THE WORLD BEYOND FEAR

This is the story of heroes who, leaving their native Portugal behind, opened a way to Ceylon, and further, across seas never sailed before.

CAMÕES, *The Lusiads*, Canto One

Adriano thought it best to start our travels in the Algarve, which is Portugal's hot foot. From there, we could follow springtime north with the flowers. Adriano always made a good case for what he meant to do anyhow. I always concurred. You would have thought that we were making sense.

Our drive south had little to do with flowers, in fact, and much to do with Prince Henry the Navigator. We would look for him at Sagres: a sheer, boot-shaped headland sticking into the Atlantic at the southwestern tip of the Algarve. Call it the hard core of Portugal's myth—by no means the oldest piece of the history, but the one that changed everything. In the fifteenth century, from Sagres and harbors nearby, Prince Henry launched the frail ships that began Western expansion. Sagres was the last piece of Europe before the discovery of the world.

The flowers that bloom in the spring were just an example of *delicadeza,* best translated as sensitivity, or courtesy. Adriano knew that I wished to do my duty, in principle (*em princípio*). The duty was homage (*homenagem*) to a hero. I was awkward at it. I was bashful about kissing ladies' hands, too. I was incompetent at many skills in which the Portuguese excelled, and among the Portuguese Adriano was a giant. So naturally he offered the flowers as an excuse for our voyage, to make me feel comfortable.

Adriano drove south and I watched, when my eyes were open. I had forgotten about Portuguese roads.

"I like to drive fast," said Adriano. Then he glanced at my face and added "conditions permitting, of course." The roads south of

Lisbon do permit high speeds, by comparison to the roads north of Lisbon. Adriano, moreover, is a good driver by comparison to some others. His virtue is steadiness. He settles on an appropriate pace and maintains it like a Portuguese admiral disdaining an infidel fleet in the Indian Ocean.

On the right shoulder was a cart occupied by an old gray couple being pulled to the market by an old gray donkey. Overtaking the cart was a motorcyclist, spare tire looped over his chest like a bandoleer, two-cycle engine screaming with effort. Overtaking the motorcycle was a truck, stake body jammed with squealing pigs. A person of little courage might have considered three vehicles side-by-side on a two-lane road to be enough, for the moment. Such a person might have applied the brakes or, if in the passenger seat, might have braced for a lapful of pigs. Not Adriano. He pulled around the moving traffic jam with velocity unperturbed. No problem. The truck did not swing out to give more room to the cyclist; the cyclist did not swing out to give more room to the donkey; the donkey did not swing out to avoid a dead cat on the shoulder. There was a gap in oncoming traffic that allowed completion of the maneuver with yards to spare. Thus does true faith reward those who have it.

Aside from my lack of confidence in the angels, the day was bright. The donkey carts were bright too, yellow and red. The donkeys were shorn over the top halves of their bodies but not the bottoms, which made them look half happy, halfway between January rain and July sun. We passed a thin little gypsy girl riding a spotted donkey colt. She was trying to keep up with seven carts, all drawn by mules or donkeys. A bigger girl with a sack was trotting along beside a cart already so overflowing with gypsies that I supposed they had to take turns riding. The girl and her sack swung up, somehow, and Adriano explained that she had been dropped by an earlier cart to collect snails for the market.

The gypsies, Adriano lamented, had not been assimilated. The Moors had been absorbed, and black Africans and Hottentots, even Indians and a few Chinese, but the gypsies right here in Portugal still lived as they wished.

The secret, I surmised, was that the gypsies were not residues of

imperial ventures, like the rest. They had arrived without encouragement at the end of an ancient voyage. They had become "syn-
onymous, to the world at large, with the reputation of Spain
herself"[1]—but not with that of Portugal. This makes it difficult for
the rest of humanity to conjure up Portugal. Spain is accompanied
by flamenco music, crisp as the contrasts between white walls and
dark shadows, ¡olé! Every travelogue on Spain ever produced in
every other country has the same music, and no wonder. It is good
stuff. It stops playing just like that, at the Portuguese border. There
is no more ¡olé! either. Adriano and I are left with the responsibility
of showing you a country for which you probably cannot supply
the soundtrack.

Gypsies are not Portuguese, in the sense accepted by the majority of the country, because being somewhat Portuguese is impossible. It is one culture, indivisible. You accept the whole package of
Portugueseness or you don't. The gypsies didn't. They trotted their
carts back and forth across the border with Spain, finding enough
to smuggle or scrounge, living as they always had, at home in a
country that considered them foreign. And they created a traffic
jam that even Adriano's angels (being Portuguese) took time to
untangle.

We passed the gypsies and the day grew hotter. Adriano put on
his sunglasses, using both hands to adjust the ear pieces till the
lenses were in exactly the right position, not too close to the eyes
and not too far, not canted down to right or left. Adriano is not one
to shove spectacles on and let nature take its course. He did let the
car take its course, however, and the faithful Peugeot kept to the
road like a donkey with loose reins.

We bounced high and fast on new paving with potholes. We
bounced low and slow on old cobblestones without potholes. (They
don't make roads like they used to.) Perhaps it was the jiggling that
made us sneeze, Adriano first. "*Saúde*," I said: "health." Then I
started sneezing and Adriano said "*Dominus vobiscum et cum es-
piritu tuo*," which means something in real Latin, and I stopped
sneezing. It occurred to me that my problem with the angels might,
after all, be merely linguistic. (They don't make languages like they
used to.)

During most of our drive south from Lisbon we passed through the Alentejo, largest of Portugal's old provinces. We knew that we were in the Algarve when we had to slow for lobsters: *lagostas* in Portuguese, northern Europeans getting their year's quota of sun all at once and all over. Of Portuguese we saw few, but perhaps they were just too drab to notice. Most numerous of the fauna were British couples who had retired under the sun. They had more clothes on than the lobsters. Thank goodness.

You may have read, somewhere, that Africa begins at the Pyrenees, which is a cute northern European way of suggesting that the Iberians are Africans. I propose a new proverb: England begins at the Algarve.

The Algarve's southern coast is on the finger of Atlantic Ocean that leads through the Strait of Gibraltar to the Mediterranean. Portugal nowhere touches the inland sea, but the climate is Mediterranean and so Portuguese houses are built in the Mediterranean style, with uninsulated walls of concrete or stone painted in some light color to reflect the hot rays of the sun. The cooking is Mediterranean, in a general sense, because the ingredients resemble those that grow elsewhere in southern Europe. The people seem to me unlike those anywhere else: not like those in neighboring Spain; not even like those in Brazil.

A Portuguese friend told me, once, that his country was a piece of northern Europe that had wound up in the south because of a lurch in the continental drift. This is getting closer. If you can picture a hospitable and impoverished version of the Swiss—which takes a stretch of the imagination—then you have a beginning concept of the Portuguese. (Once when I was staying in Geneva I heard a news broadcast that made the point. A pleasant male voice dwelt with satisfaction on drug murders in New York, earthquakes in Colombia, and football riots in England. "Here in Switzerland," the radio's voice concluded, "nothing in particular." The Portuguese newscasts have more imagination but, as to national nastiness, often nothing in particular.)

The Portuguese have another quality that used to be identified with northern Europe. It is known as modesty if you like it and prudery if you don't. Adriano likes it—conditions permitting, of course. To me, the beach lobsters look good.

We have, then, a clash of pruderies. When António de Oliveira Salazar was in charge of Portugal (from 1928 to 1968), there was a law requiring ladies to wear bathing suits with a skirt. The skirt was to be a certain number of centimeters in length. One extra-respectable woman told me of her experience when wearing a bathing skirt with hemline even lower. She was arrested and charged with swimming in a dress. Aesop drew morals from such fables and so shall I: Prudery is surrounded by lechery at all her borders.

Adriano did not like me to muse on such topics. I found it impossible to ignore lobsters grilling on the sand but they did not put me in the mood for Prince Henry the Navigator, so Adriano and I at least visited him before the beaches.

The hot wind that broils the beach lobsters is hard on the Algarve's vegetation too. Even the fig trees grovel, branches sweeping the ground, unlike their growth habit elsewhere. Of the foreign growths, century plants prosper and a few scrawny eucalypts survive, but Prince Henry would have recognized the rest of the plants. There are creeping succulents and tamarisks. In May there are yellow, blue, and white blossoms everywhere, just as Adriano had said. Even the lowest and sturdiest of vegetation quivers in the wind. There is always wind at sea and the sea surrounds Sagres.

Before corruption, the name was *Sacrum Promontorium* because the gods visited this Sacred Promontory and prehistoric peoples came here to worship the gods. No one could show me evidence of such rites but the tourist brochures were insistent. It is the kind of place where gods ought to have descended, anyhow, and where people ought to have worshiped. Prince Henry is known to have done so. In Portuguese, Sagres still sounds close to *sagrado*, sacred.

Adriano was the only adult Portuguese tourist there. We saw busloads of Portuguese children on outings from their schools and carloads of tourists from everywhere except Portugal. There was little for any of them to see, so they milled around looking at each other. Some of the schoolchildren played loud music on boomboxes, instruments of sonic aggression. The children were there because it was good for them, according to adults. (Children are never, anywhere, interested in sights.) The slightly older people were interested in each other. One American in his twenties was posing his girl for photographs—first on the rock wall above a sheer drop to the sea, and then on a *padrão*, which is a pedestal with the royal arms and a cross, modeled on those left by the discoverers when they claimed new worlds for Portugal. The girl stood on the base of the monument. She had long, tanned legs. She wore shorts and a top that exposed her navel, also tanned, when she leaned back against the cross. Her boyfriend pumped his camera's lever. When she vacated the *padrão*, I read its inscription, which said that it had been donated recently by an American naval squadron. It was the only sign of official enthusiasm for Sagres.

Adriano was pacing, angry at his government's neglect of the place most sacred to Portugal's myth. He wanted to leave, right away. I asked him to wait while I walked the perimeter of the promontory. He offered to drive me around it. I tried to explain my inability to see what I needed through car windows. I failed. Adriano strode back for the car while I hurried to find some semblance of Sagres in its wildest parts. There were the keening winds and the tortured little plants growing from sand caught in the rocks. There was a big snake—not a viper—but I caught only a flicker and will not try to pass it off as the ghost of Prince Henry. For that, I would have had to wait till the middle of the night, when he used to meditate under the stars.

There were fishermen too, and they at least were not sightseers. The fishermen knew what they wanted and were trying to catch it. Naturally they turned their backs on me; I was a tourist, lesser breed without the Law. I watched, nevertheless. One man had tied himself by a long, stout rope to the rusting relic of a medieval cannon. Perhaps he had a touch of vertigo, like me, and did not trust himself near the edge of the cliff. He put the rear half of a sardine on his hook below a float and sinker. He contorted his body as if he were a baseball pitcher winding up, then cast as far as he could with a rod about 18 feet long. His bait flew up and out. Then it fell, and fell, and fell. I had to close my eyes before it hit dark blue water.

I waited till the sinker cocked the float. The line slackened, a wispy thing glinting in the sun, and the fisherman reeled in cautiously till the connection was tight enough to let him strike a fish, should one take the bait. Then he squatted and waited. He was not Prince Henry either, but he was as close as I could come. I asked him if he had been catching anything. Without turning he said *pouco*: few. This is how fishermen everywhere answer intrusions. I asked only because, once in a while in America, someone forgets himself and imparts information. The Portuguese never get carried away. A tourist might easily conclude that no fisherman has ever been successful in the nine hundred years of Portuguese independence.

Further along the top of the cliff, however, another man hooked something that curved his rod. When the fish tired, he lowered a landing net on a long, long rope. Because the cliff sloped inward, undercut by the sea, the net dropped all the way to the water. After some maneuvering, the fisherman pulled up an *anchova*, which we Americans would call a bluefish. Sagres fishermen have worked out tricks like that—perhaps tricks unique in the world—and I would have liked to watch the netting but could not work up courage to get close enough to the cliff at the end of the world.

Adriano drove up, eyes hurling thunderbolts. He was in fact composing one, to the minister in charge of tourism. Adriano gave me the gist of the letter he would send. When, it asked, would Portugal have leaders who would remember what Sagres was about? When would the country be led by heirs worthy of Prince Henry? I shall venture a prediction: Adriano will get attention. He will, if necessary, beard the minister in his den, and when you visit Sagres, you will see changes that will please everyone except the fishermen, who would prefer to be let alone.

The second millennium has seen three revolutions, as distinguished from brawls. The most recent is the Information Explosion, which started in 1971 with the invention of the microprocessor.[2] Two centuries earlier, the Industrial Revolution began in England with the steam engine. And in the 1400s, ships called caravels launched what I think it fair to call a Geographic Revolution. The Portuguese sailors were not the first humans to see, or occupy, most of the lands that stuck out of the world's oceans—but "discovery" means more than that. The Portuguese took their sphere's measure, found the relation of its pieces, and tied them together with maps.

It is hard to picture the discoverers, as hard as picturing Ulysses. They show up in old engravings with decorator beards and finery that would have been suffocating in the armpit of Africa. The real explorers would have been burned—not lobster-red but leather-brown. Most would have been small (the better to live on short rations) and shriveled (from meager draughts of filthy water). They would have had tired faces, like great men everywhere. Heroism is elegant only in retrospect.

Prince Henry's picture, on the other hand, inspires confidence. It shows the plainest face that ever launched a thousand ships. The face is topped by an ugly black hat bearing no resemblance to Indiana Jones's. Henry was not out to impress the ladies. He also lacked political sensitivity (as we say about people in Washington who are bent on solving problems). Given a choice between the luxurious court at Lisbon and the Sacred Promontory at the end of Europe, he spent time—and by some accounts founded a school of navigation—at Sagres. As far as anyone knows, he died a virgin, and when his body was dressed for burial in 1460, he was found to have been wearing a hair shirt.

You must excuse Henry. He was half English and half odd. His mother was the daughter of John of Gaunt, Duke of Lancaster. She is best remembered for having cleaned up lax Mediterranean morals in the court, administering a dose of northern rectitude. Shows how times change.

Strange mix, Portugal and England. There is this in common, though: The people break loose. Maybe tight spaces produce a yearning for big ones. While the Russians were finding enough to do in their own vast country, the Portuguese and English were always getting in trouble somewhere on the upside-down end of the globe.

Prince Henry the Navigator is the human symbol of the discoveries. Some revisionist historians consider him little more than that. (Royalty had a near monopoly on the celebrity business in the fifteenth century, doing underlings the honor of profiting from their works.) Traditionalists, on the other hand, assign Henry a role in organizing and financing the early probes down the African coast. None of the biographies are satisfactory[3] and some are fanciful. He was not a navigator in the narrow sense—that title was awarded him by an Englishman in the nineteenth century[4]—but Henry may have controlled a process of exploration, which would be navigation enough for me.

The details of the discoveries were obscured by a policy of secrecy. The Portuguese saw hard-won knowledge as their leading asset, and they were right: Columbus would hardly have looked for India in the western hemisphere if he had been given access to accurate measurements of the world. But the secrecy that gave Portugal an advantage for a few decades has handicapped historians forever. Records of whole expeditions have been lost. It is the leading example of a problem that arises throughout this book: how to separate history from myth? They are equally important for my purpose, which is the discovery of a lost continent named Portugal. The history and the myth are almost always related. Sometimes the relationship is tenuous. In others, however, it is close.

The heroic view of Prince Henry appeals to a bias which, unlike some historians, I shall confess. I have walked around the Sacred Promontory and wondered what kind of person would have chosen to die there. Henry made that choice.

And besides, I watched the first trip to the moon. The investment in space made sense to me, in the sixties, even if it raised my taxes and delayed the solutions that politicians offered for our social problems. Grand ventures of the mind are a social problem too, if you don't have them. Some nations invested in cathedrals. Portugal and America were modest in that regard, but American spires reach to the moon and the Portuguese caravels to new worlds. In both cases, I suspect that the great achievements needed great individuals.

It is awkward to write of these things after a generation of revisionists has worked to prove heroism impossible. History, as you have surely heard, was elitist, imperialist, authoritarian, ethnocentric, and generally nasty. Even the books we thought great were just products of their times.

In Prince Henry's absence, I shall venture to exercise his right of reply. Twentieth-century humans, he would say, have lost touch with God, nature, and themselves. He needs no advice from voyagers adrift. He knew where he was going in his time. Furthermore, he got there.

And now, as referee, I shall opine that it is folly to judge one age by the standards of another. The Renaissance was an artistic explosion. It was also as violent and intolerant as the rest of human history. Its explorers had a pure, radiant faith that we will not see again. They propagated it by enslaving unbelievers. Back home, priests tortured bodies to save the souls inside. Neither the terror nor the beauty, however, tell us why Prince Henry kept sending ships down the coast of Africa. That was a story for all ages.

In Henry's youth, Europeans did not know whether there were really antipodes where people walked upside-down. Finding out took voyages more speculative than the trip into space. We Americans knew that there was a moon and that it could be reached, if we were up to the task. Even so we needed both a John F. Kennedy to mobilize the nation and a NASA to organize the enterprise. Prince Henry was in a position to play both roles. The only contemporary account of the fifteenth-century voyages suggests that he seized his opportunity.

> The noble spirit of this Prince was ever urging him both to begin and to carry out noble deeds. . . . He had also a wish to know the land that lay beyond the Isles of Canary and that Cape called Bojador, [because] up to his time, neither by writings, nor by the memory of man, was known with any certainty the nature of the land beyond that Cape. . . . It seemed to him that if he or some other lord did not endeavor to gain that knowledge, no mariners or merchants would ever dare to attempt it, for it is clear that none of them ever trouble themselves to sail to a place where there is not a sure and certain hope of profit.[5]

The key phrase is "sure and certain." The discoveries were of course driven by the hope of profit. In time they produced it, on a scale beyond any that seems likely from the space program. But the risks were astronomical and the losses enormous. The largest of the rewards were deferred for more than sixty years. As a percentage of the national economy, the Portuguese investment was probably greater than the American.

Fifteenth-century research was primitive, but it produced nautical instruments that relocated little islands in the Atlantic, guns that sank bigger fleets, and ships that gave new worlds to the world. The process was not always scientific, but it caused the scientific method to be invented, or reinvented. The explorers moved step-by-step from a few known facts to circumnavigation of the globe by Magalhães (Magellan). It could have happened, would have happened eventually, without Prince Henry. But it didn't.

One wonders how his personality was affected by the clash of science and religion. He achieved, on the one hand, his time's most striking achievements in applied science; and on the other, he drew personal strength from religious mysticism. His empire spread its faith, like all empires from the Olmec to the Soviet. Its religious leaders took refuge in ignorance and made the ignorance part of the faith. It is all hard to imagine, today. You have to suppose the American creationists more successful than the Iranian ayatollahs. You have to imagine science outlawed, evolution revoked, books banned for parents as well as schoolchildren. Even then the knowledge would be hidden somewhere, remembered by someone. The knowledge did not exist in Henry's time. No one had dared to have a look.

The Sea of Obscurity, or Ocean of Darkness, it was called. There dwelt monsters, and the sun stood so high that the water boiled. The men who lived on the outermost edge of the African shore were known to be burned black by the sun, so how could men go farther without being roasted alive? . . . The pitch would boil in the seams, the caulking would be lost, and the ships would sink. If you escaped these hazards, worse was to come. As you neared the outermost limits of the earth, you would be caught in the steady flow of water that poured day and night over the edge.[6]

The bare facts are these.[7] Gil Eanes—a daring and experienced captain sent by Prince Henry—tried and failed fifteen times to round *Cabo Bojador,* the Bulging Cape. It does not seem far down the West African coast on today's map. Until 1434, it was evidently a technical barrier for sailing vessels. Worse than that, it was the end of the world. The coast was nothing but cliffs and dunes. Waves were high, fogs thick. Gil Eanes reported that the cape was impassable and then, on his sixteenth expedition, passed it. He brought back to Lisbon flowers collected in the world beyond fear. Seldom has such a fuss been made over a few wild roses.

It would not be literally correct to say that this was the end of fear, because sailors in wooden ships lived as dangerously as mice in a field. The rounding of Cape Bojador was, at least, the beginning of confidence that explorers could venture off the maps and return. Prince Henry may have been an old man before he foresaw the opening of trade routes to India and China, but by then there was a national commitment to the process of exploration. Henry was still alive when the *caravelas* were launched. The caravels had a name that still sings, the most poetic ever given to a class of ships. They were explorers, not frumpy merchants. *Caravelas* were lean and hungry—tiny, by today's standards—and shallow of draft so that their crews could haul them up on African beaches for repair. They sailed closer to the wind so that crews could reach home against the prevailing northerlies. And they sailed farther south each year.

In 1488, Bartolomeu Dias rounded the Cape of Good Hope. His success dashed Columbus's hope of Portuguese sponsorship for an expedition that would attempt to reach India by sailing west. The Portuguese knew by then that India was closer for ships sailing south around Africa, then east. Dias had proved that this route was feasible.

It seems clear from references in old journals that the Portuguese also knew of unexplored lands in the western Atlantic. Two noblemen had apparently reached the "Land of Cod" (Greenland or Newfoundland) before 1474. This is not to say that America had been "discovered." Columbus did that by insisting that it was India.

New places were interesting and perhaps profitable in the long term, but trade with India was what mattered.

> On October 12, 1492, ... [Columbus] hit some islands, exactly where he'd calculated they would be, and told the Arawaks of San Salvador that they lived just off the coast of Japan so they had to be Indians. They were agreeable. They didn't know anything about Europeans yet, and by the time they found out it was too late. . . .
>
> Presently Amerigo Vespucci declared that the whole place was nothing but a New World, so it got named after him, because everyone was tired of Columbus crowing about his Garden of Eden when all he'd actually found was a New World.[8]

Columbus's landfall got ample exposure, which is discovery in the archaic sense. He also deserves credit for seamanship, courage, and persistence. He would have strengthened his claim on history—but perhaps not his claim on his royal sponsors—if he had understood his achievement. According to my dictionary, discovery in the modern sense means "to obtain knowledge of; arrive at through search or study." It is not clear that a thing has been discovered until one begins to grasp its meaning.

By the same token, Columbus cannot be held accountable for the long-term consequences of the deed he failed to understand. If he had indeed landed in India, he might have achieved a colonial trading relationship like that of the Portuguese. Native peoples would not have been wiped out by diseases from another continent. There might have been no slaughter of the Incas, no cavalry hounding the Nez Percés. I want to let Columbus off the hook. He was a hero, and I am grateful to have been discovered. But I could wish that the holocaust had not begun while he was still on Hispaniola. What happened was not condoned by all Spaniards, even at the time.

The voyage of 1492 was, in any case, the best example of serendipity in all history. India was still half a world away, but there was a misplaced continent waiting around for the Columbus's caravels as a consolation prize. Luck is a great quality in explorers.

* * *

The Portuguese avoided impossible dreams. Vasco da Gama followed Bartolomeu Dias's route around Cape Horn and kept going all the way to India in 1498. He was at sea once for ninety-three days, as opposed to thirty-six for Columbus, and the whole trip lasted more than two years.

What happened next ought to increase your faith in heroes and shatter any confidence you may have had in the philosophy of determinism. The population of Portugal was small even for those days. The society was less sophisticated than some in Asia. The culture and history could not compare with those of China. The domestic economy was rudimentary; the military forces were weak; the supply line was impossibly long. So what happened? Portugal became the dominant power in the Indian Ocean.

The achievement belongs to an extraordinary viceroy called Afonso d'Albuquerque, "perhaps the single greatest strategic planner in the history of European imperialism."[9] He fought Arabs, Malays, and the Moghul empire in India. In the Red Sea, he destroyed an Egyptian fleet built by Venetians. He seized Ormuz and Muscat, controlling the mouth of the Persian Gulf. He claimed Malacca. He established stations in Sumatra, Timor, the Moluccas, and Ceylon. By 1513, his forces were in China, where Portugal obtained the enclave of Macau.

Albuquerque had better ships and guns. His method of colonization made the most of Portugal's diminutive population: He married his lower-class sailors to upper-class local women and founded generations of patriotic Catholics. It was not the harshest of methods, and it worked. But I think one must concede that what Afonso d'Albuquerque had, above all, was daring. He was compared to Alexander the Great. I would like to know more of him as a man, but the reliable facts are as thin as those on most of the other heroes in this book.

Spices now came to Europe via Portugal, eliminating Arab caravans and Venetian middlemen. Lisbon boomed, though life scarcely changed for the majority who were peasants in the countryside. And of course the dream time could not last. Stronger European nations got in on the act—England, Spain, France, and

Holland. The first three of these, in particular, had enough people to colonize large areas. The Portuguese were from the beginning interested mainly in navigation and commerce. Even so, they wound up with the Azores and Madeira, which are still part of Portugal. They got Angola, Mozambique, Goa, the Cape Verde islands, and a few other bits and pieces. They settled half of South America—the half we call Brazil. Their language grew from one less important than Irish Gaelic to that with the fourth largest number of native speakers in the world.

While Adriano was driving me around, the Cannes Film Festival was in process and the critics were praising the Portuguese entry by Manuel de Oliveira. He had written a series of novels on frustrated love—a subject on which he may have been an expert, judging from what happened next. Pay attention, now: For the film's script, he converted his novels' failed love affairs into Portugal's failed attempts at imperial conquest. Of failure there was enough, as we shall see; imperialism always turns to impotence in time. While Portugal's period of expansion lasted, though, it was a performance without parallel.

It is this mythic history that must be grasped. You cannot see Portugal without it. In America, we assume that we will go on and on forever, to bigger and better things. In this assumption we are certainly wrong, but the twentieth century has been ours; children in a thousand years will be obliged to remember the moon landing and the War to End Wars. Of the fifteenth century, they will remember the discoveries.

What remains is a sort of historic self-esteem. When they found the passage to India, the Portuguese also discovered who they were. They still feel no pressing need to be anything else. It is hard on new generations to learn that they cannot live up to their ancestors, but I do not detect the desperate pains of the Latin Americans, the brilliant dysfunctions of the Irish, or the collapsing aspirations of the French. The Portuguese never intended to run the world—just to buy it cheap and sell it dear. They got away with that in their time. Back home, their society still works. They are in Camões's words a "land never subjugated," so that with their offspring they can afford to be parental rather than competitive. They even think that I might amount to something when I grow up. Their passions are gone but still good for the dreaming.

Let's define the dream time. For America, it is now, and we have movies to tell us so. (Odd that no one has filmed an epic on the discoveries. Maybe it would be too difficult for non-heroes.) The best of the Portuguese myth began in 1385, when a perfect hero named Nuno Álvares Pereira won the battle of Aljubarrota against the odds, ensuring his nation's independence from Spain. (Nuno Álvares's battle will come later. I warned you that this trip would follow geography rather than chronology.) The myth reached its peak in the fifteenth and early sixteenth centuries when explorers discovered the world. The end of the dream time came in 1578, when Sebastian the fool got himself and most of the Portuguese Army slaughtered in Morocco (another battle coming up). Portugal and Spain then came temporarily under a common crown in 1580. It was not the end of independence but it coincided with the end of prosperity, and myth. Ever since, the Portuguese have been traveling in little poem ships called *caravelas*.

And so have the rest of us. We have used different names but they have been the same ships on the same voyage. Even a boy born in Iowa wanted creaking masts, dance of Saint Elmo's fire, and rattle of anchor chain in harbor never plumbed. Tahiti was paradise but anyplace would do. The important thing was to watch a bowsprit slicing through a sea beyond fear.

Well, there are some little frontiers left—enough to see me out. But I am looking for the last places now. Prince Henry's captains found the first.

His caravels frighten me, not because they existed once but because they survive only in replica. My son's Starship Enterprise is just virtual reality, magic realism, the creation of a microprocessor. In the natural universe, light sets my speed limit and binds me to this solar system. I want to "explore strange new worlds, to seek out new life and new civilizations, to boldly go where no man has gone before." I shall not be given the chance.

My home world is better now that it is round. No reasoning person would doubt that, and I am rational. I would have been a threat to the flat-earth faith. Inquisitors would have tortured me; demons would have fried me. While I lasted, I would have enslaved others or been enslaved myself. I would have been a true believer in something, and it would have justified any nastiness I cared to perpetrate. I would not go back even if I could. I am too enlightened now.

And maybe I am too comfortable. I can afford to get my thrills from interactive software. It is a nature as imaginary as that of the fifteenth-century clerics, but it can be explored with less danger.

I regret that body and soul have been slow to get with the program. They evolved during what Joseph Campbell calls the Great Hunt[10] and became set in their ways at least thirty thousand years ago. The natural world has become irrelevant but I still want to sail into it. I am torn between nature and nurture. Old faiths and new have me split down the middle, like Prince Henry.

· 5 ·

MIGRANTS

In England, that great northern kingdom of perpetual snow, the spirit of discord was sowing its evil seeds, that were to redound to the greater glory of our native Portugal.

CAMÕES, *The Lusiads*, Canto Six

Adriano did not want to visit any more of the Algarve's tourist places. He feared, I think, that lobsters on the beach would be as counter-mythic as boom-boxes at Sagres. But research is research, and I insisted. We toured a small piece of sand hidden between much rock. Scattered around were bikinis, and monokinis, and nokinis. The designers of clothing insist that nudity is not sexy, but that depends on who's doing it. For those of us in the moral majority, nudity is not sexy because we don't look good with our clothes off. Those who do look good bare, however, look better that way than any other. They prove it on Algarve sand. Some of the proofs were speaking the pure Portuguese of Prince Henry. Alas for the explorers. Discovery today is a caravel that never gets off the beach.

The Portuguese, however, were a minority among the sun lovers. English was the lingua franca among peoples without costume—the language that one assumed would be understood when they wore no cultural evidence to the contrary. There was little to learn of Portugal except that it had been invaded, so I did not tarry on the tourist territory. No. (Such sights are available even in Montana, during the years when summer falls on a weekend.) I walked instead to the section where fishing boats were hauled up.

No vessels in the English-speaking world ever looked like these—not even when we built with wood instead of polymers. The Portuguese must have learned their marine designs in the dream time, because they clash with national character in this sober country. The boats were handmade of planks painted in the brightest of reds, whites, greens, and blues. At the prows were stems that arched high, lacking only dragons' heads to complete the effect. The rest was functional. High gunwales and transoms were what you would expect for small craft in ocean waves. Each boat had one or two sets of heavy wooden oars with thole pins for oar locks at the gunwales and transom, the latter for a sculling oar. There was always an iron anchor and a couple of rusty bailing cans. Some boats had small power winches for hauling nets. Most had outboard motors—occasionally American but usually Japanese, and fueled by kerosene. These seagoing motors had one-tenth the power used by Washingtonians to pursue black bass on the calm Potomac.

I talked to a man working on his winch. "How's the fishing?"

"*Fraco,*" he said: weak. Big trawlers—he mentioned Russians—were working so close to the beach that there was little left for the local "artisanal fishermen." But the trawlers' frozen catch did not reach Portuguese customers. The restaurants demanded fresh fish unloaded from the boats every morning, and the prices were so good that even a small catch made an overnight trip worthwhile. The fisherman gave no more details, so I imagined the lights of Sagres appearing on the horizon, then bobbing out as the boat slipped into the midnight trough of a wave. The winds whistled down from that great northern kingdom that Camões imagined covered by perpetual snow.

Adriano drove me through the town of Sagres, at the base of the headland. We passed the Navigator Hotel, the Caravel Disco, the Last Chance Saloon, and the Gift Shop. We passed signs for "Rooms—Chambres—Zimmer." On the outskirts we drove up hills networked with new roads, looking for a place that Adriano wanted to show me. There were dozens of driveways, maybe hundreds, and at the ends of some, foundations were going in. A few houses were almost finished. They were for British expatriates and the odd Dane or Dutchman—one of those English-speaking nationalities, anyhow. Each house would have, if not a view of the ocean, at least a smell of rotting seaweed when the wind was right. Gulls and rooks were hopping around and swallows were on the wing, looking for insects disturbed by construction.

Adriano did not find the place he remembered. It was a high spot, he said, where he used to drive after visiting Sagres, for a look back at the promontory and the town. He talked about those days before the revolution of 1974. Back then, the place was treated with respect. The giant wind rose of Sagres was kept clear of weeds; you could walk along the lines of rocks laid down by the discoverers, lines 50 yards long pointing north/south, east/west, and to continents in between. There were employees to maintain order and explain what had happened at this place. Then, when you had paid your respects to Prince Henry the Navigator, you looked up a fellow in town who would guide you out over the hills. He had a pointer, a partridge dog (*perdigueiro*) of the old Portuguese breed. The hills were steep but there was the sea downslope to look at, and Sagres. You could get a bird or two for dinner, if you had legs enough to catch them. They were on these hills. Just a few years ago. Real partridges, fat and beautiful and violent of flight. Here, right here.

Adriano and I could talk about partridges. They were common currency, valued at the same rate of exchange. Either of us would have traded the Last Chance Saloon for one red-legged partridge and tossed in the Disco Caravel for good measure. Both of us would have applauded if, while we were watching from that hillside, a man of conviction had stridden into the temple of Sagres and overthrown the discos, scattered the boom-boxes. After that we might have differed. Adriano would have marched into town and embraced the new leader. I would have sat on the hillside and wondered what kind of maniac I had been cheering.

Adriano was as steadfast in his politics as in his driving. He had spent most of his adult life under a regime that defended the good, old, eternal things: partridges and modesty and wine of the country, as opposed to discos and monokinis and Coca Cola. That regime was led by the dictator Salazar, who had replaced a frivolous, incompetent system of political parties. His organization resembled that of prewar Italy. The comparison does not get one far, however. Fascism (for me at least) was Mussolini, and Mussolini was grotesque.

António de Oliveira Salazar was not grotesque. He abhorred swagger, bombast, and pretension. He was a professor of economics who did not seek power but found it pressed on him in 1928. He created a stable but stagnant domestic economy. He took no money on the side. He had no bank accounts in Switzerland. He invested the whole of his salary in his modest family farm. He was, in short, the distilled essence of Portuguese virtues, which made him successful enough for long enough to do serious damage.

Let me give you a device to imagine Salazar. In order to keep ideology and social class out of this, I shall compare him to another leader of the right: Ronald Reagan. Both men had exceptional qualities—but not the same ones. Reagan provided fantasy, Salazar substance. Reagan delegated not only authority but knowledge; Salazar knew everything and took all the decisions. Reagan led without governing; Salazar governed without leading. Reagan encouraged the greed of his decade and got his share of the spoils. Salazar died with no personal property but his farm and a few dark suits. (The legislature had to appropriate money for his funeral.) Reagan left office popular. Salazar left office discredited.

Reagan was a product of Locke and Salazar of Hobbes. Reagan saw Americans as rational, with little need of state control; Salazar saw in his people passions that needed oversight by Leviathan. In my view (not that it matters), both leaders got carried away. In almost everyone's view, Locke came out of it better than Hobbes.

There is another way to explain Reagan's success and Salazar's failure. Reagan was part of a mature political system that got him out of office before his bills came due. Salazar's popularity actually lasted longer, but he lost touch with public opinion at least a decade before a stroke removed him from office in 1968. His power had forty years to corrupt itself. He censored the press till Portuguese thinking, and writing, fell behind those elsewhere in western Europe. He set up a police-and-spy network to control his people. And then he took on an endless war to defend African colonies that he never visited—not even in passing. He did not need to do so because they were, by his lights, part of Portugal: The Portuguese constitution said so. The war therefore had to be won. Only victory could defend what had begun at Sagres. It was precisely what the Africans wanted to get rid of, and did.

The endless, futile African wars were largely responsible for the Portuguese revolution of April 25, 1974. The troops came home; the ex-colonies foundered in Marxist rule and tribal conflict. It was what both Adriano and I would have expected. Each of us, therefore, thought that history had demonstrated the wisdom of his beliefs. For Adriano, the American blather about self-determination had undermined Portugal's valiant fight in Africa. For me, Salazar's treatment of the colonies had pushed them into thirty years of violence and left them poorly prepared for independence. Ours were not so much different opinions as different views: Adriano saw Africa from Portugal, while I had lived in Angola and seen the issue of independence through African eyes.

The revolution led to chaos in Portugal too. For a time, it seemed possible that the old repressive right would be replaced by a regime of the repressive left. With help from the United States, Germany, and other Western countries, however, the economy was rebuilt. Meanwhile the Communist party did poorly in a series of free elections. Within roughly a decade of the 1974 revolution, Portuguese leaders had consolidated democratic government. I can scarcely imagine a people better suited for it: unified, sober, and critical. Portugal was a democracy waiting to happen. By 1991, its economy was growing faster than that of any other country in the European Community.

Adriano and I saw this from different angles, too. Adriano's was philosophic. He did not defend all of the old regime's actions. He had refused a high appointment under it. At the least, however, it had maintained values that modern vote seekers lack courage to defend. I acknowledged the appeal of that argument but saw no evidence that despotism could work, even under a despot who came as close as most to being a philosopher king.

It might sound, from this, as if Adriano and I spent much time discussing politics. We did not. The gap between us was too wide to close, and we generally had enough sense not to try. On one important angle, however, we were agreed. In a world that had its priorities straight, there would be partridges.

On an autumn Sunday ten years earlier, I chased partridges in the old Algarve, the one beyond beach lobsters and roads. Three friends guided me. Manuel Ribeiro was an air force sergeant, young and keen and within 20 pounds of his ideal weight, thanks to a month

of weekends afoot. Zeca Tabuada was a Lisbon businessman who
appeared unfit for our hike, thanks to his wife's superb cooking, but
always managed to go the distance. I was the team's ectomorph, as
hungry as I looked and good for hill climbing. My problem was a
pair of trick knees which, at the time, forced me to hike downhill
backward.

The fourth member of our hunting party was the owner of a
small farm (*quinta*, not *quintal*). He was middle-aged, lean, and
brown as bark—fittest of us all, except that he brought his handicap
with him in a large paper bag. This was the expedition on which he
earned his nickname: Figs.

We all partook of the fateful fruit during our drive from Lisbon
to the Algarve on Saturday night. Manuel and Zeca and I each ate
half a dozen. Perhaps, in self-defense, we should have had more, but
fresh figs—especially if you fail to peel them—unsettle the digestive
apparatus. You will know about this if you have ever sipped syrup
of figs for constipation. Our friend Figs finished off the fruit in the
bag except for a few at the bottom that were overripe, which he
tossed to our dogs in the back of the station wagon. My dog
Trooper, being bigger and faster than the rest, must have got more
than his share of the discards. I figured that out later.

We spread our sleeping bags on the floor of a village house in
the town of Zambujeira. We were asleep, or at least prone to sleep,
before midnight, and we congratulated ourselves. Had we driven
down on Sunday morning, we would have been obliged to get out
of bed at two A.M. Now we would have six hours of sound rest
before our ordeal. At least we would have had, but for figs, and
Figs, and Trooper. My dog had a gastric event when I let him out
of the station wagon after dinner. I guessed the cause and decided
that Trooper had best not spend the night in the wagon—which
happened to be mine, with a new-car smell that my wife prized. So
Trooper came inside and slept with us humans. Manuel's dog Monkey joined us too. She seemed to have had her share of rotten figs,
Trooper being a natural gentledog with members of the opposite
sex. (I start with this virtue because Trooper had fewer virtues than
figs but I nevertheless remember him kindly.)

Now, dogs do have a sense of humor, but it is appropriate

humor. They do not brag about their indiscretions like certain humans. Our ex-friend Figs thought himself amusing. His sleeping bag served as a sort of muffler, but it could not cope with multiple mellifluous methane emissions. We opened the room's one small window. Portuguese village houses, unlike those in America, try to shut themselves off from the street, and this one succeeded too well. Manuel said that he needed a cigarette but feared explosion.

If this sounds like a teenage pajama party, you have grasped one of the reasons why we had sneaked off on a purported hunting trip to a place with no game. ". . . 'tis ever common that men are merriest when they are from home," and was, I suspect, for millions of years before Henry V.

Zeca informed me, with urgency, that Trooper wanted to go outside. I had to wake up to absorb this information, so there must have been some sleeping after all. Trooper and I rushed out with one pair of undershorts between us. I had to keep Trooper on a leash because, if he had found a cat, he'd have chased it up a telephone pole and barked the whole town out of bed. By the time I got back inside, Monkey wanted to go out. Manuel and I decided that Figs ought to suffer too, and Zeca was awake. We dressed and fed our dogs and went off to look for breakfast before dawn. None of us had shaved and Figs was the worse for wear, a shriveled husk of last night's bloated comedian.

Breakfast revived us. My three friends ate a small loaf of bread apiece, plus a cup of strong coffee and a shot of brandy. The smell of brandy before dawn made my life flash before my eyes. Once on another occasion I had tried such a hunt breakfast and, while I had not expired during the morning's hike, I had wished that I might. This time I ordered a liter of mineral water and three loaves, one with a thick slice of cheese, the others spread with *marmelada*. (I commend this to you. *Marmelada* is the source of our English word for marmalade, but we've got it wrong. The real thing is made from *marmelos*, or quinces, and it is not put in a jar. Never lasts long enough. It comes from a deep dish and is so thick that you can slice it for your bread.) It was the right fuel for the purpose, which was partridges.

By dawn we had formed our line of skirmish. Manuel was our

constable, being a sergeant in real life. He put me at the far left—partly because we would be swinging to the right, which meant that the left flank would have to move fastest, and I was eager. But I think Manuel's real reason was that Trooper always got in trouble, and the left wing would keep him as isolated as possible. Manuel was next in line because his bitch Monkey would not get in a fight with Trooper. Then came Zeca. On the far right, our pivot was Figs, who needed sympathy. The disposition of forces was important because Portuguese partridges have been hunted for so many centuries now that they are too clever for any single hunter, no matter how good his dog. They run and flush wild. They have to be pushed on a broad front, and surrounded if possible, in the hope that they will swing close enough to one gun or another during flight.

This kind of hunting makes military organization inevitable. No doubt my ancestors had a constable and formations when they set off to slay mammoths, or something, in that great northern kingdom of perpetual snow. And perhaps they organized in the same way when they set off to fight invaders from a more advanced Celtic culture. The exercise therefore has resonance. It is not the best kind of hunting because it relates man to man instead of man to nature, but any kind of hunting is better than any kind of not-hunting. I was at least doing instead of watching, part of a Portuguese bestiary predating the tourists.

My friends down the line seemed closer at a distance than they did when in the same car. I felt benevolent even toward Figs. I shouted "*Santiago às perdizes*," a request for St. James to take our side against the partridges, but my voice lacked stentorian quality. Constables and kings of old must have had trouble sounding valiant in the wind. They entered frays shouting *Santiago aos Mouros*—"St. James at the Moors." The Moors called the Portuguese "the bravest of the Christians" in some old accounts. There was a battle not far from here at Las Navas de Tolosa, in Spain, and a Castilian chronicler reported that the Portuguese allies "rushed into battle as if at a feast."[1] My bleat was the echo.

It was not a long walk, as these things go: a couple of miles south and a mile west and then back, with some loops off around hills and into promising territory. During one of the side trips we passed through a eucalyptus grove with sweet-smelling bark on the ground, and Figs got lost for three hours. It was pretty clear by then that there were no partridges around. Manuel's intelligence had been impeccable, no doubt—a good friend had told him of some other good friends who had found a covey hereabouts—but the birds had moved on. We would have had a dull walk, but for Trooper.

Trooper was in top form. It was a cool day, for the Algarve, with intermittent drizzle that kept dogs and hunters from overheating. Scenting conditions were good too. Trooper pointed, then flushed, a hare that had wanted to stay in its lie. The hare ran in front of me, an easy shot. I did not take it. Hares have to die sometime, but not when I'm watching. Manuel and Zeca groaned. Their anguish rang louder than my appeal to St. James. Hares are big game, in Portugal. I was letting my team down. My companions knew of my American theory that a pointing dog should not hunt fur but looked on this as a feeble excuse, which perhaps it was.

Trooper pointed again, one hind foot raised and muscles trembling. Zeca and Manuel moved in, determined to get this one. I waited. Trooper held firm. Good old Trooper. He was a German shorthaired pointer on his pedigree, a product of American field trials in fact; and when he pointed, he was not fooling. I moved in for the flush. There was no flush. Hedgehogs don't fly.

Trooper lunged and plucked his prickly prey from its bed under the windrowed leaves of a cork oak. I opened my gun, laid it on the ground, and wrestled the dog for the hedgehog. Normally Trooper lost our matches, but in this case I was handicapped by the hedgehog's spines. I fancied that the animal inside them was watching the struggle with detachment. In time I forced Trooper's mouth open and shook the hedgehog loose, unharmed. Then I dragged Trooper from the scene of battle and resumed the chase with as much dignity as I could muster, given the tasteless nature of my companions' remarks. (European hedgehogs, thank goodness, do not disable a dog like American porcupines.)

We began to hear shots in the distance. They sounded, at first, as if several hunters were missing partridges, but the shooting went on longer than partridges would have hung around. Perhaps the targets were grasshoppers or pine cones. This was in the aftermath of the revolution, remember, and the clerks and factory workers who had always wanted to go hunting in the worst way were doing exactly that. They had demanded that all hunting everywhere in Portugal be opened to everybody. It was. Everybody went, or at least everybody of voting age who happened to be male. I don't know whether hunting is sex-linked genetically but something very old must have urged those hordes on a pursuit so foreign to their experience. Pot-bellied professionals behaved like students at a boys' school.

(I ought to know. During occasional dances with the pupils of girls' schools, our skill was not equal to our enthusiasm but we behaved ourselves, more or less, constrained by the presence of certified females, and I suppose the new hunters would have figured out what to do with partridges if there had been any around, but there weren't.)

Trooper found a water hen, eventually. It was edible. In Portugal, this entitles a bird to be shot and I might have risen to the occasion, just to salvage my reputation, if Trooper had not forgotten his training again. The water hen was in a pool so covered with floating leaves that it looked like solid ground. Trooper sighted his victim and jumped. (This direct approach never works. I recall one boy at school who pounced on his date and was severely reprimanded.)

The dog landed in a geyser of leaves and panicked. As a puppy, he had been deprived of water except in his bowl, and he never got used to the stuff. Just couldn't get a foothold. I waded in, gun and all, and pulled him out. I did not laugh. Dogs have feelings. Trooper showed his by shaking so vigorously that my top half got soaked too.

We had completed our loop and were back at the car by now. Manuel and Zeca got in it and honked the horn to guide Figs in from his voyage through the alimentary canal. I did not want to sit down wet but mooched an apple from Zeca. It was of a variety named *riscadinho* that was almost as good as figs, and safer. Then Trooper and I wandered off by ourselves, which is what I had been wanting to do from the beginning.

We headed for a bog that would not have partridges but might have other good things. Trooper came to heel. He hated that but I insisted, because snipe would seldom hold for his fierce points. The snipe wouldn't hold for my bog-trotting, either. I hiked through the mud for a mile or so, trying to land on tussocks instead of the soft places where my boots made sucking sounds. Two or three snipe flushed wild. By then I was winding down, so I slopped back to solid ground and sat on a high spot.

The occasional snipe was passing back and forth over the bog: Trooper's hungry eyes showed me where to look. The birds seemed to be landing on an open mud bank beyond a sluggish stream. Dog and I sneaked closer and hid in some reeds. A snipe flew by and lit, beyond range of gun but not eyes. The bird poked its bill in the mud and caught things too small for me to see. This, mind you, was in the middle of the day. I had read that snipe feed only at night. Their entrails are supposed to be empty, and therefore edible, during the day. It may have been true in some places, but not in Portugal. I had wondered why the entrails here were more piquant than usual.

While the bird had its beak down, I tried to sneak close—a dirty trick, but not dirty enough to work. The snipe flushed out of range. Another then appeared unexpectedly over my head, saw me, and veered off. I dropped it right on the open mud. Trooper plunged to retrieve before I could stop him. I followed. He got to the scene first and was looking busily for the snipe when I arrived. I was puzzled. The bird had seemed dead. Even if it had run or flown, I would have seen it. But it was not there. Two feathers marked the spot. I called Trooper, who approached me warily. I opened his mouth and found another feather. He had somehow slurped that bird—the only thing I had shot for my family's dinner—like an oyster from the half-shell, but more quietly. I grabbed his collar and shook him. He knew why. He tried to look repentant but he wasn't. The snipe was worth it.

Trooper had not forgiven me for taking away a perfectly good hedgehog which, no doubt, he would have managed to open in time, just as I had learned to open oysters. It was all my fault. From the snipe, he wanted only the entrails, which he had learned to extract by a simple squeeze and slurp. Nothing to it. Delicious. And then I always came along and scolded him. No consideration for the other guy. Trooper had therefore experimented with a new way to hide the evidence. Didn't taste bad, either—not as good as innards, but not bad.

We headed back for the car, wherein I intended to imprison my dog till he repented. He looked too content with his snack of snipe. I was hungry myself, and tired, and angry. I glared back at the offender. He was not there. He had sneaked away from his position at heel to do something more creative. I blew a blast on my whistle, a shrill, aggravated, no-fooling blast. Trooper did not come in. I stalked back in search. The dog was easy to find: He was on point. He had stopped while I walked on, then crept a few feet and pointed a dense little tangle of brush. It was gorse, mostly, with a lattice-work of brambles and two of the scraggly little wild olives called *zambujeiras*. Just the place for a rabbit. Trooper was not supposed to point rabbits. I kicked the brush firmly to vent my feelings. What flushed was not a rabbit.

A woodcock twisted off through the limbs. My barrels swung through the bird and bucked from recoil just as the woodcock disappeared behind vegetation. I did not see the outcome, but the shot felt right. Trooper, having perhaps considered the force of my arguments, stayed right where he was pointing, just as if he were showing off in a field trial. He did not even try to lunge in for a nibble of the most delicious entrails in the animal kingdom. I picked up the bird and promised the world's best dog a three-course lunch (two, after the hors d'oeuvre of snipe).

The woodcock, my woodcock, was dressed in soft red-browns. Its big wings draped over my hand. Its small feet curled in my palm, gently, as if brooding a chick. Its odd ball of a head hung down, eyes empty and shiny as black marbles. Big head and eyes are signs of a juvenile, among mammals, so a mammal like me wants to hug a woodcock, though it was not built for the purpose. It was built to satisfy some Pleistocene fantasy by a government like Reagan's, not Salazar's. Its eyes are at the top of its skull, providing good vision even when the long beak is plunged to its hilt in the ground, seeking succulent worms. To make room for the eyes, the brain has left its normal position, rotating backward till it is upside-down. Woodcock migrate to Portugal like other confused creatures, forsaking Scotland or County Kerry or some other place in the lee of perpetual snows.

There are woodcock in America too. On both continents they breed in cool, shady, mythic places and migrate to boring southern resorts. The American bird is like the Eurasian but smaller. The woodcock that migrates from Russia to Portugal is greater than a mastodon. I have chased both woodcocks so you can trust me. My scales, however, weigh virtue. Of all creatures great and small these are the most meritorious, especially when one of them comes so far to feed me.

Hunter and hunted are "aspects of a single power," according to Joseph Campbell.[2] Raise your barrels to a woodcock and you aim also at yourself.[3] Hunting is life and death, yours and that of the bird that consents to be eaten. Omit to aim at yourself and you shoot for amusement. If I seem to be reaching for cosmic reasons, it is because this is not meant to be a game but violence, my violence. Steinbeck warned men not to "trade their violence for the promise of a small increase of life span"[4] and I aim to take his advice, so long as there are ancestors migrating from the Pleistocene to help me.

My companions fondled the woodcock lustfully. (The Portuguese defer to the French on woodcock lore and perhaps we all should, because they hunt and eat these birds with more respect than anyone else. They call them *bécasses*, by the way, and use exactly the same term for dizzy young women in monokinis on Algarve beaches.)

Manuel drove us to a small restaurant for lunch. It was not fashionable. There were no *bécasses* strolling the sidewalk where we sat. There was a metal table with a white paper on top. There was an orange-yellow sun that felt good after eight hours in wet clothes. There was a *presunto* ham hanging from the ceiling inside, suitably moldy. A waiter cut thin slices and brought them to us with fresh goat cheese, garlic-cured olives, and little loaves with brown crunchy crusts. We rushed into the feast as if at a battle.

After lunch, we pretended that we were hunting but found no more game. There was one other hunter out there, not of our party. He was bent and fragile. I asked if he was lost but he wasn't, or at least no more lost than he wanted to be. I fancied him working six days each week under a green eyeshade and going home in the evenings to his wife, Tiny Tim, and a wee dog of mixed terrier and poodle blood. The dog at least was not fantasy because it waddled at his heels, puzzled. He was carrying an antique shotgun with hammers and very long barrels. In his other hand he carried an open umbrella, black like every other umbrella in Portugal. Even in fantasy I could not imagine what he would do with the umbrella if he had to take a shot. There wasn't much danger of that. He was wandering in search of the dream time, ready to settle for any cracked shard of his violence.

WALLS

Look at this knight climbing down from the watchtower by the aid of his lance, with the heads of the two men who were on guard as a trophy, and returning to the ambush where he had left his followers. See how, by a combination of subterfuge and daring, he gains possession of Evora. It was in memory of this unparalleled feat that the city afterwards adopted as its coat-of-arms the figure of the stalwart Giraldo the Fearless, with the two heads in his hand.

CAMÕES, *The Lusiads*, Canto Eight

Adriano wore his lunch jacket of good brown wool till we left the Algarve and entered a province less frequented by foreigners. He pulled off the road, then, and into the *Retiro dos Caçadores*. The Hunters' Retreat was as clearly part of the Alentejo as the Disco Caravel had been part of the Algarve. The door was open and the customers (or ex-customers, or potential customers) were standing outside, waiting for something to happen. Adriano got out of the car, smiled, and stretched. There was not a tourist in sight. He took off his tweed coat.

The place was a *tasca*, meaning that it sold wine, beer, *aguardente*, and some exotic drinks to make the tipsy feel creative. It was not, however, a bar in the American sense. Bars are for those who wish to bar the light. Bars are wombs, dark and thick and fluid. Bars have small doors that close automatically and no windows at all. The *Retiro dos Caçadores* had big windows like a grocery store and the door was propped open. Inside, it smelled not of beer and urine but of the whole Alentejo, dust and sun. The place served more than alcohol, too. It wa's like Alice's Restaurant, where you could get any doggoned thing you wanted.

I wanted a cup of tea. It may have been the only one sold in the *Retiro dos Caçadores* that month, but the owner showed no surprise. I knew that he was the *patrão* because *tascas* cannot afford adult employees—just *patrões*, bosses without subordinates, entrepreneurs who work sixteen hours a day. This one was pleased to see us. He had built up some kind of business in Mozambique and lost it when Portugal lost the war. He was working just as hard on his second career. He was making less money and growing less hair, but his attitudes had not shrunk. If I had ordered cocoa or maté instead of tea, he would have rummaged around for what his customer wanted. He was Portuguese and had discovered the world.

Adriano and I continued north on back roads, avoiding the main route between perpetual snows and beaches. We both relaxed. I did not even depress my imaginary brake pedal when we approached a boy pedaling between somewhere and nowhere. He heard us coming, jumped from his bicycle, and pulled it off the road. Clever as a village pup, that lad. He'd live forever. I waved at him and he waved back.

We swept around a motorcycle on a curve. It was barely visible beneath a couple carrying groceries home from the market. The man was in charge of the handlebars and the woman was in charge of the sack. I reckoned that they got much of their food from the earth, not the market, because each was strong of arm and leg. Each, however, had a belly in the shape of a basketball. The woman had the sack perched on top of hers. One would have thought it was impossible to accommodate three such food containers on one scrawny seat.

The Portuguese motorcycle is a counterfeit donkey. It carries as much as the animal and does it faster, but with more complaining. Fuel consumption is in both cases inconsequential. The cycle's engine is tiny because almost no one has a motorcycle for fun. For sporting purposes, the appropriate two-wheeled vehicle is a racing bicycle, the kind with a human engine.

(The American motorcycle is a counterfeit charger. My first had a thumping side-valve engine bigger than that in most Portuguese cars. The machine had been built for carrying messages during World War II, a romantic purpose, and by the time I got it much later, someone had made it into a "chopper," which is to say that he had cut off most of the fenders that he had probably wrecked at the same time he put the dent in the fuel tank. I added a coat of metallic red paint. The engine was hard to start. I would bounce up and down on the lever, producing whuff-whuffs but no vroom-vrooms, and once some guys in a gas station laughed and said, "You ain't got enough ass on you." When she was running, though—I gave her a gender when the engine started—she would throb between my knees and do anything I asked of her, though we never quite found what I was looking for.)

Adriano took me to the city of Beja first, and the part I remember is his story. Its hero was Gonçalo Mendes de Maia, nicknamed O Lidador: The Battler. He had earned the title by celebrating his birthday with a foray at the Moors. This was in 1170. The Moors were glad to oblige and The Battler took on the King of Tangier twice in the same day. On the second scuffle, The Battler lost his life and won immortality. If that seems like a poor trade, consider that he was ninety years old.[1]

I have a modest proposal: We should restock Moors like trout, raising them in a hatchery if necessary. Think of the money they could save us on nursing homes.

The Moors were in Portugal for almost five centuries and in Spain for two more—longer than Americans have been in America. When the Moors were expelled, however, they were not ennobled like the last of the Mohicans. I detected no more interest in Moors than gypsies. Moors were just the generic bad guys who made heroes of one's ancestors. Of course Moorish genes were left behind, but the genes of the human species count for little without culture.

The Moors do seem to have changed the way the land was used. You can still see noras—waterwheels that dip with buckets and discharge into irrigation ditches. These may, in turn, water terraces built by the Moors.

I would like to know whether Moors had anything to do with the mattocks. They and other tools of the hoe family are invariably used for tillage—big ones to break the soil for spring planting, little ones to do the weeding later. All are of heavy cast iron with handles handmade from peeled limbs. Any peasant woman in the Alentejo can do what would be impossible for me, bending from the hips till her trunk is nearly horizontal and swinging the heavy implement for hours. Mattock is an Old English word and the tool it describes must have been used in America too, at one time, but we invariably prefer spades now. Perhaps we got too tall for the old ways.

When Mark Twain visited Portugal in 1867, he saw "not a wheelbarrow in the land—they carry every thing on their heads, or on donkeys."[2] I saw no wheelbarrows either, but the donkey carts struck me as a better idea.

In one remote Alentejo village called Salto, I saw women—and only women—carrying water from the fountain on their heads. I do not know whether the men were culturally forbidden to help, as they are in the Arab world. Perhaps they were just following the universal male policy of doing nothing that a woman can be persuaded to do instead. The Alentejo women did not need much persuasion. They were the most vigorous housekeepers I have encountered, fanatical by comparison to those in northern Portugal.

The weather may have something to do with it. In the Alentejo, the winter is not cold enough to demand huddling. You keep warm in pursuit of cleanliness. You iron, cook, bake, and scrub—especially scrub. You use a solution of water and bleach everywhere: floors, walls, and furniture. You scrub till the grain of the wood stands out. Then you go out and whitewash your house. At greater intervals you paint its base with one of the bright colors used for boats and donkey carts. You turn a low, rectangular, mud-brick dwelling into a model of simplicity and cleanliness. It is the best of architecture, a place for good dreams, elevated from squalor by energy pure and simple.

If you are male, the routine is different. You work the fields and vineyards. You herd your pigs to forage on the acorns of the holm oaks. Time permitting, you take your gun and do some foraging of your own, and this is the part of the routine that I know best. You hike out before dawn and come back at midday to bread from the clay oven, cheese from the ewes, and water from the fountain. You watch sun filtering through shutters and listen to women outside talking about shiftless men. You nap on ironed sheets.

In the afternoon, there were people all over the sides of the rural roads. They had parked their cars and cycles. Some had walked from their houses on foot. Perhaps, Adriano thought, they were collecting pine nuts, but then we saw people far from pines. Perhaps they were collecting snails, but no, snails are not active (even for

snails) in the afternoon. Ah—it was the *Dia da Espiga*, Wheatear
Day. The religious term is Ascension Day, but the people were
collecting symbols older than those of Christianity. Each family was
picking, first, the ear of wheat, which represented an abundance of
bread. Next was an olive branch for peace, and then wild flowers
(poppies and daisies, I thought) for happiness and love. At home
these growing things would be dried and kept from one year to the
next, blessing the house. We did not spoil the mood by running over
any of the seekers of happiness. Adriano slowed and we craned
down the windows. The scents of plants for the bouquets drifted
into the car. We decided to stay for the night in the small town of
Vidigueira, where people were committed to bread, peace, happiness, and love.

In town, Adriano pulled up beside a woman carrying a basket of
laundry on her head. The thing looked like an athletic feat to me—
always does—and I would not have bothered her, but Adriano
knew better. She was glad to talk to us and the weight of the basket
was as nothing compared to the burden of gossip seeking an audience. She told us that there were two *pensões* in Vidigueira, and
which of them was best, and who owned each, and a little of the
family history.

A *pensão* is, literally, a pension. Call it a boarding house in
American terms. Call it anything but a motel. Adriano and I wanted
a *pensão* because it would be cheap, would have no foreigners but
me, and would be in an old house near the center of town. It would
have good home cooking, too, and we had worked up an appetite
deploring the Algarve.

We drove to the best of the pensions (according to our laun-
drywoman's guide) but found it crowded. The people seemed to be
in the bar listening to the blare of a football game. Adriano shared
my dislike (both un-Portuguese and un-American) for crowds. We
drove, therefore, to the other *pensão*. On our way, we passed the
local headquarters of the Socialist party, which seemed abandoned.
Posters peeled from dirty walls, a window hung ajar, and the party's
flag drooped in tatters. Adriano paused and deplored. The decadence of the headquarters violated his sense of propriety but not, I
am sure, his opinion of the party. We had talked about that.

For Portuguese conservatives, the Socialists are doubly hard to accept because, after the revolution of 1974, it was they who mounted effective resistance to the Communists. The right had been knocked out of combat. Imagine how it feels not only to be threatened by Communists but to be saved from them by Socialists.

Our *pensão* of choice was on a narrow street opposite a town park. As we stepped from the car, a skinny partridge dog in the park was working on a plastic bag with remnants of a sandwich in it. She watched me, fearful, and hurried to lick the bread and meat out of the plastic. I guessed that she had more experience with garbage than partridges.

My room was small but it had a good mattress resting on a wooden platform, not a box spring. (Box springs are a sign of decadence. They sag, no matter how firm, and the spine sags with them. I have this from a physician who attributes a portion of American backaches to box springs.) The bathroom was down the hall, as it is to be expected in pensions, but the room had a sink and bidet. (The bidet, like the platform bed, is a product of advanced civilization but considered vaguely sinful by Anglo-Saxons. I wonder whether the British in the Algarve have figured out what to do with the bidets in their new houses.)

Adriano and I intended to walk around town, but first we ordered dinner from our host. There was no choice of dishes: The butcher had been closed on this holiday, and the pension had in its refrigerator only *bifes* for a main course. *Bife* is pronounced like beef, more or less, and derives from that English word, but the meaning has drifted. A *bife* is a boneless strip of meat, usually from a cow too old to give more milk—the dish of last resort all over Latin Europe. Our host, when grilled by Adriano, assured us that these particular *bifes* were exceptions to the rule.

Adriano then raised the sad affair of the Socialist party headquarters. Someone, he said, ought to do something.

Our host agreed, but he blamed the Socialists for setting up headquarters in Vidigueira in the first place. This town, he said, did not want Socialists. "I am a Communist," he explained.

I tried to conceal my enthusiasm. My collection had been in need of a Communist. The Portuguese version was the real thing,

devoted to good old Marxist ideas that did not work and at passionate odds with the reticent, conservative national character. The
two main Portuguese parties—Socialist and Social Democratic—
were your standard center-left and center-right groupings, much
like Democratic and Republican or Labor and Conservative. Dull.
Portuguese Communists, on the other hand, were devoted fans of
Stalin, an endangered species.

Adriano and I took our walk and found the residents of Vidigueira remarkably interested in Ascension Day, for a bunch of
Communist atheists. Bells were ringing and the whole town was
drifting toward church. Everybody had time to look at everybody
else. (Things like this must have happened in America once; we had
an old song about the "Easter Parade," though I never saw one.)
The boys of Vidigueira were dressed in neat suits but the stars of the
soft spring evening were the little girls, all fluffed out in pale dresses,
skipping a few steps and then slowing down and trying to look like
ladies. It would have been worth running for political office if you
could hug those children.

Adriano walked me back to our *pensão* by a different route. We
passed by Vidigueira's *Casa de Saúde* (House of Health). It was, if
I understood correctly, a junior-grade hospital with some official
involvement. Anyone could get emergency care there at any time. I
asked Adriano, a lawyer, if the physicians were not pulling out of
small towns like this because of problems with liability suits. I did
not manage to explain myself across the culture gap. People did not
sue physicians, Adriano said; they were there to help.

"Here you are," said our host when he brought the *bifes*: "ten-
der enough for a suckling babe." They were as tough as the genuine
leather soles that Adriano demands for all of his shoes. I yearned for
chicken sandwiches in the Burger King. When our host asked how
the meal was, Adriano said nothing. Adriano does not tell lies. I
said the food was fine. (Well, the fried potatoes were all right.) I
was sure that even a Communist would not serve such a dinner on
purpose. He simply believed that what he wanted to be good *was*
good—a matter of Marxist training. He suggested a bottle of red
wine. His cellar, he said, had the world's best. It was the wrong
thing to say but we ordered a bottle anyhow, in desperation. It

arrived and was excellent, for five dollars. The bread was good too. We nibbled and sipped and the meal would have been saved, but for the television in the dining room. It was playing the evening soap opera.

Even Communists get the soaps. Portugal is too small and (so far) too poor to produce *fotonovelas* on its own, but it imports them from Brazil or America. The Brazilian version has the advantage of being in Portuguese already. It is Brazilian Portuguese, which has undergone more continental drift than, say, Boston English as opposed to London English, but the Portuguese are eager for corruption. Each evening for what seems an eternity but may be only an hour, the country immerses itself in lather. It is the real thing. There are good guys and bad guys who are distinguished by the music that accompanies them, like cowboys with white hats and black hats. The main function of the guys is as in classical ballet: to give the girls a spin. The good guys languish over the girls and the bad guys make trouble for them. The girls have all the fun, which is remarkable, considering that they are not even bright enough to tell the heroes from the villains.

Our host turned out to be the owner of the partridge-and-garbage dog. She sneaked into the dining room, took one look at the *fotonovela*, seconded my opinion, and crawled under the table to eat the *bifes* I offered. Then she curled at my feet and went to sleep. I kept my back to the screen and tried to turn down the volume, but everyone else wanted to hear the suds bubbling. The place reminded me of America in 1950. I had crossed the ocean in search of the Noble Savage and found him square-eyed.

The news came next. Lead item: An English Desdemona had offended an Angolan Othello who had disposed of her body near Lisbon. I knew all about it. It had been the main news item since I arrived, unfolding day by day as the courts did their meticulous, salacious business. Portugal was making progress in petty crime but still had so little of the violent stuff that the casts had to be imported, like those of soap operas.

Except for our Communist host, everybody in Vidigueira had a good time for the rest of the evening. I lay in bed listening to fireworks popping, dogs yipping, girls squealing, and boys shouting. Hannibal, Missouri, must have sounded like that a long time ago.

By the time I came down to breakfast in the morning, Adriano had hiked out to a newsstand for his copy of O Dia (The Day). It was the morning newspaper of those Portuguese who remembered the days of serious, decent government, the days when papers printed good news instead of trash. I admired the steadfastness of character required to read this paper. It was as hard to chew as leather steaks, but that was not the point. O Dia was a part of life, a consistent element, an agent of coherence, a statement. In Portugal, a serious man was expected to have a project of life, and to live by it without equivocation. The alternative was to make a declaration of error, resign any public positions (which was called "taking a walk in the desert"), and return later, chastened, with a new project. Adriano had undergone no such change of heart. He therefore unfolded O Dia at the breakfast able to make his position clear—politely, perfectly clear.

I have a debt to Communists that ought to be acknowledged. It was incurred on a rainy day in 1981, when Zeca Tabuada and I tried to go hunting in the Alentejo. We bounced down a dirt road and stopped at a stream that we had forded on other occasions, but this time the water was high and brown. I wanted to park, cross the stream on foot, and walk the extra mile or so to the hills where we weren't going to find any partridges anyhow. Zeca wanted to chance the ford. He had great confidence in the car (my car), and while he was willing to take some exercise while hunting, he saw no point in exaggerating. I must have been drowsy, because this line of reasoning persuaded me. Halfway across the ford, the air intake sucked in water and stopped the engine instantly, with a clunk. The cylinders were full of water.

We opened the doors to step out. Brown water rushed in over the car's new upholstery. We waded ashore and looked back damply at the vehicle. I walked for the nearest farmhouse. Before I got there, a tractor came along, headed for the fields. It was driven by a man. It towed a large, open trailer occupied by a score of women in long peasant dresses. They came from the Communist cooperative that had seized the land from its old owners after the revolution of 1974. I explained my predicament. They would have seen it anyhow, in another mile. You may be sure that I displayed humility: It's easy to do that, with water running down the back of one's neck. I kept a tight upper lip, showing that the humor of the situation was not lost on me. My shiny new car sure looked funny out there, leaving an oil slick.

The women stood there in the trailer and looked at me, faces blank. Then they drove on to the ford and everybody jumped down—everybody except for the male driver of the tractor. The women waded into the stream and half dragged, half carried my car back to dry land. The tractor driver chugged across after them, lifting his feet above the flood. (The revolution of 1974 had nothing to do with relations between the sexes.)

Many farms in the Alentejo had been seized by their peasants after the revolution. In 1975, there were some 550 cooperatives, many really communes. By 1990, when Adriano and I took our trip, the number had shrunk to 210. "The land reform has been destroyed," one of the leaders of a cooperative had said to a journalist. "We were given no help by the governments that followed the revolution." The cooperatives were, for the most part, labor-intensive and inefficient, driven by every motive except profit. Even cash crops went into a decline. By the late seventies, it was hard to find good-quality olive oil in this nation of olives.

There will not be many communes in Portugal's future. Adriano told me that there was even a new law returning some of the hunting to private control. Maybe one of these years I'll go back and find a partridge.

Adriano looked bouncy. He had enjoyed reading O Dia while a Communist served breakfast. He had needed a spirit-lifter, after Sagres. With an infidel trounced so early in the day, Adriano was eager to show me other battlefields, repositories of the Portuguese soul. He drove through Vidigueira smiling, and when Adriano smiles, the world smiles. Cars coming onto the main road stopped when they saw him coming. He doffed his cap to the drivers. He stopped at a pedestrian crossing (a startling event), waving his hand graciously at a *menina* waiting to cross. She laughed and trotted to the other side. I may have commented that she would uphold the honor of the *pátria* on any beach in the Algarve. Adriano said that he had noticed. He made a point of noticing, even when out with his wife, and she encouraged him, wise woman. "I always look at the *meninas*," he said.

Menina is a useful word. It is polite for unmarried females of all ages; one does not have to choose between "girl," "woman," and "lady," as in English, which avoids trouble when one guesses wrong. *Menina* implies only femininity and eligibility: current, prospective, or retrospective. A female baby is always a *menina*. A female at eighty is a *menina* if she has never married. I surmised that the females Adriano preferred to watch were in between those extremes.

Adriano insisted on driving me to Monsaraz. I was not keen to go. Monsaraz is a sight—what tourists see. We went, and I was wrong. I had not realized that Nuno Álvares Pereira's tracks run through Monsaraz. He had been military commander there before he led the battle for Portuguese independence at Aljubarrota.

I would follow Nuno Álvares wherever he went, except that woodcock and trout lead me off the track. They are heroes too. It is easy for them—their natural condition—but for humans, heroism is hard even once. Nuno Álvares got it right every time. His path is marked by battles and fortresses (of which Monsaraz is one), and his deeds are attested by multiple independent witnesses, some of whom were his foes. He can, therefore, be followed physically, unlike Sir Galahad.

The Alentejo countryside near Monsaraz is the kind of place where you would expect things to have happened long ago, even if you had not read the history. In America, only the deserts of the southwest feel so old, and for the same reason: There is not enough vegetation to cover ruins. Monsaraz is rocks on top of rock, a walled city on a hill too big to be called a boulder. In the middle of the city is a castle built after the Moors were pushed out. I suppose that every fortification on this hill for millennia was built on the ruins of earlier defenses. It was where anyone defending the countryside would have put his headquarters, looking eastward into Spain.

Walls define Europe as roads define America. Walls helped to avoid nasty surprises, gave defenders time to muster their forces, and let the burghers sleep more soundly. Walls never worked forever, but they worked while Nuno Álvares was in charge.

Adriano parked outside the walls of Monsaraz and we walked in. There had been no obtrusive progress except for television antennas: The rest had been preserved by poverty and, more recently, by tourist dollars. The houses were still of stacked schist. The streets were little more than donkey paths, and three men with hammers were repairing one of them with new cobbles. Adriano watched the masons while I climbed the old castle's tower and looked out over the dream time.

A gust from the Atlantic stirred the hair on the back of my neck. What passed below was only what wind-blown clouds chose to reveal. Shafts of sun spotlighted tumble-down farms, flocks of sheep, and a lonely shepherd. The walls of a village flickered white. Beyond them, a highway shone in the sun and vanished, blown out by the breeze.

Cavalry from Spain moved along that road once. With help from the sun, I would have seen flashes of armor soon after the knights crossed the Guadiana River. At my alarm, Nuno Álvares would have rushed to meet the invasion. His troops were minutemen, mostly, peasants and burghers. The Spanish forces would have disdained such "badly armed peons" till the horses hit "a wall of lances glued to the earth."[3] The invaders, not the defenders, would have been impaled.

A church bell rang ten times and a dog yapped in reply. I climbed down from the tower and walked the rest of the town with Adriano. Twice more the hair on the back of my neck felt as if the wind were blowing it. The first time was in the street by a little house marked "Saint Constable." Nuno Álvares was said to have lived there. A constable, in his time, was the highest military leader appointed by a king. Nuno Álvares had been the best of all and I'd have wanted to sleep in his room if I'd known, even if the place was for tourists.

The second place that felt odd was the church of St. Mary of Lake. I could not have explained why I walked in, but the doors were big and open to the morning. No one else was there—not even a woman in black on her knees. Columns with fading paint stood beside me like old comrades. Most of the place was plain and worn and scrubbed, which helped. The fantastic gilt carvings on the walls kept their distance. The smell was not incense, not dust, not Alentejo sunshine, not anything else I could recognize, but it recognized me. Call it the odor of six hundred years of prayers. Some of them had been offered by the Saint Constable before his battles.

We made it to Évora for lunch. This was too much sightseeing for anyone in a day, more than I would want in the average century, but we were in a hurry to move on to things that were not sights and Évora stood in the way. During the four years when I had lived in Portugal, I had driven around the great walls dozens of times without entering. I made excuses about not being a wall person, but Adriano did not let me get away with that nonsense. The Évora wall is (I imagine) the only feature of Portugal that would catch the attention of commuters in space. We traveled around the fortification for miles. It was a monument to the ferocity of Christians, against whom the Moors built it.

The wall stopped the Christian armies, so *Giraldo Sem Pavor* (Gerald the Fearless) took it on. During the autumn of 1165 he assembled a few good men on a dark, rainy night and urged them over the top. They decided that they were not quite *that* good. He then shamed them by climbing the wall himself, beheading two guards, and scrambling back down with the evidence. Faced with bloody proof that the thing could be done, his men followed him over the top and slaughtered the sleeping Moorish defenders. This is what happens when you count on walls for defense.[4]

Conquests are hard work, especially when the last full meal was inedible, so Adriano and I rushed for lunch. He parked the car outside the great walls and we walked inside.

Évora is laid out on the original, narrow, twisting, cobbled streets; and the churches, of which there are said to be forty-eight, are built on the foundations of mosques. The whole town, for that matter, is stone and brick stacked in infinite ways over infinite years according to the infinite whims of Romans, Moors, and Portuguese. There is a visual interest that cities built with machinery cannot approach. Tourists, of course, view the whole as a hypermarket of handicraft. Every little winding street has a brace of restaurants and a covey of sidewalk tables to serve the crowds. The place Adriano found was good just the same.

Each of us started with a bowl of thistle soup. I wished that it would catch on in Montana, which is the thistle capital of the world (and we control them by spraying). Next Adriano had fricasseed pork tongue, considered better than beef. I ordered the plain-sounding *carne alentejana*—Alentejo meat. It violated the dietary laws of at least two great religions, so it was sinfully good. The meat came from free-ranging pigs fattened on acorns. Mixed in were tiny clams in their shells. Adriano had enough sense to skip the next course, but I had a piece of almond cake, heavy and dense. We both had deep sighs.

Adriano had another sight in mind but I was tired of walls, surfeited with sensations, bored by splendors built long ago with no sweat of mine. The best thing in Évora was a crowd of preschool children linked hand-in-hand so that none could stray. One little girl was crying because a grasshopper the size of a sparrow had lit on her temple. It must have flown a long way to provide torment, because grasshoppers have no business in stone cities. I wanted to brush off the insect and give the child a comforting pat, but Adriano beat me to it. "It's just a *gafanhoto*," he said. The children walked on, giggling now. I glanced at Adriano, who was beaming, and realized that I too was smiling all over.

Adriano led me to the Church of St. Francis. I did not want to enter. Adriano guided me in. We wound through shadows and bought two tickets from a quiet old man. Our destination was the Chapel of Bones. The bones were human. Stacks of them formed the walls, stacks with bits of femur protruding and skulls, big skulls and little ones. I touched them gently. They were textures of lives, rough in most places. I comforted a child's temple, almost smooth.

"There was plague in those days," said the quiet old man. That might have put the date in the fifteenth century.

The bones were bare and disconnected but for one skeleton. It was of a young person, I thought, but with narrow waist and womanly hips and shreds of flesh left in a dress brown with decay. The dress exposed her pelvis and what was, or had been, her sex. Leave it to the padres.

Near the doorway were hanks of women's hair. They were *promessas*, vows from those still living. One read "*promessa* from Rita Batista when she had a bad headache." I did not have a headache, but I put the remaining coins from my pocket in a collection plate, little pieces of brass and nickel tinkling a soft plea.

My body reentered fresh air before my thoughts. What strange mind had built that chapel? Why? One skull on a philosopher's desk represents mortality. A thousand skulls represent atrocity.

We walked the cobbles of the walled city toward our car. The narrow streets were all contrast at that hour, sharp-edged shadows and low shafts of sun.

SUNLIGHT

Veloso in his astonishment gave a great shout. "Men," he called, "what strange game have we here! If it be possible that the ancient pagan cults still persist, this is a glade sacred to the nymphs and we have stumbled on something beyond man's farthest desire. It is obvious that there are greater and more excellent things to be discovered in the world than we unthinking mortals dream of. Let us follow these goddesses and find out if they be real, or only creatures of the imagination." And with that they all set off, swifter than any deer, and gave chase along the banks.

CAMÕES, *The Lusiads*, Canto Nine

Some bishop with a higher level of consciousness would have razed Évora's Temple of Diana, if given the chance. It is bright, simple, and open. The city's other places of worship are dark, ornate, and confined—what you would expect from medieval humans within medieval walls. The Temple was built before the Dark Ages. Romans occupied the Alentejo, then, and when they left, the Portuguese turned the structure into a fortress, preserving it till it could be excavated. No one knows whether it was originally dedicated to the goddess of the chase. It just looks as if it ought to be Diana's Temple, marble columns standing like trees up there on a hilltop in the sun.

The Alentejo has always been Diana's territory, anyhow. Human hunter-gatherers arrived at least a million years ago. Modern (Cro-Magnon) humans moved in from Africa some forty centuries back,[1] replacing the primitive Neanderthals. The woolly rhinoceros and giant deer did not last either. Perhaps they could not survive the end of the ice age, or perhaps the latest human arrivals were too clever, and too well armed. It would be good to know.

This was when the myths began. Of all times forever, this was when European man was most naked, easiest to see. We were physically and emotionally identical to what we are now. We were as intelligent, obtuse, artistic, crude, devoted, and violent. That much is clear from the paintings and burials. Of contrivances, we would have had little more than we could hack from wood or chip of stone. We would have had more heroes because it took heroism to keep a family safe and fed. We would have had more villains because there would have been fewer restraints. Some of the villains and heroes would have been the same. They would have died with no record but a wild bull painted on a wall, a mammoth's tusk carved in the shape of Venus, or a spear interred with human bones.

Arabs and Berbers followed the same route north in the eighth century A.D. By then, the glaciers had retreated and the flood they released had become part of the creation myth. The latest wave of immigrants could no longer walk from Africa into Iberia on dry land, but the voyage was a short one in ships. The Rock of Gibraltar had been beckoning humans northward since time began. It is still visible from Morocco.

The Moors were not organized like hunter-gatherer cultures. They invaded a region in which agriculture had made a start already, then guided the Alentejo's scarce water onto its wide fields. Food was produced so efficiently that some people were freed from the labor of subsistence. Their leisure was, depending on your point of view, either original sin (the apple of Adam) or the foundation of civilization.

The Moors distributed their wealth through a structure of social classes. I am skipping over a lot of history—but perhaps not distorting it—by suggesting that the old ways persisted through different societies at least until the revolution of 1974. Christians replaced Moors during the reconquest and the change seemed important to both sides, but the lives of the peasants would not have been much altered when Évora's mosques were converted to churches.

One universal feature of the class structures was this: The poor got the farming and the privileged got the hunting. Portuguese falconers succeeded Moors without missing a wing beat. It was paradoxical, in a way, because hoes were vastly more efficient than falcons at producing food. One has to conclude that Diana was more appealing than Ceres. Two of the earliest works in the Portuguese language were on falconry.[2] In the fourteenth century, King Fernando's retinue included fifty falcons and hawks. Keeping even one of them happy was an endless job for a skilled attendant, but this was the best and purest of sports, the one fit for a king.

Fernando's successor was João I. He was an energetic ruler who, among other things, backed up Nuno Álvares at the battle of Aljubarrota, prevailed against five-to-one odds, and secured Portuguese independence from Spain. (More on that in chapter 10.) People today write autobiographies with less cause, but Dom João dedicated his last years "to literature and to composing a book on hunting."[3]

Harsh medieval laws make it clear that nobility and peasantry clashed over the hunting privilege. (One keeps hearing of "the oldest profession," and I suppose that the reference is to poaching.) The peasants won the argument in the revolution of 1974. So did the clerks and factory workers. For purposes of hunting, private property was abolished and the countryside was overrun—literally. To grasp the scale of the thing, imagine a world in which sex had been repressed for a thousand years, which may not take much of a stretch. Imagine, next, that anyone, anywhere, was encouraged to do anything that felt good. The parallel is not perfect, but it gives some idea of the enthusiasm and inexperience of most who poured into the Alentejo's fields on the opening day of partridge season. As spectacle, it resembled an American decade that most readers will recall.

As hunting, it was the tragedy of the commons.[4] Everyone had an incentive to consume what he could before someone else beat him to it; no one had an incentive to conserve the resource. Fortunately, the partridges were not like other kinds of communal property. They did not consent to be consumed (which is one definition of game). As they grew somewhat scarcer, they grew much wiser. When private management became possible again in about 1990, partridge populations rebounded in one breeding season, showing more resilience than, say, the olive groves.

The bigger problem, for me, was a dearth of the taboos that govern America. Our ancestors gave us rules and self-respect in the same package, one nation indivisible. The list of what we may shoot is short; the list of what we may not shoot is the rest of creation. Songbird slaying is the moral equivalent of child molesting, and less frequently practiced. I therefore found it hard to stomach a saying of postrevolutionary Portuguese man: *O que vem à rede é peixe.* Literally, it meant "What's in the net is fish." In the field, it meant that anything remotely edible was in trouble.

*   *   *

On the eve of opening day 1981, I drove south into the Alentejo with Manuel, Zeca, and Figs. There was an American greenhorn with us too—an air force sergeant named Earl who had recently arrived in Lisbon. He thought that the walk would be pleasant, poor lad. Manuel and I took it upon ourselves to advance Earl's cultural education.

We began at the beginning: olives. They tasted interesting, we reminded him, even in California, where they are picked green, cured in lye, turned black by oxidation, pitted, canned, and heated to a high temperature—all by a sophisticated industrial process designed to remove as much flavor as possible.[5] Olives are better still when cured everywhere else in the world by older processes. In Portugal, most olives are picked ripe for maximum flavor, then cured at home. Sometimes the cook adds herbs or garlic. The color is natural. There is no cooking. The pits are never removed. The vats or jugs are always open.

For the best in olives, however, one must seek them out where they grow. One must pluck them from their tree, bite into them, and roll them around on the tongue before their subtle flavor fades. So we told Earl. By a happy coincidence, as we pointed out, olives reach their peak of succulence when partridge season opens in autumn. On our drive to the Alentejo, we smacked our lips at the sight of neat gray-green rows of olive trees stretching, sometimes, for miles beside the road.

We stopped at the shepherd's yard near Vila Boim where we intended to camp. It was not in an olive grove, but there were a few gnarled, old olive trees anyhow. (There usually are, in Portugal. An Alentejo family can make it through the winter on olive oil, bread, sardines, wine, and a little mutton.) Earl asked if the shepherd would mind, and he didn't, so Earl took his first taste of fresh olive. It was not what he expected; we could see that by the color of his ears. But Earl maintained the sangfroid expected of an American soldier, spitting the fruit out casually and shaking his head.

An uncured olive is bitter beyond belief, even when it comes from a tree developed for large, mild fruit. I do not understand how humans first guessed that the thing might be eaten. Hunter-gatherers seem to have made the discovery by 6000 B.C., during the

Old Stone Age. Later they domesticated the fruit and developed the advanced curing methods that made it rewarding. I suppose that the secret was not genius but time, and hunger.

The olive tree is not on the Portuguese flag, but it should be. It is old, small, and twisted but it survives on dry, rocky ground. The fruit is bitter if you taste it wrong. You ought to try a nibble, just the same.

There was a big lean-to shed with piles of loose hay that we shared with a newborn lamb. It had been rejected by its dam, so it decided to join the human race. (Lambs are almost clever, but their brains atrophy as they grow.) The five of us took turns mothering it: more rewarding for us than for the lamb, perhaps, but it lived as long as we were there, which was better than the shepherd had expected. Its soft bleats smoothed our fragrant beds in the hay.

The Portuguese were up before dawn, boiling coffee and drinking it with shots of brandy. I delayed the operation by eating a huge bowl of muesli. (Brandy rampant on a field of coffee is another Portuguese national symbol, showing a fierceness beyond lions and unicorns.) Then we slopped off in wet grass, headed for a pale streak in the eastern sky. My dog Trooper, at my heel, was shivering; he had hated wet skin since his escape from pneumonia. At least one of the humans—me—wondered why he was not home in bed with a warm wife. The sky was gray by the time we formed a line and started hunting, each of us 40 yards or so away from the next.

The birds were there. We heard the beat of wings flushing ahead of us in the dark: probably a family group, or covey. Like other gallinaceous (chickenlike) birds, most partridges die before they are a year old, whether they are hunted or not. They are in that sense an annual crop, prolific as wheat. To make up for the high mortality, hens may raise two broods of a dozen or more chicks each. It is hard to believe, in October, that so many large, fat birds issued from one source.

Another bunch flushed wild ahead of us, dark shapes skimming over the top of a hill. The light was still dim when our chance came. A covey appeared over a rise and was upon us. I saw one fall and heard Manuel's shot, in that order. A bird crossed in front of me and I swung the barrels ahead of it. I did not hear my shot but the bird fell. Trooper raced me for it and got there first, but before he could munch I shouted "whoa!" He pointed instead of grabbing. I picked up a perfect partridge.

You could get an idea of the feeling by taking a cold shower and then toweling off under a heat lamp. Within seconds, you turn from cold and wet to warm and dry. You had feared that you might hike all day without a partridge, and now you are illuminated by the knowledge that you will, thank God, bring home a worthwhile meal. You have not had to *trazer o chibato*. (It means literally, "bring the goat." My friends no longer recalled the origin of the expression. I surmise that the hunters of once-upon-a-time were expected to buy goat when they failed to shoot something of merit.)

The sun woke up, then, and fluffed itself out like a partridge after the dews of night. We walked faster to catch it while it was still sitting on a ridge top. The sun had not risen for a year, not so close and plump and friendly.

The Hunter's Moon is invoked, occasionally, by poets who have not done their field research, but in fact the moon is a goddess of settled planters. Roaming hunter-gatherers ask for the sun's help.[6] When it comes, it is better than herb-scented sheets, better than crushed strawberries with red wine. The Hunter's Sun turns goat into partridge. The warmth fills me like a balloon and I float up to the red lines in the sky. I will not die at dawn because it is a beginning, but when my body is worn out, I will come back at sunrise as a partridge for some other hunter. I will be a hero after all.

There is no explaining the happiness explosion that comes at dawn. It is too old and simple to fit these dark, ornate, inward-looking times. It is a relic of the time when all of us faced the sunrise on foot. Some expectation in us is frustrated when we turn our days on with a switch and commute to the same damned climate-controlled job. We try to switch ourselves on too, but the stimulants don't work. And then we do something ridiculous, like chasing partridges in the dewy grass, and rapture flies by.

At dawn, we were believers against the odds. There had to be game in such country. It was never desolate and never sublime, never endless and never cramped. There was space in the prairies and shelter in the trees. There was time for long steps.

We walked over open ridges and dropped into evergreen oaks—*sobreiras*, mostly, cork oaks planted by jays dropping acorns, then midwifed by humans. If you looked closely, you could see that most had been pruned long ago into three or four wide-spreading branches. The trees were twice as broad as they were tall, and we walked through their shade when the day warmed. The oaks' trunks and bigger limbs were almost smooth because their bark—the cork—was peeled every nine years. Scattered as individuals and in small grove are *azinheiras*, holm oaks that produced big edible acorns instead of bark. Most of them had been pruned too. They were considered fruit trees, as good as chestnuts for flavoring pork. I gathered a few acorns for roasting.

Human touches were either subtle, like the pruned oaks; or ancient, like the remnants of windmills on breezy rises; or tasty, like the ripe figs, of which I also gathered a few. There were no walls, no roads, no bad smells. But there were too many hunters who were innocent in all the wrong ways. We heard them where we could not see them, popping away at anything that hopped or fluttered. The tasty hares made sense. The jays may at least have been edible. The hoopoes, though: Would anyone cook a hoopoe? They are birds of small body and spectacular black-and-white plumage, migrants from Africa like humans, and they share with humanity another characteristic: They foul their nests.

It was time to get lost in the rough stuff, anyhow, time to escape the line of skirmish. And so I did. Manuel was kind enough to call a meeting of the general staff first. Zeca and Earl volunteered to go back for the cars. Manuel, Figs, and I decided to separate and thrash around for a while on our way to the place where we would meet for lunch. I listened carefully to Figs's directions. By now I knew enough of Alentejo speech to be aware that, in this nation that perfected navigation, there still existed a system of directions so primitive that I could not comprehend it. There was no left and right, upstream or downstream, north or south, sunrise or sunset. Figs used only the terms *sobe* and *desce,* translated literally as "climb" and "descend." They described turns on terrain that might be perfectly flat. I had to use sign language, which made me feel childish. I understood that I was to avoid the pasture of the *gado bravo*, which are the kind of cattle used for bullfights. I learned that we would meet for lunch at a *monte*. This, as any fool would know, is a mount, which is something like a mountain but lower. It was not visible yet, but it was there in the northeast, a couple of hours away. Figs said so.

We strolled north, Trooper and I, while Manuel and Figs swung east with their dogs. For the first hour my passage was as close to wilderness as the Alentejo gets, which is to say that even the Portuguese could not profitably exploit it. It had the look of the African highlands where my ancestors and I had left our footprints, some 3 million years apart. By this I do not mean that there were buffaloes, tsetse flies, or francolins. The scrubby trees just seemed familiar, and the tousled grass and aridity.

The backward climate helped. It was wet in the summer when crops do not want to grow, dry in the summer when they do. Grazing was unrewarding because the slopes had developed goat-proof vegetation. The soil was too rocky for oaks. There were occasional scraggly "wild pines," as opposed to the umbrella pines planted near houses and along main roads. There were scattered tangles of wild olives. Mostly there were shrubs: patches of gorse in humid spots, wild lavender and broom where it was dry. Haw-thorns and wild pear trees grew a little taller than the rest. Where nothing else could make it, rockroses were turning thin soils back into cover for wildlife.[7]

And there was light, light everywhere—light brushed by the pines, light drunk by the herbs, light washing my insides even as my skin accumulated strata of dust. The sun's light was my felicity.

The light is feeble where most of us live. Londoners and Berliners are accustomed to seeing the air before they breathe it. In America, industrial haze stretches without interruption from the Atlantic to the Dakotas, then starts again in California. People accustomed to life under a gray filter are startled by the sharp edges of Montana, even threatened by mountains that pounce from a

hundred miles away. The Portuguese are Westerners too, and prevailing winds from the open Atlantic sweep their skies. In the north,
you scarcely notice because hills cut short the horizons. In the
Alentejo you notice. The altitude is low and the air dense, so there
is not the bright, crisp quality of the American West. You need a
visor to shade your eyes but not a cowboy hat to keep your ears
from burning. The air is golden like that of Italian renaissance
paintings—the warmest and oldest of lights. You keep thinking that
you must have been here before.

This, then, was the place to look for Noble Savages.
    Please understand that I did not undertake the search like a city
boy bagging hoopoes. Neither was I guided by Jean-Jacques Rousseau, whose uncorrupted natives were located beyond the Western
horizon, accessible only to the imagination. Rousseau sent Europe
and America off on a wild-goose chase. Margaret Mead even persuaded herself that Samoans were innocent about sex, demonstrating that anthropologists can be as gullible as the rest of us. Later,
seekers of truth found it in Nicaragua, but the Sandinistas spoiled
everything by holding an election. You might argue that these Savages *would* have been Noble if we had not poked around in their
affairs (or vice versa) and corrupted them. This argument fails.
Rousseau was wrong and Voltaire was right: People everywhere are
capable of corrupting themselves without foreign aid.
    And still, there are peoples with little opportunity for corrup-
tion. At least there used to be. In Angola, back before its wars, I
reached the place called Lands at End of the World. There I went
hunting with the Bushmen, who were Africa's largest remaining
group of hunter-gatherers and therefore my heroes. In the short
time I had with them, they did not disappoint me. That is another
story and it lacks a happy ending. By now there may be no Bushmen
left who live in the old ways.
    The problem is that I (and you, perchance) still want Noble
Savages. If they are extinct as facts, they remain as needs. Our
spirits fly with the Bushmen's along threads of spider silk to the sky.
We beg them to show us a time before smog and walls, when our
work was not drudgery.

It occurred to me that the place to look might be in the oldest part of Europe. The Alentejo was marked by the paths of Neanderthals and Cro-Magnons and Moors and Christians. A people at the crossroads of history would not be innocent, but it would at least be accustomed to getting trampled. In some incoherent way, the food led me on too. Never mind the romance of "premodern purity and closeness to the soil."[8] I was not looking for ambience. I did not care for the way that Portuguese peasants haggled for their produce. It simply tasted good. Carrots and oranges and beans and the rest: They were small and dusty, like the Bushmen, and they tasted better, every time, than their big, scrubbed, waxed cousins in my supermarket back home. The people who grew such stuff might have another secret, if I could figure it out.

A man cutting hay with a scythe ignored me, showing admirable resistance to corruption. A group of peasants hoeing a rice paddy tried to ignore me too, and when I insisted, they claimed not to know the whereabouts of the *monte* where the luncheon fire would, by now, have been lit. A shepherd leaned on his staff, hunched into his sheepskin cloak, and pretended not to see me till I had almost passed. Then he shook his head slowly. I did not blame him. He knew better than to let confusion into his life.

At the bottom of the partridge hills lay what looked like a woodcock valley, a strip of matted brush and trees along a sluggish stream. Trooper waded into it belly-deep, trying to guzzle it all. Then he lay down, sighed, got up, and rolled onto his back for a slow writhe in the mud. When he got up next time he indulged in a perfect shake, teasing it down his spine to the tip of his tail, then finishing with an all-over shudder that sent droplets flying from flapping ears. I envied this debauchery but could not imitate it. The *alentejanos* have a saying: *"Agua corrente não mata gente,"* meaning (without the rhyme) "running water won't kill you." Maybe not, but even Trooper used to get indigestion after these hunting trips.

We worked through a eucalyptus grove and into the thick stuff. It had an outer barrier of whitethorns, then tall gorse under the pines. Trooper shortened his range. He seemed almost afraid to get out of my sight, which was curious in a dog so bold. Perhaps he was losing his violence, like me.

He skirted the edge of a gorse bush and pointed. It was a remarkable point—back humped, brow wrinkled, hair bristling even on his tail. I angled to the side, trying for a clear shot. Trooper was pointing a tall, black, muscular animal with shiny horns. It would have been what Ernest Hemingway called a brave bull, except that it was a cow, which was worse. The bulls were seldom bellicose, I had been told, and even if they did charge, they lowered their heads and closed their eyes. You just skipped to one side and yielded the terrain. But you had to stay away from the cows, which kept their eyes open. They would not settle for a brave show. They wanted to do you in.

Footsteps followed my retreat so I broke into a weaving run, interrupting the line of sight with as much brush as possible. The footsteps were just Trooper's, in the dry leaves. He did not leave my heel till we were back across the stream.

An American farmer who saw me heading into a field with violent cattle would have warned me. The Alentejo's peasants probably got a kick out of letting me go. So much for Noble Savages.

I won't be treated like this. I have fabricated society and will fabricate nature if it won't cooperate. I'll have a Noble Savage painted, buy him in the mall, and hang him in my house. I'll purchase books about him by nature fakers. I'll watch television programs on him. I'll dress him up as a wolf and film him till he learns who's boss around here.

Or I could look inside myself. I am still sapient man—a species not domesticated by selective breeding. Those bursts of bliss and terror must mean that the dream time is down inside me somewhere. When I said that I wanted to keep my violence, however, I did not mean that my sacrifice should upstage that of the partridge. Any interest I might have had in provoking brave bulls and liberated cows was long gone, by then. My taste for trouble was limited to sleepless nights, sore muscles, dry throat, wet shirt, banged shins, scratched face, rumbling belly, the occasional tumble, and getting lost.

Joseph Campbell's findings[9] might have saved me a futile search, if they had been published at the time. He found that the Noble Savage does not exist among peasants. When nomadic hunter-gatherers become settled planters, everything changes.

The hunter identifies his life with that of the animal he kills. He sees it as a "reasonable, pragmatical, commutative" transaction: The partridge dies so that it may feed him and return in another season, "according to the order of nature," to feed him again. The bird is venerated, furthermore, as a teacher of "the way of life." The transaction "is consistently of the light world, Apollo's realm." This is of course human, like all myth, and in my scientific mode I am sure that no individual partridge wants to provide my family's dinner. As a species, however, they do return to nourish me, and I accord them the respect that teachers deserve. I had therefore guessed the mythology, and felt it in Diana's Temple, before reading Joseph Campbell.

The rest goes beyond what I would have let myself think.

The planter's sacrifice (says Campbell) is of a different order from that of the hunter-gatherer. It is dark, Dionysian. The planter believes that he has fallen from Righteousness. Outside of Eden all nature, including his own, is corrupt. He kills not to put himself in accord with the world, like the hunter, but to redeem its evils. To this purpose he sacrifices human flesh, not that of an animal. Sometimes the sacrifice is of his own body and blood. Sometimes it is that of other humans. At its core, however, the symbolism is the same all over the planter's world, in all tribes and nations.

And that's what had oppressed me in Évora's Chapel of Bones.

The sun had drifted nearer to the western horizon. I wanted water a lot and food a little, so I climbed a hill and spotted a white house. It was down in a valley and out of my way, but the people inside would know where to find the Mount of Lunch. As I walked closer I began to make out vehicles, probably tractors. They turned into cars, and then into the cars of my friends, down here as far as one could get from a mount. And then the smell of boiling *bacalhau* hit me.

Bacalhau translates as codfish, but in Portugal it is always salt-cured. The Portuguese have been learning the technique of curing and cooking this dish since (it would appear) before Columbus's first voyage. *Bacalhau* used to be cheap, the "Faithful Friend" of urban poor who could afford little else but potatoes, eggs, garlic, olive oil, greens, and wine. Salt cod is almost as expensive as lobster now, and worth it. The flavor is unique, with a hint of fermentation. When boiling, it has a "divine and slightly suspect odor, like everything that smells really good."[10] I always carried sardines and crackers, mind you, but was never allowed to eat them. The same tin of sardines lasted for four years.

If you have not walked since dawn and approached a Portuguese hunting lunch upwind, you have missed something. You smell only the *bacalhau* and garlic, but you think that you smell also the potatoes and olive oil and bottles of red wine and bread wrapped in cloths. And if, by chance, you come bearing partridge instead of *chibato*, you are as content as a human is allowed to get.

As to the *monte*, well, I should have asked. A *monte* in the Alentejo is the house of one who owns an *herdade*, which is a large landed estate. Often the houses were built on hills, so they all came to be called mounts. This one was inhabited by peasants. My friends did not know the history and we did not inquire: something to do with the revolution, perhaps, or just the old story of an estate going broke. It takes a lot of dry land to support a family.

There was *bacalhau* in excess and we ate all of it. Then we attacked the apples, figs, and cheese. Finally we savored the *filhós* sent by Zeca's wife. *Filhós* are what doughnuts ought to be, but without the holes.

We took photographs of the expedition. They showed four men hidden under strata of sweat and dust, four moribund dogs, and a very few partridges that had lost their fluff. Never mind. Photographs are a form of statistics, not to be relied upon.

For my wife I dug a bush of wild *rosmaninho*. It signifies love everlasting, and a supply of that comes in handy when a woman is called upon to massage the cramps out of your legs in the middle of the night.

While we were basking, the woman of the *monte* came out and picked up the cans and papers that my friends had thrown around.

She seemed glad of an excuse to meet new people. I imagined the reaction of an American farmer's wife to refuse in her front yard.

We leaned against cork oaks, then, spongy bark cushioning our backs. We immortalized in fable the partridges we had shot or missed. I slid down and rested my head on the grass and went to sleep with sunlight dripping on me through the leaves.

It was Saroyan, I think, who wrote of lying in hotel rooms and wondering how much of himself would remain behind when the time came for the rest of him to leave. And I wonder how much more of me is still sleeping under a cork oak, bathed in droplets of light.

HOME

. . . degeneracy, beyond a doubt, there has been, and a withdraw-
ing from the lustre and valour of their forerunners, in a generation
so depraved in its pleasures and vanities. . . . . notwithstanding,
some descendants of noble families and rich houses may be found
who worthily maintain the great name they have inherited, pur-
suing a way of life that is at once distinguished and beyond re-
proach. And if the torch of their forbears does not burn any more
brightly in their hands, as least it has not gone out nor grown dim.

CAMÕES, *The Lusiads*, Canto Eight

Adriano loves home. Furthermore, he likes to spend time there, which is not the same thing. He needed home's solace after our tour of the Algarve and Alentejo—a trip that he had taken in generosity, just to show me around. The places that had seemed like fragments of the dream time, to me, had for him been disappointments, victims of disrespect and neglect. But some of the world's good things were secure, and he wanted a meal from his wife.

We got back to Lisbon late in the evening, a day ahead of schedule. Finding a public telephone and getting a connection might have delayed us for another hour, so we gave no notice, but Maria Tereza was happy to see us. She made for the kitchen at once. In America, I would have helped out, but Adriano does not cook. He and I sat in the dining room and waited for the food to arrive.

Visually, the scene was nothing like that in my childhood home. Everybody lived in the kitchen, in America. Five children flipped pancakes, raided the cookie jar, and stored angleworms in the icebox—all more or less at the same time. My mother loved it. What struck me in Lisbon was not the difference in environment but the constancy in feeling. For Maria Tereza, as for my mother, there was no such thing as a family late for dinner. The brood was a problem only when it was not there. Tolstoy got it right when he said that all happy families resemble one another.

As assortment of Adriano's children and grandchildren drifted in. One of them—I do not remember which—asked what Americans thought of Portugal. It was the kind of shallow-profound question that pops out of young people. No longer a diplomat, I told the impolite part of the truth: Portugal was not on the American globe.

Many of my countrymen did not know quite where it was, or what language it spoke, or that the same tongue was spoken in half of South America. I did not mean to be brutal, but Adriano was hurt. He had swum eight hundred years in mother Portugal's amniotic fluid and Americans scarcely knew that she existed.

Over the strawberries, Adriano said that he would head north in the morning. We would move our center of operations to his old family home in Anadia, three hours north of Lisbon. From there we could take day trips into the central mountains. After Anadia, we would work our way to the northern border. At Sagres we had seen the age of discovery; we would now visit the rest of the dream time. We would watch Portugal become a nation during the Middle Ages and win its independence from Castile. We would see birth and feisty adolescence and contented old age.

We could tarry a day or two in Lisbon, I said. There was no rush.

Yes there was, said Adriano. Even if we hurried, we could not see half enough.

We hurried. Next morning we loaded the car while the blackbird was deploring the state of his cage. We were in the same mood—and then we added a little fishing gear, just in case. The airline had found my two missing duffel bags. Next to them, Adriano stowed three rods, a creel for trout, another creel for lunch, a collection of reels and fly boxes, and two sets of hip-waders. Under these items were cloth bags for provisions collected in the fields or bought in the streamside villages. Might as well be prepared, Adriano said. We'd be in the right parts of the country. Maybe we would have not time for foraging, but maybe we would. One never knew.

I knew. We would sneak off for a couple of hours during a couple of days. We would see the best of worlds, because trout live in the best of places. Just thinking about them changed everything. We stopped whining with the blackbird and started singing with the larks. If we were going to fish a little, then we could talk about fishing a lot. We might even take our minds off National Highway 1.

Adriano's ancestral home in Anadia lies just off the main road between Lisbon and Oporto, the major industrial city of the north.

Picture U.S. Route 1 between Washington and New York. Shrink it to two lanes in width. Add a range of hills and tortuous curves. Insert diesel trucks groaning uphill in clouds of noxious fumes. Dodge the sparkling piles where tempered glass windshields have shattered over the pavement. You see now why I was trying to put off this voyage.

It was Salazar's fault. The old dictator had given the people what was good for them (efficient public transportation) instead of what they wanted (a good road). He was, among his other virtues, ahead of his time as an environmentalist. I suppose that I would have supported his priorities. I would have approved of a policy aimed at forcing almost everyone to take the train, except me. That's where the fuel taxes came in. The price of gasoline in Portugal was roughly four times that in the United States, which should have been enough to discourage the public from driving and perhaps did, in some imperceptible degree. But the whole nation seemed to be on the road with Adriano and me. The main effect of expensive fuel was to alter the vehicles in which—or on which—people traveled. The motorcycles had engines smaller than those of American lawn mowers. Most cars had smaller engines than American motorcycles.

The last Citroën 2CV was manufactured in Portugal during 1990, forty-three years after the first. It was never the most abundant car on the road, but it seemed to me the most Portuguese. (Of course it started in France. To design a national car would have been folly, which is not a Portuguese trait.) The pancake wheels, flap windows, pop-eyed headlights, and canvas top were so ruthlessly stingy that one could not even call the vehicle cute, like a Volkswagen beetle. (The Portuguese did not admire cuteness in adults.) But the 2CV got twice the mileage of the Volkswagen that seemed so frugal in America. I would have liked to own such a car to annoy the Philistines. Unfortunately, there would not have been enough room in a 2CV for the paraphernalia of two fly fishermen, let alone the breads and cheeses and fruits that the fishermen would gather to accompany the trout that they would probably not catch.

There was room in Adriano's Peugeot. It was a big station wagon with four doors and three rows of seats, two of which were folded down for our cargo. And yet for each American gallon of fuel, the car took us 35 miles at speeds that would get my driver's license revoked in Montana, let alone Pennsylvania.

The difference between American cars and Adriano's Peugeot was the difference between Reagan and Salazar, once again—between fantasy and function. The Peugeot had no sound system, no velour upholstery, and no metallic paint. It had no vinyl-covered roof or electric windows. There was a diesel engine that made some noise but did not smell bad. And there was a five-speed manual transmission.

All cars are, or should be, designed from their gear boxes outward. (This is known as Proper's Principle because it is certainly not General Motors'.) Automatic transmissions work best with lots of torque at low speeds, which comes from engines with large displacements, which require sturdy running gear, which makes the car heavy. You can forget fuel economy. Manual gear boxes, on the contrary, work best with lightweight, high-speed engines. Vehicles built around them do not have to be cheap, but efficiency is usually better.

There now. You thought that shiftlessness was a simple technical development but it turned out to be original sin.

You can take a car designed around an automatic transmission (which is to say an American car) and pop a manual gearbox in it, but you won't gain much economy and your spouse will burn the clutch out. Or you can take a car designed around a manual gear box (which is to say one made anywhere but America) and give it an automatic transmission, but you will lose some of the qualities that made you buy a funny foreign car in the first place: thrift, control, and dependability. Instance the Peugeot. I tried to buy one like Adriano's in America and couldn't get it. Peugeots for the American market had doodads, including automatic transmissions, and cost half again more than the same basic cars sold in Europe. The American version also had a reputation for needing expensive repairs. Adriano's model was considered a *carro forte*—strong car.

American car manufacturers will tell you that their clients demand automatic transmissions. No wonder: For years you could not get an American car with a manual gearbox that was any good.

We had forgotten how to make them. But it was easy to sell European and Japanese cars in America, even at the usual high markups. And it got harder and harder to unload American cars anywhere, even for cut-rate prices.

The decline and fall of American vehicles had an impact on broader European perceptions. Innocence had been appealing when it was the rugged naivete of a cowboy roping cattle. Something seemed wrong when people would not shift for themselves.

Adriano pulled into a roadhouse—my first in Portugal. During my years in the country, I had made a point of snacking on sandwiches at the steering wheel, taking advantage of the lull in traffic that occurs when every Portuguese citizen has lunch. It never fails. The stillness at noon is one of the compensations for miserable roads. Another is the absence of antique shops and souvenir stores, because what the Portuguese crave is provender.

Adriano's choice was *O Manjar do Marquês,* roughly translated as "The Marquis' Tidbit." The Marquis of Pombal had governed Portugal from 1750 to 1777, becoming a dictator as distinguished as Salazar, for some of the same reasons. The Marquis would not have entered a restaurant with such a name, and I was wary too. Roadhouses elsewhere in the world had conditioned my liver to twitch like Pavlov's dogs.

The front of the *Manjar do Marquês* was separated from the noisome highway by a parking lot. Inside, the place was too big and too new, but neat. Even the strings of garlic and onions that hung from the ceiling had been dusted. Adriano ordered the standard lunch without looking at the menu. Hot soup appeared within seconds: homemade, fresh vegetables, not overcooked, seasoning right. The rest of the lunch came on serving dishes from which we helped ourselves. I started with the bean salad and got a shock. It was better than any I had ever prepared, and I'd tried. There was no secret that I could decipher—just firm chickpeas, grated onions, olive oil, wine vinegar, chopped parsley, and some other fresh herbs. The mixture must have been made fresh that morning, because bean salads get mucilaginous when they sit too long.

The hot spinach salad with beans and bread crumbs was just as good, but I moved quickly to the whiting filets, codfish cakes, and *arroz de tomate*—rice in a fresh tomato sauce. Adriano was working on deep-fried filets of salt cod. We both skipped the beef, as usual. (The telephones may not work in Portugal, but the system of seafood distribution does.) We had fruit salads as a last course. The fruit was fresh-chopped, oranges and strawberries mainly, with just enough sugar.

We were out of the Marquis' roadhouse in about the time we would have taken at a hamburger parlor in America. We could have made the meal a long, warm occasion with special orders and wine, but neither of us wanted that in the middle of the day. Adriano had known what to expect. For me, the meal was not an epiphany, exactly. It was just the sudden revocation of a guiding principle of the universe. Good food, it seemed, could be prepared in industrial quantities, cheaply, and right on the highway.

I was sorting flavors in my mind all the way to Anadia.

When Adriano turned off the main road, I felt as if someone had abruptly turned off a pneumatic hammer. The relief was so unexpected that it hurt.

Some other foreigner must have visited Anadia sometime, but he did not find it in the *Michelin Guide*. The *Guide* fails to show the town even as a dot on the map. Realtors would call the place "centrally located," because there is not much else to say. It lies between south and north, highway and mountains. The land is flat. A big winery provides employment. The population density is urban, but there are no amusements like those of Lisbon and Oporto. Right in the middle of what looks like town, there are truck gardens, and on the edge of one of those is Adriano's house. The mix would be inconceivable in America. It is heartland Portugal.

Adriano swung wide on a cobbled street and drove into the *quintal* of his old home through a gate. He pulled into a long shed that also sheltered a tractor. The place was, I learned, a working farm run by his *caseiro*, which means caretaker as well as farm manager. The man lived with his family on the ground floor of the house. The details of the arrangement were not clear to me, but it seemed less a boss–employee relationship than a deal between businessmen.

Adriano's ancestral home was a square monolith. It had been built precisely as it would have been built in Lisbon, with no concession to its surroundings, and then it had eroded. What paint was left made lichen-colored patches on cement gray as a boulder. The red-tile roof had faded to the color of the pounded earth on the street side of the house. Trees had grown, people had been born, and souls had flowed like buttresses into the landscape. It was the kind of architectural effect that you get only when you are not trying for effect.

The house had a wall around it, like all respectable Portuguese houses, but the only function of the wall was separation of the half-acre farm within (*quintal*) from the larger farm (*quinta*) outside. Inside the wall grew almost everything except a lawn. The oranges were of poor quality, Adriano said, but the lemons, apples, walnuts, cherries, figs, pears, and pomegranates were fine. On the sunny side of the trees, an iron arbor covered with grapevines ran back through the *favas*—Old-World broad beans. I noticed these because of some personal history. *Favas* had looked, to my untutored eye, like the mealy New-World beans called limas. I had spent years in Portugal ignoring *favas* and then tried them and found a surprise as tasty as Adriano's roadhouse.

It started drizzling and we went inside, Adriano eagerly, me lagging behind, hoping to hear a quail call from the fields. Then Adriano lit a fire. It brought the outdoors inside and warmed it up. The triangular fireplace was like no other. Its sides angled back till they almost met in the middle, the better to reflect heat into the room. Painted tiles framed the opening and a carved chestnut mantel faced the whole. The firewood was *medronheiro*, which comes from what the dictionary calls a "strawberry tree," though the medronho fruit is no strawberry. The wood was dense and full of heat, good-smelling with a cup of tea. Adriano must have planned this introduction to his ancestors. They clustered in the smoke as souls will at their hearth.

There was a studio portrait of Adriano's parents on the shelf of the parlor. The photographer's victims were so camouflaged by the clothing of the period that they were difficult to see. Dressed normally, I supposed that they would have been much like the Portuguese of today—closer in habits and attitudes than my ancestors are to me. Portugal had more history, more resistance to change, and fewer resources for it.

Adriano did not suggest that his ancestors were aristocratic. Nobody in Portugal takes the remnants of the old noble families seriously anyhow. (Only in America does the middle class fancy coats of arms.) Adriano's people would have been a mixture of rural and urban, peasant and prince, a little old money and the kind they worked hard for. They produced four bright, hardworking children and got them to good schools. Adriano was the last of the four still alive and so the house had come to him.

He had no sour memories of his family or, for that matter, of Anadia. Of course it takes tears to turn every child into an adult, but Adriano did not mention hard knocks. Perhaps his mind, like mine, had erased most of the sobs or turned them into chuckles. He recalled mother and father and hearth, all warm, always there. I looked into the fire and saw different faces. The hearth was something we shared. Despite abundant evidence to the contrary, each of us assumed that this world was a place of homes and laps and warm encircling arms to cry on.

The Anadia home was as cluttered as any in America, but the debris was different. There were no old radios or cameras or lapsed hobbies. There were chairs that an antiquarian would have liked and a rustic desk worth auctioning at Sotheby's. There was postwar furniture discarded from the house in Lisbon. There was an old photo of a little boy in an elaborate short dress; you knew that he was a boy because he had nothing on from the waist down. The walls had local hand-painted tiles, local marble, dark wood panels, and sometimes paint. The place had never been decorated. It had been accumulated. It had no Look. It had emotions. You could always come back and find them safe. Adriano's wife was not there now but his mother had been there once, so it was still home.

The kitchen had a modern gas range and not many other new things that I can recall, but then I wasn't looking for them. What caught me was a built-in brick oven, 4 feet deep and domed. It had its own chimney and a pile of grapevine trimmings ready for the fire. The oven would do for suckling pig, which was a specialty of the region, but the raison d'être was bread. The bricks would soak up the moisture from the dough so that it could form a crust, then return the humidity slowly to maintain the right texture. Such an oven would give birth to little fragrant loaves, insides swirling like white roses where a mother's hands had twisted the dough.

Such bread takes the measure of a cook. It is utterly simple and relentlessly demanding, with no fat or sugar to trick the taste buds. There are no dough conditioners, emulsifiers, or preservatives, either. There are four ingredients only: flour, water, yeast, and salt. They are mixed, allowed to rise, kneaded, and baked at the right temperatures and humidities—both of which change during the cooking. The bread is then eaten within twenty-four hours. It is never put in a plastic wrapper, which would make the loaf go spongy.

One cannot, on reflection, hold an individual American cook responsible for flabby bread. Even a restaurant's cook cannot control everything. He can leave the beef gravy off the fish dinner, bake the potatoes without foil, and even bribe a gardener to grow good vegetables. I wish that more cooks near my Montana home would do these things, but I do not expect real bread. Getting it right takes the support of a whole culture, cooks and consumers.

"My cousin is very Britannic," Adriano said. "We'll have to be there at four o'clock sharp." We were. We parked in a driveway by a real lawn. Its trees and shrubs had been artfully planted at least a lifetime earlier: pines, lindens, a chestnut, and rhododendrons. This was a garden in the British sense, not a Portuguese *quintal*. Inside, the house had dark old furniture and ticking clocks. There were fireplaces with screens in front and baskets of firewood—oak, olive, and *medronheiro*. And there was Dona Maria Rosa.

Mary Rose. It is a pretty name in any language, and she was slim and straight. She greeted me in a low, strong voice and I thought that she must once have been the prettiest girl in Anadia. I told Adriano, later, that if there were ever a beauty contest for seventy-year-old widows, I'd bet on Ms. Mary Rose. That's when he told me that she was eighty-four. (I don't want to mislead you: Few women in Portugal can afford to maintain their looks beyond the nubile years. Adriano just has a talent for finding the exceptions. And as for me, I'm not honest enough to call anyone ugly unless he or she is ill-tempered enough to deserve it.)

We sat around a fire. A silver pot held tea from India or Ceylon—the real stuff, not the imitation that comes in tea bags and smells like after-shave lotion. Adriano appreciated the brew. Maria Rosa and I enjoyed it. She had made an orange tart, too, bittersweet like all good things. I ravished it and she was pleased by my appetite. Outside the back window, a pomegranate blossomed red. I tried to get a conversation going but my hostess was reticent, as you would expect from a Portuguese lady. She would not just rush into things like the American blonde who was fluttering between two sappy suitors on Dona Maria Rosa's television screen.

Adriano drove me to the top of the Buçaco forest to revive my appetite. He always came here, he said, when he was in Anadia. He liked to look out over the valleys that held trout streams—not the best in Portugal, but the ones close to home, familiar as the veins of his hands. He pointed to the lower courses and the inaccessible headwaters, separated by "bad passages." He recalled the handholds on the cliffs that had taken him, year after year, to water where few people dared to fish.

He sounded as if he had been in the battle of Buçaco, too, but that was in 1810. Napoleon's generals had invaded Portugal with a large force of French and Spanish troops. "We booted them out," Adriano said. I think he meant "we Portuguese and British." Portugal's forces could and did carry on a guerrilla war, but they could not have undertaken a conventional battle against such odds. The future Lord Wellington led a combined British and Portuguese force into close, nasty fighting on a "damned long hill." At the end, Portugal was still free—or at least free of French and Spanish. The British influence lasted a long time.

I saw little in Portugal resembling the Irish admiration of England. The Irish wanted political freedom but stopped there. Nobody in Ireland but a few zealots believed the stuff about economic and linguistic independence. The Portuguese believed it. They manufactured their own products even when doing so made no economic sense, and it seldom did. They ignored England's language almost as successfully as its cookery. If anything, there are fewer Anglicisms in Portuguese than in French, and there is certainly less fuss about the resistance. Adriano knows what a *piquenique* is but finds *farnel* easier to say. On the other hand, he uses the English word for whiskey and the Chinese word for tea (*chá*); they describe products for which Portuguese had no equivalents. The most interesting word imports to reach my attention arrived, oddly, from America. A few Azoreans learned whaling terms from New England back in the days of Moby Dick, and a vocabulary extinct in America still lives in the Portuguese islands. But this is trivia.

What matters is the poetry. In Portuguese—or at least European Portuguese—the baroque is elegant. In English, elegance is simplicity. The gap cannot be bridged. Adriano recites Camões. My mother sang Shakespeare.

Some British influences on Portugal go deeper. Dona Maria Rosa's garden and tea would have been hard to explain without Britain. So would Adriano's tweed coat and plus fours. His trout flies all seemed to have English names: Red Spinner, Olive, March Brown. What impressed me more, however, was his attachment to the countryside, as opposed to the city. There was nothing in the least modish about this. He felt deeply that the country villages were the source of national virtue. I doubt that the feeling went back many generations, however, because few Brazilians share it.

The English created the countryside. The rest of civilized Europe preferred the town; England built country houses. The French dressed fine ladies in shepherdess costumes; the English dressed trout flies. Rousseau dreamed up a Noble Savage; Dame Juliana Berners wrote of a real angler like Adriano.

And yet, at the very least, he will have his wholesome and merry walk at his own ease, and also many a sweet breath of various plants and flowers that will make him right hungry and put his body in good condition. He will hear the melodies of the harmony of birds. .... and if the angler catches the fish with difficulty, then there is no man merrier than he is in his spirits.[1]

Being right hungry and wanting to put our bodies in good condition, we walked to the restaurant. We passed many houses but no mobile homes. (I asked and gathered from Adriano's response that "mobile home" is an oxymoron in Portugal.) We walked past the big winery. We walked by a white-painted bench with black letters reading "Offered to Our Lady of the Fevers." We walked past another bench "Offered to Our Lady of Fátima, patroness of the volunteer firemen of Anadia." We walked past the church where Adriano attended Mass on Saturday evenings.

Catholicism is part of being Portuguese. The nation's history cannot be separated from that of the church. The reconquest, the great discoveries, the colonialism—all were undertaken, in part, for the true faith. But nationality and religion are entwined in much of southern Europe and Latin America, and the men still do not attend Mass. In Brazil, they stay away in droves.

I refrained from asking Adriano what he would have done if the only Mass had been scheduled at a time that interfered with his angling. Both were parts of his life, but the church was an iron arbor left by his ancestors and the fishing was a green vine of his own growing.

He told me of the religious ceremonies that tied his community together. They were very old, he said, and they differed from those of other regions. In Anadia, the cross came to your home at Easter. To welcome it, you spread flowers and greenery on the street in front of your door. The priest would enter sprinkling holy water. Behind him, the sacristan would carry the cross. Your friends would appear before or shortly after the ceremony—not invited but expected, obligated. Your obligation as host was to offer them specific foods. Adriano listed them in this order: *queijo da serra,* which is a cheese that we will get to know later; white sparkling wine, specialty of the region; shelled almonds; and a white, breadlike, semi-sweet cake. The food had evolved to fit together like the town. The sound of it revived my appetite.

At the Flower of Anadia Restaurant, the waitress greeted Adriano as *Senhor Doutor*—Mister Doctor, the latter a reference to his university degree. She rushed the seafood soup, which we rushed to eat. We then lingered over *Bacalhau à Flor de Anadia,* salt cod in the restaurant's own style. It had been soaked to remove the salt, briefly deep-fried, then sauced and baked over red peppers, olives, and onions. The olives had their pits and the fish had its bones. We took pleasure in sucking them dry of flavor. The waitress brought a local red wine which, in the odd way these things happen, was right with the main dish. There was bread in a distinctive shape baked only in Anadia, with meringue-like peaks on top. I had my usual liter of mineral water too, with no ice. (Ice water is bad for the taste buds or something; ask any Portuguese.) Dinner having been rich, we ended with a baked apple.

The bill for both of us was just over thirteen dollars, including wine and service. (Adriano would not let me tip more than 5 percent.) This, mind you, was a year when the dollar was so low that American tourists in most of western Europe were dining on bread and cheese smuggled into their hotel rooms.

Food and love are almost the same thing, and you should not have to pay much for them. It's a notion I got when my mother let me do the family grocery shopping, starting at age nine. This was during World War II and there were circumstances: no car, scarce money, rationing, and a house full of children. The only luxury was a baby-grand piano that took up most of the living room. I was the eldest child and I liked the walk to the store. We didn't talk about love in my family but I understood that I could help out by saving pennies. Of the many ways to do that, catfish were the best, being not only cheap but tasty and romantic. They were wild food from the Missouri River, still, not farm-raised. Mom would hug me when she saw the receipt. Then she'd laugh and fry the filets. She did not know much about fish and game but she cooked every bit of it I brought home from then on.

Maybe I took the exercise too seriously; children will do that. They all want the same thing but some learn to save for it and others to pay. Depends on the times, I suppose. The Portuguese are all frugal. I share more assumptions with them than with Americans who came along just a few years later than me in the boom times—more assumptions on food, anyhow. Lots of Yanks these days fancy High Cooking. They travel around the world looking for it, and more power to them.

For me, however, food and wine should not be destination resorts. (Neither should love, I suppose.) Flavors fade if you make a hobby of them. The more you demand, the less you get. But if you come across the Flower of Anadia in the course of some other search, you leave happy.

This is not to recommend pure chance. Serendipity might work in about half of Portugal's restaurants. In America it has worked for me just once—in Davenport, Iowa. There were two bad signs: The place was on the road and it claimed to be a farmers' restaurant, which is the next-worst kind after the truck stops. The food was good. It wasn't haute cuisine, either, so it didn't cost much. It was pot roast of beef with potatoes, sauerkraut, lots of crisp vegetables, and real pies. It was what you would get for Sunday dinner in farm country from a grandmother who knew how to cook, and some of them do. So perhaps we have a chance to build American cooking from the ground up as well as from the stratosphere down.

For the most part, the French taught cooking to this generation of Americans. The Chinese and Italians could have done it but made the strategic error of charging reasonable prices. There was no danger of that with High Cooking. It evolved from peasant practice, like all other good food, but was redesigned to extract money from those who could afford to pay. What remained was skill, good ingredients, generations of acquired knowledge—and discipline. We needed that.

I counsel foreigners in the United States and Canada to accept any invitations they get to private homes, but to be wary of roadhouses. And I give travelers from this continent the same advice for Britain. In Ireland, bring sandwiches. You might eat well on the road almost anywhere else in Europe. (Some British claim to have joined the continent, but they haven't subverted the food yet.) As for me, I shall tighten my belt till I get south of the Maginot Line of Cooking. Its defenses are invisible, but the hamburgers do not get through. Neither do the pork pies, knackwurst, and hollandaise sauce. Of course these delicacies are not lethal in the short term, assuming that you get enough exercise to work them off, but I'd just as soon keep driving.

You will not find the Line on the map. As best I can make out, it defends the Iberian peninsula, France south of the Loire, and every bit of Italy. No doubt there are other tasty places that I have not checked out. You could get scientific. You could research, say, the ecology of the olive tree, the temperatures of the seas, the boundaries of the rockrose, and the geography of the snail. (Maybe it's the Escargot Line.)

Or you could just drive south and stop where the first person tells you of a restaurant with cooking as good as it is at home. You will then, I wager, find yourself south of the Line. North of it, restaurants are fantasy, escape, destination resorts. South of it, the cooks are professional versions of Mother. She knows what's good for you.

It is probably not a coincidence that the areas south of the Line were the poorest parts of Europe, till recently. Good cooking demands a waste-nothing philosophy. When you get rich, you tend to be lazy with the hard-to-extract flavors. And you can afford to get squeamish, like British and Americans. "The great gastronomic cultures are all in the omnivorous category . . . [they] live close to the land, gag at nothing, or almost nothing."[2]

Cooking is worst in the countries that created modern democracy: England, then America and the other English-speaking ex-colonies. I want to believe that democracy made us prosperous and that prosperity, not democracy, made us squeamish. But democracy also made us safe and safety made us into something we weren't, in 1776. I wonder how many congressmen today would put their John Hancocks on a Declaration that might get them hung. Democracy encourages decisions that do not offend, like our restaurants. "If this people has so atrophied its taste buds as to find tasteless food not only acceptable but desirable, what of the emotional life of the nation? Do they find their emotional life so bland that it must be spiced with sex and sadism?" The question is Steinbeck's.[3]

I hope the folks south of the Line know what they are getting into as they form a prosperous, democratic Europe.

The walk back to Adriano's old home worked off the first false drowsiness of wine. I opened my bedroom to the night air and looked out. There was not another shutter open as far as I could see: No Portuguese would sleep exposed to the vapors and I would not sleep closed in. My dreams, therefore, would have the run of town, unjostled. I crawled into bed.

Church bells around town bonged eleven times each, though not all at the same time. Little boys would have climbed the steeples to crank up the clocks' iron weights. (I used to do that, before America's bells were electronic. Forgot all about it till Anadia.)

The chimes were answered by cocks even more numerous and varied in voice. All told, several minutes on either side of the hour were devoted to the concert. (There was crowing in my town, when I was a child. That was before the roosters were confined to chicken factories.)

Some of Anadia's voices were good. (My mother still sings at the edge of sleep. I can almost understand the words.)

WATER NYMPHS

Limpid streams flowed from their summits, murmuring over white pebbly beds. . . . A pleasant valley set between the hills caught the pellucid water. . . . the air was redolent with the odor of delicately moulded lemons, like a maiden's breasts. . . . The stalwart Portuguese, eager to be touching land once more, were now hastening. . . . The nymphs fled through the foliage; but, more cunning than swift . . . and desire, battening on the sudden glimpse of lovely flesh, grew more ardent still. One stum-

*bled, by design, and . . . her pursuer fell over her and made
escape impossible.*

*Some of his fellows, taking another direction, came upon the
nymphs who were bathing naked and drew from them a startled
cry, as though such an invasion were the last thing they looked
for. . . . There was one youth who dashed into the water fully
dressed and booted as he ran, there to quench the fire that consumed him.*

CAMÕES, *The Lusiads,* Canto Nine

Camões had been at sea a long time, I surmise, when he wrote Canto Nine. He called his desire a Nereid because, if he had called her Your Royal Highness, he would have been exiled again.

I too have been an exile and I remember what I wanted. It was a trout, a fat little pretty tasty trout. Make that two trout, which is enough for dinner with green wine, boiled potatoes, asparagus, and a pudding of fresh oranges. Camões was exiled for seventeen years and I for only the same number of days, so my ambition was smaller. I wanted to catch my trout where the Alvoco flowed from its summit, pellucid water in a pleasant valley set between the hills. I had dreamt of the Alvoco and its shy little trout even when fishing a bold big river with too many trout in Montana. I wanted my desire hard to get, like that of Camões.

The poet's nymphs were expurgated from at least one edition of the national epic. Some editor decided that readers should not be exposed to the Isle of Love that Venus built in midocean—Camões's idea of the perfect reward to Vasco da Gama and his crew for discovering the sea route to India. Canto Nine is, of course, the one that I turned to first in every edition of the poem. Illustrators over the centuries have failed to produce art as sublimely outrageous as the text, but their struggles are worth watching. Naturally, then, I discovered the deletion while leafing through Adriano's several editions of *The Lusiads*. Three or four were intact but one—that with the most wear—had been censored. It had belonged to the young Adriano when he went off to high school in Aveiro. Its covers were loose, its pages yellowed, and its flyleaves covered with stanzas written out in pencil. Here and there were good sketches of fellow students. These changes to the book were improvements, but the passages that adolescents would have liked best were missing. Young women were modest in those days, Adriano explained. It would not have been right to tell them about the sport of sailors and Nereids.

Adriano grew talkative as his Peugeot climbed the Range of the Star, and I boiled with questions. I did not bounce on the seat—as far as I know—but the feeling was the one I used to get just before my mother told me to calm down. I welcomed it back. Looking for other men's myths is good; entering my own dream time was better.

Think of the Range of the Star as Portugal's Colorado. Altitudes are lower but the *Serra da Estrela* is where water begins, forming on the peaks in little trickles, becoming clear streams for a few leagues, and then growing into the turbid rivers that water the nation's midlands. As in Colorado, water is the mountains' most important resource, though you would not guess it from casual conversation. People talk to you about everything else: sheep, cattle, tourists, trees, tillage, fish, and wildlife—derivatives of water, every one. Of them all, trout get closest to the source. Where trout thrive, there are innocent currents, clean and cool and flowing even in the dry season. To write of trout as water nymphs is to be as precise as a symbol can get.

The mountains of central Portugal remind an American of Colorado in another sense: The Range of the Star is young landscape. Most of the country, even further north, was unaffected by the Pleistocene glaciers, or at least by the last of them. The *Serra da Estrela* is a child of the ice. A Yankee (as opposed to a Southerner) feels at home. The mountains and valleys are steep but slightly rounded, scraped by the glacier. There are little roads with no cars on them. There are cloudy distances, smells of heather, diggings of boars, and slithers of vipers. There are even wolves: not many, but enough to work up a shiver if you try. This it the best place in the world. I may have told you that about the Alentejo in October, but the best place migrates with the seasons.

The parallel to Colorado does not work for the human geography of the *Serra da Estrela.* Colorado is new, even in American terms, and largely populated by refugees from the east coast or California. The people of the Portuguese mountains have been there since the glacier left.

> The *Serra da Estrela* is the highest Portuguese range, prolongation of the [Iberian] peninsula's spine. It divides the two halves of Portugal, so different in countenance and temperament. Finally, [the *Serra*] is the heart of the country. Perhaps in the breaks and slopes, valleys and mountainsides, there remains a true representative of the ancient Lusitanian. If there is a human type that is properly Portuguese, if across the happenstances of history there survived any pure example of the prehistoric race from which we can claim descent, then here is where we should look.[1]

She was climbing the road with a stack of loose hay balanced on her head. She had not looked like a Nereid for thirty years but still had the proud neck and back of a dancer. The rest of her body was square and muscular, draped in a black dress with sweat stains between the shoulder blades. Adriano pulled in just ahead of her, parking at a fountain fed by the mountain's springs. There were many such along the roads, because until recently all travel had been on foot. He and I drank a toast to the Nereids and felt better for scouring our plumbing with innocent water. Adriano filled a bottle, then, and handed it to the woman with the hay when she arrived. She drank with deep, eager gulps, hay still balanced. *Muito obrigada,* she said: much obliged. And then she trudged on into the mountains.

The road was narrow and steep with a bend every few yards. A cottage stood back just enough that a vehicle cutting one curve too tight would not scrape the stones around the door. Into this small space was squeezed a truck, its driver, a peasant couple, and a litter of pink, huddled piglets. The people must have been dickering over life and death. Before leaving I wanted one dinner of suckling pig, but I did not want to remember how pretty even swine are for a few weeks.

Adriano turned downhill onto a road even steeper and nar-
rower. It led to a village of few streets and one *praça,* an open,
wedge-shaped polygon. (We would call it a square in English. It is
the kind of confusion Latins expect of us. Square, square.) The
small end of the wedge had just enough space for parking Adriano's
car. Two houses fronted on a long side of the *praça,* and one on the
opposite end. From the remaining side, steps led up to a church.
Next to the steps but lower than the church in altitude and dignity
was a *tasca.* Outside it were tables, parasols, and an invisible waft-
age of fresh-baked bread.

Lunchtime was close and Adriano confessed that the *tasca*
smelled good, but we kept to our plan and filled our creels with
bread, cheese, and lean *chouriço* sausage. The scent encouraged one
of the seven deadly sins and I popped a chunk of *chouriço* into my
mouth, washing it down from a fountain on the square—just to
stave off hunger pangs during the hike to the Alvoco River. It was
not a long walk, but it was steep. Adriano descended slowly, paus-
ing twice to look back, worrying about the return trip uphill. Not
me. I was in a hurry to get to the bottom of things.

Trout fishing is, in Portuguese, *apaixonante.* The translation would
be "passion-inducing" in our tongue, which is shy in curling around
such thoughts. This kind of passion lets you make a fool of yourself
without witnesses. It has nothing in common with courtship except
sleepless intensity, which is resemblance enough to lead angler after
angler to the same symbolism. You like this or you hate it, but
passion it is, passion without dilution, passion without unfaithful-
ness, passion uninterrupted by commercials.

Passion was interrupted by the donkey and the miller, in that
order. The burro was plodding up the trail under two sacks smelling of ground maize. The miller was still cleaning his millstone. I
told him that his burro had gone off on a lark, at which he and
Adriano both laughed. The donkey could have been turned loose in
dense fog with no danger that it would fail to find the village, which
was more than I could claim. The miller was old and said that he
would have no successor. The trail pounded by hoofs over the

centuries would grow back into brambles soon, because no young man would work for the meager profit in this business. I tried to talk longer. I wanted miller's tales, which had been extinct in English for some time, but might as well have tried to interview a dinosaur at the Cretaceous-Tertiary boundary. My victim was as taciturn as most Portuguese and one of the poorest residents of a poor village. He had neither status nor stories.

And besides, I was in a hurry for trout.

The first came under an old stone bridge. It looked lost—the bridge, not the trout. Perhaps the local lord had ordered this construction in the time before governments, when peasants preferred a route near water. The only life there was in a small run beneath the arch. The water was not deep but every bridge shelters either trout or troll, and one or the other pulled my little floating fly down in a wink of water. There was a flashing and flopping and a fine fat fish in my net. It was a brown trout from a family going back to the time of the glaciers, here to give me a courtly welcome. I kept the trout in the water and thanked it with such gentility that Adriano, who was listening, complimented me on my command of his language. Then I unrolled my tape measure and found that this trout, this one-fish welcoming delegation, this chief of protocol for the Duke of Alvoco, was only 18 centimeters long. The legal minimum is 19 centimeters. (I do not translate this into inches because it would sound even smaller.) A single centimeter is so serious deficiency, in the minds of most Portuguese anglers, but I felt the weight of a different culture. The trout went back. Surely there would be bigger ones ahead anyhow.

Above the bridge, granite walls bounded the Alvoco on both sides, sometimes right in the water, sometimes a short distance back. The wall on the right supported the millrace; the one on the left held up the edge of a field. Little white and pink flowers grew from the chinks of the rough gray stones and tumbled over the top. I asked Adriano the name of this blossom that squeezed so much emotion from the hard heart of granite. It was, he said, a *mal-me-queres,* from the Portuguese equivalent of the English "Love me, love me not."

Mal me queres;	Poorly dost thou love me;
Bem me queres;	Well dost thou love me;
Muito me queres;	Much dost thou love me;
Pouco me queres;	Little dost thou love me;
Nada.	Not at all.

Love, then, had gradations with these flowers. They did not demand decisions, yes or no, like big American daisies (or like American anglers who want to catch a fish and move on). And besides, the *mal-me-queres* were delicate. A lover needed the most gentle touch. If he rushed, he would pluck several petals at once and merit a slap in the face.

High above us in the village, the church clock chimed once. I took this as a call to arms, or fishing rods. Adriano said "one o'clock," as if the gastronomic consequences were obvious. I fished faster. He selected a table of granite with hummocks of sweet-smelling anise for chairs. I fished on. A flock of goats trotted down the hillside and right into the pool where my fly floated, preferring grass growing on river rocks to the lush green of the hillsides. I glared at the goats. They paid no attention. Neither did their goat-herd. I gave up and retired for lunch.

Adriano and I opened our trout-and-cheese knives, each of which had a blade for dressing fish and another for lunch, if one remembered which was which. We pulled off chunks of bread and alternated them with bites of cheese and *chouriço*. Adriano produced two oranges that he had smuggled into his creel, and we peeled them with the knives. The mite of a bird called a *pintasilgo* (English goldfinch) hopped in a cluster of olive trees on the terrace behind, giving us a little day-music. Maybe he just wanted us to move on, but he made me feel benevolent even toward trout-scaring goats.

Across the Alvoco, the goatherd leaned on his staff, watching everything and nothing. He was a man of about my age—the prime of life. He wore a wool suit that had probably been brown or black once, and used with a tie for going to Mass. It was just dark, now, and worn with knee-high rubber boots. When he moved, the goats moved with him, though he gave them no command. I suppose they saw him as the head of family.

Once I had asked a Portuguese shepherd about this relationship. He was prosperous, for his profession, with a sizable flock of sheep and a few goats. He was also more talkative than the miller. The sheep, he said, were only sensate as lambs. As adults, they were just a sort of bush that walked around producing milk and wool and meat. The goats, on the other hand, were clever, the brains of the flock.

I asked what happened when they grew too old to produce kids and milk.

They had to be killed, of course. His words rushed out. It was hard, he said, but there was no getting around it. Middle-aged nannies had given what they had to give. They could only waste forage for the rest of their time, growing tougher and tougher of flesh. He was obliged to collar a member of the flock in the prime of life, roll her on her side, thrust a knife between her ribs, and hold it there till she bled to death. She would keep her eye on him and cry like a woman. She had been a kid not long before, hopping from rock to rock and running to him for a rub of the head where little horns were trying to sprout. He was god, and he was killing her. It was very hard.

It was not my image of the shepherd. Where I grew up, he had existed only in church, as a metaphor for eternal care. Portugal has the real thing everywhere, dotting the landscape like trees. It is poor man's work. A shepherd's mission is to keep himself fed, not to provide ovine geriatric care. It makes sense. I would not care for the job.

The Alvoco flock moved off uphill, away from the stream, winding in and out of invisible trails between terraces. The nannies' brass and steel bells sent ripples of sound across the valley. It was as much music as a meat-animal can expect to make before the knife.

I don't mind killing enough trout for dinner. They are beautiful and they may know something about music, because a trout stream makes it; but I am not their god and their eyes do not ask questions. They do not even look at me.

*   *   *

There is a modest claim that I may make: I have liberated myself from trophies and scores. It was not difficult—not like liberation from fear, which only a few heroes like Nuno Álvares achieve. Mostly I just grew older. Once I had dreamt of catching big trout, read books about how to do it, and chased them from Patagonia to Donegal. When I catch one now, I am still pleased. It is a gift, but it is not a triumph.

The scores were a phase too. I had learned to return most of my trout to the water, unharmed, and thought that numbers were needed to document my prowess. It was nonconsumptive consumerism, a competition without messy dead fish.

Now that my affair with trout has progressed through sophistication to the primitive, I am free to pursue a two-little-fish dinner in bliss. I take comfort in the relationship enjoyed by the first people who hunted food in these streams after the glacier. The method is different and the restraints are stronger—must be, in these days of fewer trout and more fishermen—but the emotion is the same. I feel sure of this. Fishing is a kind of anthropology, a way of excavating layers, digging into strata built by my ancestors, finding an underground river.

In the same way, I know that my trout is a Nereid. Female is nourishment, be she trout or nanny goat or Camões's nymph with breasts like moulded lemons. My trout would be male only if I had the "desire to latch onto a monster symbol of fate and prove my manhood in titanic piscine war." That's how John Steinbeck put it, and he did not have the desire. "But sometimes," he wrote, "I do like a couple of fish of cooperative frying size."[2]

The lady was not for frying. I caught trout, to be sure, but not many, and none bigger than the first under the bridge. Even the little ones demanded my best. I cast far upstream, keeping my line out of the water by draping it on boulders. I made sure to throw slack into my leader so that the fly would drift like a real beetle caught in the surface tension. I watched my tiny fly float down the edge between deep, still shelters and the currents that carry food.

The trout, such as they were, all came from places that few fishermen would have probed.

Adriano explained the problem. We were, he said, in the waning quarter of the moon, and trout do not take then.

Every Portuguese fisherman and every Portuguese farmer believes in the influence of the moon. The farmers even plant by its quarters, which shows that the old-time religion is good enough for them. The fishermen profess devotion but are not bound by it. I deplore this moral decay. It is just as bad in America, though we have several lunar theories, one or another of which offers fishing at any given time. If each angler would choose his own lunacy and stay with it, there would be more space on the streams for me. (It is true that I fish whenever I wish, but afterward I consult the tables till I find one that explains my impotence.)

Bowdlerizing Camões's national epic is a mild offense compared to the suffering inflicted on poor Ernest Hemingway for fishing in Spain. A scholar (I shall not provide her name) has written that when Hemingway threaded a Spanish worm onto his hook, he intended for the reader to understand that he was really impaling a portion of the male anatomy. No fooling. This is what happens when students deprave a noble sport. Writing is meant to be done, not spied on. It is an active pursuit like fishing or sex. When you try to pin it down and dissect it, you addle your brains.

For the record: No human male (even Hemingway) wishes to stick a fishhook into any part of his anatomy, especially the one resembling (in the mind of overwrought and underprivileged scholars) a worm. Ouch.

I am in charge of the symbolism around here and will brook no confusion. Adriano and I fished the Alvoco not with worms, for whom I find myself developing sympathy, but with flies. A fly is a representation for a real insect, but tied on a hook with silk and feathers and other materials as filmy as a Nereid's gown.

Adriano stopped casting and started looking for a trail up the hill. I fished with redoubled ferocity. He told me that he knew of a field

of wild strawberries and would have a look for it on the way back
to the village. He would just take his time and mosey along. I was
to feel free to fish as long as I wished. I did wish, for some reason
of incomprehensible hunger, but pretended that I did not and tagged
along.

The strawberries were almost as scarce as the trout. We had to
get on our knees and search through the grass for red beads. They
were good but they did not flee like a Nereid, so I lost interest.
(Adolescent males, including overgrown ones like me, are all hunters. Older men are content to be gatherers. Gathering may require
a higher level of consciousness, if by "higher" you mean older and
therefore closer to heaven. Then again, some of the things we call
levels of consciousness may be layers of platitudes.)

We worked our way up the hill in stages. Adriano, as usual, did
not remove his tie and coat; I, also as usual, worried when his face
turned from pink to red. The first time it happened, I stopped and
asked him about a *curral* built with walls and roof of shale. It was
to shelter the animals in bad weather, he said—not just to hold
them, like a corral in Montana.

The next time I really wanted to stop. A little boy somewhere
was calling for a strayed kid, urging it back to the fold before night
came, and the wolves. Closer to us, a blackbird sang to the setting
sun from a thicket of pines. There was no hint in his song of
complaint or aggression. The melody rippled out like goats' bells
across the valley, or like the bright Alvoco over its boulders. I did
not care what the ornithologists thought: That blackbird was singing the song I hum when I fish for little wild trout.

Lots of men will tell you that they just go fishing as an excuse to get
out and enjoy nature. Don't believe any of the young ones. Adriano,
however, was seventy-seven years old. He was relieved when we hit
the outlying houses, and I was sorry that I had kept him on the
stream for so long. He wanted a cold beer. Usually he did not drink
it, he said, but this evening he would savor one glass on the terrace
of the *tasca* while he looked out over the valley.

A yellow dog was rubbing his back lasciviously on a small patch
of green grass. It smelled good (even to me) and the rubbing clearly

felt good right up the spine. This was a fulfilled dog. He was of about the size and shape of a coyote, with shorter hair of the same color. He was, perhaps, close to the ancestral Asian wolf, thanks to generations of breeding at random and survival of only those ancestors who needed no attention from veterinaries. I liked this dog. He felt about his rub on the green grass the way I felt about massage by Nereid.

"Anda ca, Pirolito," Adriano called. The first part of that means "come here," and Pirolito is just a name that a Portuguese dog might well have. This one trotted along behind us, ready for adventure.

The next house but one had a *quintal* of packed dirt big enough for a two-person soccer game. One of the persons was a teenaged boy and the other a girl half tomboy and all Nereid. She could kick a ball as well as the boy but she was wearing a plain white dress and pale purple hose. She was almost as flushed as Adriano. The effect was no doubt inexpensive, in her case, but actresses spend large sums to achieve it.

"Who makes the most goals?" Adriano asked.

"I do!" the girl shouted.

"I do!" shouted the boy a moment later. He was a believer in ladies first, at least for pretty ladies.

Adriano chatted with the couple and discovered that Nereid's dress and purple hose were for church, where there was to be some special occasion of a significance lost on me. She and her escort did not exactly walk along with us, but they just happened to head for church right behind us.

Three houses later, the same thing happened, except that the new couple was younger. Ana was eight, she said, and Nuno nine. When asked who made the most goals, both shouted at the same time. Ana thumped on Nuno with an open hand, disputing his claim to equality. Nuno made no attempt to thump back. One day, I thought, he would make a good husband.

"Oh Ana," said Adriano. "You should not hit Nuno. He's a nice little boy." Ana looked at Nuno and giggled. And then we all walked to the car, Adriano doffing his hat to any lady in a doorway or window. I walked beside him, apprentice to the Pied Piper, imag-

ining the reaction in America if a couple of sweaty fishermen hiked off with the town's children. Ana ran circles around us. Nuno watched Ana. Pirolito tried to frisk with smaller dogs, which ran into their houses and yapped at him. The adolescent couple followed.

At the fountain, Adriano was taken by an idea better than cold beer. He paused and drooped. He told Ana of his long day's journey into the lower reaches. He confided the depth of his thirst. She listened. Her eyes were alternately suspicious and sympathetic, but always big and brown. And then she ran back to her house and brought a glass. Adriano accepted it with a bow, filled it, and drank deeply, eyes raised to the mountains. He sighed as the liquid quenched the fire that consumed him. He grew in height, shrank in years. He refilled the glass and raised it for a toast. The eight-year-old Nereid watched. Adriano gave her a speech of gratitude, words murmuring like limpid current over white pebbly bed.

She smiled.

A Church Called Battle

The front lines moved forward on both sides, and the doubtful issue was joined. The Portuguese were inspired to defend their country, the Spaniards to win it. First in battle was the gallant Nuno, engaging the foe and striking them down till the ground seemed in fact to belong to those who so greatly coveted it. The air was thick with arrows, darts and bolts that hissed as they flew; the earth quivered and the valleys echoed to the pounding of horses' hooves; lances shivered, and the noise of men falling in their armor was like claps of thunder. And still the enemy surged forward.

Camões, *The Lusiads*, Canto Four

Adriano took me to the battlefield of Aljubarrota, and as he drove he recited *The Lusiads* on this "land never subjugated." It was lunchtime, thank goodness, with few cars on the road, because he donned the verses and looked down the shaft of his lance, ignoring the arrows, darts, and bolts of traffic.

Aljubarrota was nothing like Gettysburg, with its cannons and historical markers. On the other hand, there was an agreeable absence of advertisements and souvenir shops. The battlefield was just a meadow and a small museum. They were south of Anadia and split by the main Lisbon/Oporto highway—same one the Spanish had marched down in 1385. Adriano and I traced the bloody work of genius, pacing out the old lines of the vanguards and wings. We traveled back to the dream time without help, which may be the only way to do it.

What if, before the battle, I had been one of the Portuguese nobles summoned by their king to discuss the Spanish invasion? Having been to other staff meetings, I can guess how it went. Someone at the table would have started with the intelligence: 42,000 men were marching on Lisbon. They included the whole of Spanish chivalry, 700 French allies, and perhaps 1800 Portuguese who supported the Spanish king's claim to the Portuguese throne. There were sixteen new high-technology weapons called canons. King Juan I led his army; in his retinue was the archbishop of Madrid to crown him king of Portugal when Lisbon fell. Such was his confidence that he had brought even his falcons, for an outing in the Alentejo once the fighting was over.

The Portuguese side might muster one-fifth as many combatants, some of them short on armor. A man without helmet and breastplate could not be expected to stand firm against enemy weapons. There was no artillery. The Portuguese high commander— Constable Nuno Álvares Pereira—had recently won the battle of Atoleiros against the odds, but this time the invaders were taking no chances, risking no half measures.

I would have been with the reasonable men at the meeting, those who wanted to make a deal. After all, the nobility throughout Iberia had always aspired to its unification; Portugal alone was too poor and provincial for grand ambitions. And besides, what good would it do to fight hopeless odds? Why not live for another day? Everyone would have suspected that there would be no other day— not for an independent Portugal, at least—but good company men don't say that kind of thing. Disrupts staff meetings.

Nuno Álvares said it. He, by God, was going to fight. If Portugal had men of courage, they would join him. If not, he and his own few troops would take on the invaders. Camões later imagined Nuno Álvares saying that "This nation has shown the world how to fight. Can there be among its sons those who would deny that it still knows how to defend itself?"

I want to believe that I would have swung to the Constable, but I would have been afraid of fear, afraid that I would be of no use. The fear would have been worse than the dying. Sooner or later I would have to leave this life anyhow, and a brave death in battle would at least get me promoted to Heaven. The experts were sure of that. Perhaps we would even win, because Nuno Álvares was always winning against hopeless odds. Perhaps I could skewer some invader of distinction before he skewered me. My king would then bid me kneel. He would pull his sword through a tussock of grass to wipe off the blood of our enemies. He would tap me on the shoulder and bid me rise, Sir Datus. I would be loyal forever.

My Aljubarrota and Adriano's are different, as you see. His is the site of the battle that secured for his country a glorious, improbable independence. Mine is a yearning for what I used to be, or should have been. My Aljubarrota is a fairy tale that by chance occurred.

I need a hero. Spare me from people who model roles like

fashions. Most of the role models are athletes and other entertainers, anyhow, and they have enough money to dispense with my support. Give me instead the courage to join Nuno Álvares's vanguard or Pickett's charge.

On the other hand, it would make no sense for me to face death with a rebel yell, would it? Who would take care of my family? There is too much invested in me. And besides, I am not quite sure that I'd go to Heaven. Now that we've won the war to end wars, the conflicts are inside me.

Let me drop my excuses and risk everything to find what a human is capable of achieving. Nuno Álvares achieved perfection. He would have made a good drama for Shakespeare—except that he lacked flaws.

Selfishness? Once, during a campaign in the Alentejo, food was so scarce that he had to trade a horse for dinner: six small loaves of bread. Just then a group of his allies, six English knights, came along looking for food. He gave them the loaves.[1]

Debauchery? The young Henry V ran around with Falstaff. Nuno Álvares, age thirteen, ran around reconnoitering Castilian forces before an earlier battle. He reported "many men badly led; and they can be routed by [our] few men well led by a good captain."

Whims? Achilles tried to dodge the draft, and later he sulked in his tent while battle raged. Nuno Álvares missed a bit of fighting only during the battle of Valverde. He had gone off alone to pray for guidance and may have got it, because he came back and won the day.

Lust? Lancelot seduced the king's bride. Nuno Álvares married the king's daughter and seems to have lived happily ever after.

Pride? He was born a bastard, became a count four times over, but never used the honorific title of *Dom*—equivalent of Spanish *Don*.

Cruelty? Under wartime conditions, Nuno Álvares fed hungry Castilian populations near the Portuguese border at his personal expense.

Greed? He customarily refused his commander's share of the spoils of battle.

Recklessness? He had Custer's zeal but no last stands.

Hatred? Once he received in friendship ten squires from the enemy forces who had heard his growing myth and "just wanted to see him," like me.

Well then—fear? Nuno Álvares confessed that he had seen nothing to frighten him. Once, when Castilian ships were blockading Lisbon, he went out at night in a skiff and entered their squadron. Then he ordered trumpets blown to give the enemy a bad sleep.

You may have heard that a hero is one who conquers fear to do what he must, but such courage is episodic, the best most of us can get. We call it heroism because, being in the majority, we cowards write the histories. Real heroes are made of better stuff.

"Nothing disappears forever, and less so our deeds."[2] Nuno Álvares's deeds are still there at Aljubarrota, and I mean to witness them. He's a saint now, "Saint Constable" as his countrymen call him, though I'm not sure that the Vatican concurs. (You cannot rely on an organization that made a fuss even about Saint Patrick.) I commend Nuno Álvares to you not as history but as a hero saint to get you through every night before every day's battle.

Dame Edith Sitwell said that "historians are such liars." When asked why, she replied: "I don't know. They just are."[3]

I could make a guess. There are two kinds of histories: first, the dull, objective, scholarly kind. They are dull because they are accurate, more or less. Give me such histories (though they put me to sleep) for my sources. The other kind of history—the kind that wakes me up—is a report on meaningful, exciting things, things that had consequences. The facts are selected as a robin picks worms, overlooking wide expanses of lawn. The problem is that different robins pick different worms, or worse yet opposite ends of the same worm, leading to battles. No harm is done (except to the worm). This is the kind of history that I enjoy. Give me knights shouting "Saint George!," horses neighing in panic, and a standard bearer holding his flag high with bloody stumps after his hands are lopped off. Then give me also a safe grandstand.

Before the battle, it must be said that King Juan I of Spain was

correct in claiming the Portuguese throne. Most Portuguese noblemen agreed. They were obliged to uphold the medieval principle
that every man had a lord. Portugal's lord was Juan because he had
married the legitimate heir to the throne, and his personal right was
the only one comprehensible. Nuno Álvares and the Portuguese
claimant to the throne had to go around conquering many of the
castles of their own country before they could face the Spanish.
Nuno Álvares then had to face two of his brothers at Aljubarrota,
because the Spanish had placed Portuguese nobles loyal to the right-
ful heir in the first line of battle. Like many wars of independence,
this was also a civil war.

It is time, now, to introduce the Portuguese claimant. I shall use
the title he earned at Aljubarrota: João I. (His name and that of
Juan I, the Spanish king, both translate as John, which is more
confusion than we need.) João was young and a bastard, like Nuno
Álvares. João happened to be a better leader than Juan: decisive,
popular, and tough. João also had an eye for talent and an extraordinary willingness to delegate authority. Many a modern executive
with training in such matters would be unwilling to put a twenty-
five-year-old in charge of history. Not even one like Nuno Álvares.

Aljubarrota was no sporting event, no choreographed contest of
chivalry. Aljubarrota had consequences.

The battle was a thing of the spirit, romance and horror. It was
fought with blades, points, and bludgeons. The cannons fired rocks
plucked from a river's peaceful bed. Pity the shepherds who got in
the way and oozed to death. Pity the tinkers who drowned in red
mud. And if, instead, these "small people" won their battle, there
was no reward but what spoil they could tear from the bodies of
their enemies—more gear for the next battle. Well, there was one
other thing, for the Portuguese: nationalism, a territorial claim satisfied, like the blackbird's. For two years there had been a revolt in
Lisbon against the pro-Castilian aristocracy by the lower classes.
When the bishop of the city had seemed insufficiently nationalist,
the crowd had stripped him and thrown him from a high tower.

What did they dream of the night before the battle, the men and
boys at Aljubarrota? Did they sleep at all? (I do not sleep much

before opening day of hunting season, wondering if I can go the distance, fearing that my dog will meet a viper instead of a partridge. How much worse would it be to spend the night with the prospect of a crossbow's quarrel in my guts?) Nuno Álvares would have said his prayers, rolled up in his cloak, and slept with the angels. The rest of us would have tossed and whimpered, missing mothers' cool hands on hot foreheads. The worst Portuguese casualties the next day would come from the *Ala dos Namorados* , Wing of the Lovers, so called because they were impetuous, romantic youths. Many would go sleepless into death.

The Portuguese were on the field at dawn, claiming a defensive position that Constable Nuno Álvares had picked the day before. It was just above the confluence of two small streams, a wedge of high ground pointed north toward the approaching invaders.

The Spanish had expected no formal battle till they reached the walls of Lisbon, if then. Their intelligence and scouting must have failed, because they first sighted their enemies in late morning and fought in the evening, tired and hungry from a long march. Instead of attacking head-on, uphill against arrows, they skirted the Portuguese position. Nuno Álvares must have feared that his adversaries would decline or postpone battle. That would have been shameful for the Spanish and perhaps disastrous for the Portuguese, who had only one day's food with them. But the Castilians had simply decided to attack from the opposite direction, slightly downhill and with the sun over their shoulders—both tactical advantages. Endless files of men and horses and wagons moved by all afternoon, listening to Portuguese jeers. The Constable had time to reverse his battle formation, facing it southwest; and to dig a trench and make barricades of tree trunks, which would have made it difficult for the Spanish to use horses even if they decided to refuse the challenge to fight man-to-man, on foot. They did not refuse.

This is no shapeless melee. The combatants on the Portuguese side are ordered in three formations, one behind the other.

1. In front is Nuno Álvares's command of 2,850 men. He further divides them into:

a. A center called the Vanguard. Its 650 lancers are in three lines, each 200 yards long—perfect spacing for medieval arms. Each man has almost a yard at each side in which to swing his weapons and sidestep blows, and yet his fellows are close enough to support him.

b. A right wing angling forward. It contains 100 Portuguese crossbowmen and 100 English archers with longbows. The latter are experienced professionals, mercenaries in the pay of the Duke of Lancaster. They have the world's best long-distance weapons and know how to use them, but they must be shielded from hand-to-hand fighting. This is the task of the 950 Portuguese and Gascon soldiers in the front lines of the wing.

c. The Lovers' Wing on the left. The Spanish will predictably swing right, some running into this Portuguese left wing; men with weapons in their right hands always fight to the right. The Lovers have been placed where they will share with the Vanguard the brunt of attack. They are among 850 combatants with "white arms," lances and swords of polished steel. Behind them are 200 crossbowmen.

2. Two hundred fifty yards behind Nuno Álvares's vanguard and wings is the second major Portuguese formation, with just over 2,000 troops. It is commanded by the future King João. He too will fight on foot with his men.

3. At the rear is a third formation composed mostly of men who are, or hope to be, noncombatants. This is the train or *curral* of wagons and livestock, reinforced by 200 crossbowmen in case some Spanish sneak around to the rear. (They will.)

Spanish King Juan is not well (perhaps afflicted by malaria) and does not join the battle. His organized combatants number some 1,750 more than the Portuguese. More could not fit at one time in the confined battlefield chosen by Nuno Álvares. The element of surprise has therefore helped to even the odds.

The Spanish are divided into:

1. A vanguard and wings numbering 3,250 altogether. Many of these front-line fighters are French allies and Portuguese noblemen supporting King Juan.
2. A reserve of 5,000.
3. In the rear, a great mass of noncombatants and of troops who are not organized for battle.

Constable Nuno Álvares will dismount to fight (being a hands-on manager) but for now he is "riding a horse before his Vanguard and wings from one side to another . . . and this to see that each one [of his fighters] is correct in the good and wise order that he first established; bidding them advance very slowly when the Castilians approach and on joining battle to stand firm and plant their feet well, holding their lances straight."[4]

Before the battle, a Castilian delegation approaches to parley. Nuno Álvares knows that it is also observing the disposition of his forces. He tells his enemies "to leave at once lest he order his crossbows to bid them farewell." He is, as you see, the kind of executive who has no trouble with decisions.

Sundown is near and the Spanish are in a hurry to attack. They see a chance to achieve a decisive victory with their superior forces, ending what might otherwise become a drawn-out, inconclusive guerrilla conflict. Besides, the unexpected boldness of the Portuguese challenge has put Castilian prestige at stake.

The attack begins with volleys from the sixteen canons. They do little damage, but they make a noise that terrifies some Portuguese peasants at the rear, in charge of the livestock. Thirty of them flee downhill across a stream and try to hide in the brambles. The Spanish light cavalry runs them down and spears them like pigs. Their screams concentrate the minds of their companions back at the wagons.

The Spanish vanguard and its wings advance. Bad terrain on their sides squeezes them into a shapeless mass. Quarrels and stones from Portuguese crossbows fly low and fast into its edges. Arrows from the English longbows arch high, wink in the evening sun, and plunge into the center of the crowd. This is the image of battle that

I see most clearly. The rest is close, sweaty, grunting stuff, but there is a purity to the flight of arrows and I do not see their victims. The curve of any missile fascinates, transcends gravity. And of all the engines behind the flights, the longbow is the only one that sings like a violin.

The attackers step over writhing comrades but do not falter. Now Nuno Álvares's vanguard advances in its planned slow cadence, lances straight, trumpets blaring. Listen.

The 650 troops of the vanguard face about 2,000 of their enemies. The heaviest fighting surrounds the flag of the Constable, because it represents immortality to any Castilian knight who can seize it. None can. The Portuguese hold for ten minutes, then yield slowly, swinging back from each end in good order. The Spaniards spot the Portuguese royal standard in the second formation and rush to win the day. The Portuguese front lines close behind the Spanish. It is, probably, not a maneuver planned in advance but an opportunity seized by troops of extraordinary discipline.

King João shouts "Forward, St. George of Portugal!" His men drop their lances and take up shorter weapons for fighting at close quarters. The Spanish are surrounded by an enemy now greater in numbers, better spaced, and less tired. There is, however, no difference in sinew or courage, and the attackers keep fighting, condemned by their bravery. Most are dead within half an hour. The Spanish flag falls. Of its warriors, only some 500 escape, fleeing back toward their lines.

You wonder what the Spanish reserves are doing. They are 5,000 strong, enough to overwhelm the Portuguese with a fresh assault. What they lack is a Henry V to order them once more unto the breach, dear friends, once more. The 500 who have fled from hell arrive with Nuno Álvares's vanguard right behind, chopping them down. Their panic demoralizes the reserves. The Spanish king's guards see the confusion, worry for his safety, and hustle him away. The retreat becomes a rout of individuals without a leader.

If you were on the winning side, what would you do in a case like this? I would shake for a long time, have a drink of water, and wait for someone to pat me on the back. Not my hero. Nuno Álvares and his few men seize any horses they can find and pursue tens of thousands of fleeing invaders, preventing them from re-grouping and mounting a counterattack. The Spanish king barely escapes. In all, some 6,400 enemy combatants die and another 5,000 are taken prisoner. As pursuits go, this one has few parallels in the history of warfare.

King João of Portugal stays on the field of victory "for the customary three days," by which time the stench is hard to take. He thanks God and promises to build a great church near the site. The promise will be kept, though the church will take more than one lifetime to complete.

The Portuguese used to invoke St. James when they charged the Moors. They did not call on him at Aljubarrota because the Spanish were doing so, and identical battle cries might have caused confu-sion—among the combatants if not the saints. "Forward, St. George of Portugal!" cried King João. And at Agincourt thirty years later, another king said, if we may believe Shakespeare:

> Follow your spirit; and upon this charge
> Cry "God for Harry, England, and St. George!"

The English connection went deeper than that, deep as an ar-row. The longbows were just earning their reputation in the four-teenth century. A trained English archer could shoot twice as fast as a crossbowman and hit an enemy soldier often at 200 yards. It took the fun out of being a knight in shining armor. I have seen no good account of the archers' performance at Aljubarrota but at Agin-court, thirty years later, they seem to have been decisive. There are other similarities between the two battles. In both, the winning side was "Like little body with a mighty heart," winning against a force five times larger. I could wish that Shakespeare had noticed Al-jubarrota's hero. Shakespeare's drama speaks to me with more force than Camões's panegyric. Today, however, the important things about Agincourt are the play and the myth. Aljubarrota changed the map.

England was there for balance-of-power reasons. England was often in a war with France and Spain, while little Portugal chopped at their knees. If Shakespeare did not notice, C. S. Lewis[5] must have done so; Reepicheep the mouse won the day at Aljubarrota. But these wars are antique now. In the new European order, they may become incomprehensible. Aside from football tournaments, what's the use of nationality?

Well—Portugal may be one of the few European nations with internal unity. It has no equivalent of Catalonia or Languedoc or Wales. Better said, it is a Catalonia or Languedoc or Wales that managed to make nationalism stick. Portugal lacks even the communities that increasingly feud with each other in America.

There is a puzzle. When the Portuguese and the English coordinated tactics, talking of Morlaix and Poitiers, did they also speak of poetry? Camões would celebrate Aljubarrota in meter; Shakespeare would later write of Agincourt in meter. The Spanish could have used meter but did not; the French language is not adapted to it. Mind you, I am just a robin shaking my private worm. For what is may be worth, however, meter does wonders for the martial spirit. You would believe me if you could hear Adriano reciting at the steering wheel.

If you learned about Spain from Ernest Hemingway, you know about the brave bulls and the trout. If you did not learn about Spain from Ernest Hemingway, that's your misfortune. He won all his battles but the last. What you get from him, however, will not help much in Portugal. They don't kill the bulls in Portugal. They don't do much of anything in the same way as the Spanish. Aljubarrota decided that.

Once I went to a Spanish bullfight because of Hemingway. The conflict required much courage from the man with the cape, some from the bull, and a little from me. The moment of truth was not hard to watch—not as hard as professional boxing—because I am accustomed to thinking of cattle as beef. But I closed my eyes when the picador weakened the bull's neck muscles with a lance. This is a personal reaction, not a statement.

(You should not trust me on anything having to do with spectator sports. For my money, the emperor should turn the gladiators free and toss the spectators to the lions, though I would not want to watch that either.)

For some other reason of duty, I also saw a Portuguese bullfight. There was no picador. The bull's neck muscles did not have to be weakened because he had two opponents: horse and man, in that order. The horse was of a special breed called Lusitanian. He violated my concept of horse. I had spent a couple of summers playing cowboy, climbing on horses and falling off, concluding in the end that they were all spectators. Their walnut-sized brains could do nothing but react to stimuli. They got satisfying thrills from mice, ropes, dried deer skins, and stumps in the trail. When the occasional real danger arose, my horses would consider their options carefully and chose the worst of them. The Portuguese bullfighting horse was, by comparison, a hero. He danced within inches of the bull's horns. He bobbed up and down, taunting the bull to charge, then swiveled out of the way and taunted some more. This horse was gladiator, not spectator.

As to the bull, he was not given a pension, but his slaughter took place offstage after the fight, which made the tourists (though probably not the bull) feel better. All things considered, that bull had a better deal than your average Hereford steer.

I do not maintain that the Portuguese bullfight has more or less merit than the Spanish. It is just one more difference between cultures. Of course there are no good generalities on such subjects, but bear with me while I draw some bad ones that might be useful.

In Portugal, the truth does not fit into a moment.

Castile is a castle. Portugal is a port.

Spain in grand. Portugal is modest.

Spain is black and white. Portugal is shades of gray.

Spain was blood red during its civil war. Portugal was flower red in 1974, when revolutionaries sported carnations in their rifle barrels.

Spain conquered half of South America with the sword. Portugal conquered the other half with a different male instrument. (I won't vouch for this, but it is a fair condensation of the Brazilian myth.)

Spanish males still use *Don* as an honorific. The Portuguese still don't use *Dom* for anybody but kings.

The Spanish take siestas. The Portuguese don't.

Spanish food is excellent, but dinner is served when I am asleep: maybe 11 P.M.; maybe midnight; who knows? The Portuguese eat early.

Portugal is a frustration to Spain—a failure of history to complete itself, an absence of symmetry. Spain is an admirable country to Portugal—as long as there is a border in between.

The Spanish answer "*¡sí!*" or "*¡no!*" with two exclamation points each. The Portuguese answer "perhaps," or "that would be rather difficult." I am not sure that they have exclamation points on their typewriters.

A Spaniard looks right at you, sizes you up. A Portuguese would consider that impolite.

In Spain there is a distinctive swagger and proud carriage of the head, even by people who are not balancing burdens on it. The Portuguese walk inconspicuously. If there is one Portuguese in an international group, you have to ask somebody to point him or her out.

The Spanish have celebrities, like Americans. Portuguese celebrities are as scarce as Portuguese fast-food outlets. I would like to tell you the secret of avoiding celebrities and other hot dogs but no one could explain it to me.

The Spanish caricature themselves. The Portuguese try but do not lend themselves well to the art.

Spain is strong and episodic, Portugal weak and persistent. Spain produces picadores and picaros, Portugal neither. Spain produces Quixote; Portugal produces Henry the Navigator.

Quixote would not visit Portugal, though I needed him as much as I needed Nuno Álvares. I wonder: Did they need each other?

Spain has cathedrals. Portugal will not admit to having any, but you ought to see the church called Battle.

It is not easy to make a space like this. Humans worked as high as they could, stretching altitude as they had stretched their forces at Aljubarrota. They achieved something that may or may not be an illusion, depending on your faith. You walk inside, wait for your pupils to dilate, and discover that you are in a place of infinite height. The ceilings pull you up on wings. The wings turn out to be real. They belong to sparrows, cheeping somewhere up near the ceiling, flying among the arches.

My ears, like my eyes, were slow to separate illusion from reality, and the birds made me feel as if I were standing in Adriano's *quintal* expanded a thousand times. No saintly claustrophobia here. The Venerable Bede used sparrows flying through a banquet hall as a metaphor for human life. I would volunteer for adoption by sparrows building nests in the church called Battle.

Adriano told me a story proper to the place. Its old Portuguese architect went blind, so a foreign expert was hired to finish the largest of the vaulted ceilings. When his scaffolding was removed, the ceiling collapsed. The new man tried again, and again the ceiling tumbled, tons of masonry shaking the earth. The old architect said that he could complete the job without sight. The king acceded; perhaps he had no choice. When the scaffolding was removed next time, the blind man sat in the center of the floor, betting his life on his work. The ceiling held. It is still holding. And Portuguese professionals like Adriano are still given the story with their degrees.[6]

I looked for a good engraving of Battle but found none. The edifice is too big for artists, let alone cameras. If you step outside and walk a long distance, you can finally take in the whole church. By then it looks human in scale, though it is not. Up close you see only pieces of wall and column. Each is fantastically intricate, each saint individual in features. But what you see is detail, not Battle. You have to walk around it and through it, absorb it through the lens of your brain, get used to the fact that it is taller inside than out.

Just outside there is a big equestrian statue of the Saint Constable with his sword. He looks as young as Saint Joan, by no coincidence. He deserves a permanent bronze horse if anyone does, but I'd have put him on foot, as he fought at Aljubarrota. I do not remember the inscription but this is what it ought to read:

*   *   *

"Advance slowly when the enemy approaches, and on joining battle stand firm and plant your feet well, holding your lance straight."

Guiding your dreams is not difficult, when you get the hang of it. You picture what you wish and find yourself in the picture as you drift off to sleep. The only trick is that the picture must be accepted by whatever part of your subconscious makes such decisions. Base desires do not pass inspection; I've tried them.

Aljubarrota works. You line up on a meadow at the edge of sleep, comrades a yard away at either side. You grip your lance in sweaty palms. Your armor hides a frightened little boy. You might lose the battle, even if your name is Hemingway. You advance slowly when the trumpets sound. You take comfort from your fellows on each side, and in the corner of your eye you see the banner of your hero.

Bless us, Saint Constable.

A SERIOUS PEOPLE

Venus . . . was attracted to the Portuguese, seeing in them many of the qualities of the ancient Rome she had loved so much: their stout hearts and favouring fortune—witness the conquests in North Africa—[and] their tongue, which may so easily be taken for a Latin once removed. And there was another reason. The Fates had given her clearly to understand that, wherever this warlike race extended its sway, there too her praises would be sung.

CAMÕES, *The Lusiads,* Canto One

Camões met Venus in old books at the University of Coimbra. Young men had an incentive for classical learning in those days: It was racy stuff, at least by comparison to the rest of the texts that the good fathers thought appropriate. The young poet must have managed a closer look at Venus, too, because his erotic verses were his best. He would have met a girl in town. To get there, he would have hiked down the footpath known as the back-breaker, like every other student over the centuries. In Coimbra, downtown is really down.

Somebody, sometime, must have given serious thought to the university's location. It is away from the biggest cities, near the center of the Portuguese littoral, and perched on a hill overlooking the lower reaches of the Mondego, longest river with its source in the fatherland. It is a view that could not have just happened. It was calculated to broaden the sweep of young minds.

Adriano and I climbed the hill of learning, scuffing red and gray cobblestones that looked as if they had been there since the sixteenth century, perhaps because they had. Adriano had accepted the responsibility of showing me his country and would not shirk. He would ensure that my tens of millions of readers grasp his language and culture. If he had any concerns about the skill of his interpreter (me), he did not display them. If he doubted that the subtlety of his language could be rendered in the bluntness of mine, he did not let on. He just led the way up the back-breaker. It was crossed by cobbled streets barely wider than the path, from which baby Fiats burst at speeds suitable for a grand prix. We stopped often and pretended to admire the views, breathing heavily. I remember an ancient house with wildflowers growing from cracks in the tiled roof. It had a manicured garden down below, tall cabbage woven into the scheme of colors.

Progress had reached the university before we did and filled it with building as ugly as those that my own university is still building in Ithaca, New York. But there was an old library, too, and in it we asked to see the oldest books in the Portuguese language. The librarian did not seem to know where they were. They should have been on display under glass, as the Irish display the *Book of Kells* at Trinity College. No language is worth more than the history invested in it.

Take English: It is a conglomerate of foreign investments. Its several Indo-European founders set up business at different times and contended vigorously for my trade. The Celtic tongue of the native Britons was unable to compete and went bankrupt. The others, after hostile mergers, formed a consortium known as English Limited. They cut costs by simplifying gender, splitting infinitives, and extirpating case. (Good riddance, say I.) On the other hand, they built a great inventory of words by pooling the stocks of all the constituent companies. They then put Shakespeare to work turning out vocabulary on an assembly line. Modesty aside, I invent a word myself now and then. The old business is English Amalgamated now, world's largest producer of word-processing software, lingua franca of business, science, education, war, art, and probably Venus. Some 330 million people even speak English as their native tongue.[1] We still make decisions without committees, though. No *Académie* for us.

There is another way to put it: Had English evolved anywhere but in Europe, it would be called a creole, chaotic in its vocabulary, convoluted in its etymologies. On the other hand, creoles are logical in word order and economical in syntax. When you stay in a Portuguese hotel, have a look at the list of regulations posted on the inside of your door. They will be written in four columns: one each for Portuguese, French, German—serious languages all—and then English. The English column will be the shortest. Shakespeare wrote not for the court, like Camões, but for a rowdy audience sitting around a stage. The customers were short of patience. They still are, it seems.

The Spanish language has 260 million native speakers. If Sir Francis Drake had not sunk the Armada in 1588, the tongue of Castile might have spread even further. Its victory would have been a perfect disaster: retrograde politics coupled to the ideal lingua franca. Spanish is crisp and precise, as sharp-edged as printing on good stock. The language is easy to learn, too. Vowels and consonants have logical values that scarcely vary. When you see a Spanish word, you know how to pronounce it. A scholar who did not understand the workings of the world once invented a universal language called Esperanto, and of course it sounded like Castilian. Why bother? If you stay in the original, you also get a great literature.

(Linguists, by the way, may try to tell you that all languages are equally easy. Pay no attention to this foolishness. All languages are easy for children born into them, but children are instinctive linguistic geniuses. Adults, on the contrary, are logical linguistic dolts, and for us some languages are very much easier than others.)

With 150 million native speakers, Portuguese fits right here, after English and Spanish. I have passed over the dialects of Chinese, which should have come first, because they form a sea that I cannot navigate. And I shall do French before Portuguese in order to make the French feel better. For the record, though, French has two-thirds as many native speakers (100 million).

French culture and literature are as good as the French think. The people are as rational as the Portuguese and have more resources to work with. Life's little chores—those the rest of us brush off—are analyzed and then done right. This is why the world uses French recipes. For one frustrated with the rest of a slipshod universe, Gallic logic always comes as a relief. Well, almost always. When it comes to language, you must deal with this proposition: (a) French is the only acceptable world tongue. (b) It must be kept pure. (c) Ergo, only the French can be trusted with it.

If you try to learn French, you will have to pass muster or your interlocutor will walk away. The British understand this kind of behavior—perhaps because they, like the French, remember Agincourt. Americans find it all puzzling. The French won't tell you what we did wrong, so I will.

We frustrated destiny. We made English into the language of textbooks in Beijing, T-shirts in Prague, and even movies in Paris. But for North America, English might have been roughly equal to French in both native speakers and world presence. With us in the game, there is no contest. Our ebullient presence has been known to discomfit even the British (who feel a residual responsibility for us), and for the French (who don't), our language is original sin. The guiding principle of French policy has been to find out what the English-speakers want and then propose something different.

Portuguese-speakers everywhere are as polite as Americans (as opposed to Parisians and New Yorkers). If you learn only "good day"—*bom dia*—your hosts will say, with great sincerity, "You speak our language so well." With that kind of encouragement, you will indeed find yourself speaking it before long. The hardest part is forgetting English. Your hosts are logical Latins and would not tolerate a word like *slough*, which means three different things and is pronounced in a different way for every one of them. In other respects, however, the Portuguese language evolved like ours, fighting its way into existence, colonizing regions where it was not native, and then civilizing itself in universities.

Once I asked a Portuguese diplomat how he negotiated with his brother Iberians. "They speak Castilian," he said, "and we understand. Then we speak Portuguese and they pretend not to understand." But they understood once.

In the "time of the troubadours during the Middle Ages, the language adopted by all Peninsular poets . . . whether from Leon, Castile, or Aragon, was the Galician-Portuguese tongue."[2] It was considered "suave and sweet," appropriate to love songs. Castilian, on the other hand, was for war. Camões would have been aware of this history when he wrote of Venus's penchant for his countrymen.

Camões's tongue is one of great subtlety. You will be told this of every language you don't know, from Eskimo to Irish, and it is always true, but they are subtle about different things. The Eskimos specialize in snow and the Irish specialize in words as words. As for Portuguese, I am not about to argue with the troubadours. Its sounds are soft, even indistinct to those unfamiliar with the language.

Consider the word *Coimbra*: It derives from *Conimbriga*, a Roman city whose ruins lie not far from the university. *Conimbriga* sounds like a military command, sharp and clear, pronounceable by a legionnaire from any part of the diverse Roman Empire. The Portuguese *Coimbra* drops the consonants *n* and *g*. The *m* and *b* are indistinct. You could change the vowels *o* and *a* to *u* and *e* without hearing much difference. In the whole word, then, an English-speaker might be certain of only the hard initial *C*. No wonder the Portuguese seem reticent: Their very language is shy.

The way to learn, of course, is to go where Portuguese is played and get involved. (When you study language instead of doing it, you addle your brains. Look what happened, for example, when a lot of bright people who should have been writing English went about deconstructing it instead.)

Brazil is the easiest place to get the hang of Portuguese. Americans who believe that they have no talent for language are pulled into slangy Portuguese after a few weeks in Rio de Janeiro or São Paulo. Part of the difference is a New-World attitude shared with North Americans: Language is supposed to be fun. But there's more to it than that. Mother Portugal was too small, poor, and distant to have much influence on its giant ex-colony after independence. The Brazilians went off on their own with an innocent disregard for rules, much like the peasants who blundered into the English language after 1066. Brazilians sharpened their vowel sounds, stopped pronouncing *s* as *sh*, changed rhythms, and added an irresistible enthusiasm. The living is better in Portugal but I'll always be a foreigner there. In Brazil I was a Brazilian.

Don't misunderstand: The Brazilians speak Portuguese, but it is further from that of the mother country than American usage is from British. Until I was a teenager, it did not occur to me that Robin Hood and Tom Sawyer came from different countries. Brazilians of my age were not so lucky. Their own writing was in flower when that of Portugal was stagnant under censorship.

When in Lisbon I heard Portuguese-language music on the radio, I knew instantly whether it came from Portugal or Brazil. When I heard popular music in the English language, however, I could often not decide whether it was from England or America.

Irish, Scottish, and Australian accents are identifiable in song, but English-English and American-English frequently are not. The only explanation I can find is that they originated in the same dialect of medieval English. Something in music digs deeper into origins than everyday speech.

There are real women in Shakespeare's verses but not in those of Camões. The English poet wrote drama, which required humans, and the Portuguese wrote an encomium, which required super- and subhumans. Perhaps Camões thought that he was treating females in the only way possible. Then again, he might have been able to turn Venus into Portia if his audience had wished to look into her head instead of under her gown. I am not leaping to conclusions.

What is clear is that Portuguese history was about men. We know of Camões's education at Coimbra. We have his bones, buried in a great tomb. We have his verses on pretty green eyes. We have the effects without the causes. If the green eyes belonged to a princess, did the poet fancy her just because he could not have her? How about the others at Coimbra who were not so hard to get?

Camões certainly did not worry about *machismo*, because the word is a recent construct. Neither my Portuguese-English nor Spanish-English dictionaries contain it. They do have the noun *macho*, translated primarily as "male." The Portuguese-English dictionary adds some secondary meanings, all of which would be used as compliments: "(vulgar) lover . . . (popular) strong, virile, robust, manly." The Spanish-English dictionary offers nothing similar but reports these secondary meanings for *macho*: "stupid fellow; foreigner, Anglo-Saxon; (colloquial) blonde."

So. We Anglo-Saxons borrowed a Latin word that the Latins, or at least the Spanish, use to describe Anglo-Saxon blockheads. Let us take this as fair warning that the subject has its pitfalls. Portuguese familiar with the term *machismo* have, I think, picked it up recently in Coimbra or some other university, from American writing.

Well, never mind what the Iberians think. I know what *machismo* means for us Yanks. It afflicted one of my wife's friends in Washington—a hardworking, pretty Uruguayan woman who married a hardworking, ugly Ecuadorean man. She took him and their new baby home to meet her family. Her sister had to fight him off. The marriage broke up. Now the woman had to work harder than ever to support both herself and her baby daughter. When the child grows up, she will be told to look out for men. Girls have been ignoring that warning for years (as witness the increase of the world's population), but it remains sound advice, Lord knows. If I had a daughter she would hear lots of it from me.

The Brazilians had a different angle. At least, the Brazilian men I knew preferred romance to conquest. The romance was a kind of lie in which both parties colluded, for a time—love as a nonce word. Portuguese is the language of Venus, remember, not Mars. A Brazilian man did not sweep a woman off her feet. He "sang" her—a literal translation of *cantou*, though he might not literally resort to music. The women listened, anyhow. An endless stream of them moved from country to city and found short-term male companions. The women had not heard that being a sex symbol was a bad thing, and they played the role with extravagant success. Girls are as clever as boys, remember, and faster-starting. I was not quite sure who was seducing whom. I was not even sure whether the problem was the game itself or the general powerlessness of women. Both sexes had fun but the men moved on. The women could not follow.

I lived in Portugal longer than in Brazil but learned less of Portuguese women. The difference is that women were, by far, the leading subject of conversation among Brazilian men. Portuguese men, on the contrary, followed a rule that I had thought Anglo-Saxon: Gentlemen don't talk. They do not kiss and tell, anyhow. If discretion is a virtue, the Portuguese serious man has us out-virtued.

And besides, Portuguese women are just emerging from their black dresses, which are as close to a chrysalis as anything in the Western world. It's hard to identify a butterfly till its wings have dried. Montana girls were riding and shooting in the nineteenth century, affrighting the dudes, but respectable Portuguese maidens still did not go out unchaperoned in the 1950s. An American male invited one to the movies and found himself taking her mother too. When I heard of this, I tried to have a chuckle with my friend Miguel, who told me that I did not understand the problem. "If we

Portuguese are alone with a girl," he said, "we try it, every time."

I guessed that girls knew how to cope, every time.

"They know how to cope with Americans," Miguel said. "We do not give up as easily." This was in Angola, where European men perfected their technique with African women and European women were easily cloistered. The code was not fundamentally different in metropolitan Portugal, however—just more difficult to enforce.

What is astonishing is that so much has changed. My wife and I knew Portuguese professional women whose lives did not differ from those of Americans. There was, on the other hand, a booming market for True Romances. My wife found herself consoling pretty young Emília, not very bright, who had let a slubberdegullion climb in her window because he sang of his devotion as ardently as a blackbird. And then there was Maria, old enough to know better, who had walked out on a good husband in order to look for what she called "the man of my life." He turned up in a bar, and he barely hung around till dawn. I called him Sir Lancelot till my wife brought me up to date: He was the phantom of the soap opera. It is true that Maria had started using Brazilian slang.

The Portuguese male code has gone through fewer changes, and I know more about it. It has less to do with inciting the sex drive than managing it. Come to think of it, males need little incitement, anywhere; our hormones make fools of us whether or not they are encouraged. There is a notion that sex is for conception—padres of certain respectable religions will still tell you so—but nothing could be further from the truth. The purpose of sex will be clarified when we meet a young couple named Oomph and Whoopee a few pages from now. For the moment, it is enough to say that young males in pursuit of sex look on pregnancy as a kind of social disease. It invariably spoils the fun and can lead to serious consequences, like marriage.

The link between sex and commitment must therefore be forged by culture. A culture that cannot do the job has broken down, and its babies are deprived of fathers. Americans will not have to look far for examples. For the most part, though, our culture works. Portuguese culture, being more uniform, works more predictably.

Young males gather their rosebuds while they may, and then one day the florist's bill comes due. Sounds Victorian, but the message is older than Queen Victoria by a few million years. Of course some men are hard to convince; Don Juan is their archetype. Do you remember his fate? Monks killed him, on behalf of society.

Someone is going to accuse me of failing to recognize *machismo* when I see it. Allow me to introduce, as a witness for my defense, a scholar who worked across the border from Portugal in Spanish Andalusia. But remember that the Iberians do not share even the word with us. Let's use *manhood* instead: author David Gilmore's term.[3]

> A real man is one who provides for his family, protects his dependents, and produces babies. He is not a bully, never a wife beater. . . . The brutal *machismo* of violent men is not real manhood in these cultures, but a meretricious counterfeit—the sign of weakness. . . . "Real" men are those who give more than they take.

Boys do not become real men just by growing older. Boys are born but men are made and what separates the two stages is a trial. It was highly organized in some societies that Gilmore studied. In the Kalahari Desert, boys of a hunter-gatherer culture earned manhood by stalking and killing a large antelope single-handedly. In Melanesia—a culture of planters, not hunters—the trials involved brutal beatings. The human sacrifice was not shared with an animal.[4]

Modern societies seem to me different from those of both hunter-gatherers and peasant farmers. Some of us boys get to choose our own rites of passage. Perhaps this is why (when we are no longer boys) we describe ourselves as self-made men. We are either self-made or we are not men at all.

The key to the trials of passage, Gilmore thought, "lies in the inherent weaknesses of human nature, in the inborn tendency of all human beings, male and female, to run from danger." Manhood is "the moral force that culture erects against the eternal child in men, that makes retreat impossible by creating a cultural sanction literally worse than death: the theft of one's sexual identity." A few heroes like Nuno Álvares are unafraid to defend their tribes, but the rest of us would rather make love than war. We find ourselves standing in the Wing of the Lovers just the same, gripping our lances. But when—as in the America of the Vietnam War—women tell us that what used to be manhood is now nasty, we are easily turned from lions into lambs, or at least rams. (A biologist whose name I have lost commented that males are a vast breeding experiment run by females.)

Gilmore must have understood what manhood means in Iberia, because he described Adriano without meeting him. Adriano had made himself a man at university and in life. He was not a fake, not a shell, but a construction of his own choosing. I knew little of the underlying Adriano. I knew nothing of his youthful dreams, excesses, and failures. For me he was Adriano the Fearless, no more or less. In this sense he was myth—not all of history but the part that mattered.

Adriano did not know exactly where the playing fields of Coimbra were: somewhere below the hill of learning, he thought. The university had athletic teams but sports were voluntary. And I recalled that there had been no college games on television.

I tried to explain American college sports. Adriano did not at first comprehend the connection between students and athletes. When he understood, he maintained a polite silence. The serious person is *ponderado*; he ponders before he speaks. He must neither lie nor be gratuitously hurtful, so he often chooses to say nothing.

Of course the Portuguese have no monopoly on seriousness, but they perfected the art as the English perfected fly fishing. Portugal could never afford France's *hauteur* or Spain's disdain for commerce. The Brazilians think of the Portuguese as "sad, formal, even repressed."[5] Camões had an effervescent innocence, almost American, but it has long since boiled off from his fatherland.

At risk of making this sound like the Scout's Honor, I shall tick off the serious person's other qualities. And come to think of it, Adriano would approve of the Scout's Honor.

The serious person believes in:

Himself. When I asked what distinguishes a serious person, Adriano replied, first, that he is *com mérito*—with merit. It is not a flexible concept. It must be proven in academia or by some other rigorous test.

Values. The serious person makes judgments—after thought—on what is meritorious or worthless, lasting or shallow.

Culture. The serious person does not pursue all of the arts; that would be dilettantism. But he respects them. More important, he accepts his society's cultural rules.

Intelligence. He prefers bright politicians to those as thick as the rest of us. He debates intellectual matters. He may watch television, but he does not talk about it.

Modesty (or perhaps it is circumstantial humility). The Portuguese have fallen short of their own history: Who would not? They have failed to keep pace with the rest of the world, too; Salazar chose for them to be "proudly alone" in their African wars, and in the end they were humbly alone.

Organization. It is a feature of Portugal that amazes foreigners, especially if they have experienced Latin America. Despite a third-world standard of living, things work in Portugal. The springs are tested for pure water, the children get an education, the mail is delivered, and the police maintain order.

Looking the part. Remember the fancy edition of Camões? The sailors are in tatters, Venus's gown is slipping, and the Nereids have lost their raiment entirely, but Vasco da Gama is in impeccable armor, steaming.

Coherence. The serious person works out a thesis and guides his life by it. He expects that it will triumph *in the long term.* He does not expect a fat bottom line in a year or even a decade. This is the great gap between the politics of Latin Europe and America: We cannot imagine why they fuss over theses instead of getting on with the job; they cannot comprehend candidates who stand for whatever is necessary to get reelected.

Group identity. Americans wear clothes that demand to be looked at. Portuguese clothing is meant to disappear in the crowd. It is not just a matter of taste. America holds individualism in high regard; Portugal prizes collective identity more than any other European nation, with the possible exception of Greece.[6] Adriano fights his country's battles, wants no language but his own, and flies the Portuguese airline as far as it goes.

My wife and I gave him sound advice before he visited us in Montana. Take an American carrier, we said; it will get you all the way from Lisbon to Bozeman in one day. We will meet you at the airport. Think of your comfort.

We were thinking of his safety. Production of Adriano's model ended before most Americans were born. On an American street, he would stand out like a Duesenberg. What he did, of course, was what he had always intended to do. He flew to New York on his own country's wings. He made no onward reservations because he was determined to cross America in a Pullman car, seeing the villages along his route. It was a good idea except that passenger trains do not come this way anymore. He got here on wait-listed flights after two overnight stops in cities that he could not pronounce. He said that he had enjoyed the whole trip but that the best thing, for him, had been the helpfulness of every American he met, even if he could not understand what they were saying.

He was not tired by the last short flight, so we drove the long way to our house. We watched the farmers harvesting their first cutting of alfalfa, half-ton bales bumping off the back of machines the size of European cottages. An ocean of wheat was still rippling. Around the plain were purple mountains. I tried to translate the song we used to sing in school right after the pledge of allegiance, back when that sort of thing was encouraged.

"Please keep on driving," Adriano said. "*É lindo.*" It's beautiful.

But if he reacted to the countryside as we did, he saw a different town. We drove through the late-Victorian houses of the Historic Preservation District; he thought it a modern suburb. We pointed in pride to the old storefronts on Main Street; he was amazed that cars actually stopped at stop signs. We paused to show him trout streams under the bridges; he wondered why so many businesses and houses chose to display American flags.

And then there were the people. I thought that Adriano would like the joggers, after the square women in black dresses back home. But it was not the joggers that he mentioned.

He started pointing out *senhoras gordas*. The fat ladies were inconspicuous among the young and fit, but equally numerous. He had never seen so many, he said, except perhaps in Germany. He hoped that we would not be offended. He had simply noticed something that must have a meaning. A serious person had to move from observation to comprehension.

My wife and I had not seen the *senhoras gordas* till they were called to our attention. Portugal produces a sturdy average; America produces the beautiful and the invisible. And women, it seems, run to extremes more often than men. From there we let Adriano work out his own synthesis.

At our house, he unpacked and hung his six wool suits in the closet (where they remained for the rest of his stay). Then he pulled a stack of fifty-dollar bills from the breast pocket of his coat and asked my wife to hide them. He explained that he did not trust credit cards.

Over dinner, he told us of his excursion in New York. He took a taxi to Harlem to see how grassroots America lives. From there he tried to hike back to his hotel, but he does not use maps and he got a little turned around. Another taxi pulled up, this time unhailed. The driver turned out to be a Portuguese from the Azores. Instead of wandering lost through Harlem, bale of banknotes bulging his vintage foreign jacket, my friend got a guided tour and a dinner at the driver's home.

Just before his first sleep in Montana, Adriano asked if there were any rattlesnakes in the state. He had seen them in cowboy movies.

There were plenty of snakes, I admitted, but not up in the mountains where we would be fishing. He need not worry.

He was not worried.

I saw my duty and I did it. I drove him to snake country. What happened was not my fault: Somehow rattlers never show up when you are looking for them.

Adriano the Fearless had to return to Portugal without meeting anything venomous.

· 12 ·

SECRETS OF NATURE

So, you daring race. . . . You have come to surprise the hidden secrets of nature and of its watery element, that to no mortal, however great, however noble or immortal his deserts, have yet been revealed. Listen now to me and learn what perils have been laid up against such excess of presumption.

CAMÕES, *The Lusiads*, Canto Five

The Mondego River plunges from the highest range in Portugal, cuts through the steepest gorge, and dawdles past the oldest university. The flow sections the nation's land and people: granite and shepherds at the top, then terraces and peasants, bottomlands and farmers, streets and students, salt marshes and shipyards. This stream is to Portugal's natural history what Sagres is to its human achievements.

Adriano and I wanted to drink from the Mondego's source and cower in its canyon. We were in no hurry, however. I was working up courage for the passage—a translation of *passagem*, meaning a place on the gorge's cliffs where one passed or one didn't. Adriano the Fearless just wanted to work up to the best part gradually, enjoying the preliminaries.

"I like to watch the brooks," he said. It was what he had said about the *meninas* back in the Alentejo, but for streams we got out of the car and stared without shame. Had we rushed, we might have driven from Anadia to our lodgings near the upper Mondego in three hours, but Adriano chose to spend the afternoon admiring nature.

We were not disappointed. The rocks below the bridges were round and smooth. At their bases, fringes of grass shaded the dark places that we coveted. Upstream, arms of water spread out into the hills. Two or three times Adriano told me that he had caught trout in some hidden pool. At the other crossings, we speculated that the rivulets must be big enough to fish, judging from their topography; and then we imagined unplumbed pools protected by hidden passages. Few anglers would be man enough but we were sure that *we* could pass, if only life gave us time.

You might think that the topic would run dry. It doesn't. Not even when the river shrivels. Men see nature's sculpture on women, women's bodies in nature. We are not deterred when the notion is ludicrous. (There was a movie, once upon a time, that compared Marilyn Monroe to Niagara Falls, and I went to see it anyhow.) Nature is always female. This confession is embarrassing, today, and we might be persuaded not to talk about our vision, but in the dream time we paint her on our cliffs, up beside the mammoths and elands. There is no future in father nature—not for men, at least. Women may have any vision they wish, though I hope they won't stick fishhooks in it.

We had better call on Oomph and Whoopee to untangle this. You did not know that there was a tangle? Well, look at Sigmund Freud's twisted sheets. Not that he didn't do good work. The problem was that he lived in turn-of-the-century Vienna. What was a nice Jewish boy to do in that decadent town? Not fishing, surely. There was scarcely a chapter of Trout Unlimited in the Austro-Hungarian Empire. Freud was squeezed into the only re-creation permitted: sex. No wonder he got carried away. In that hothouse, everyone was steaming the windows. But here is what Freud would have seen if he had wiped them off.

There are two drives: hunting and sex. Hunting came first. Our forefather, Oomph, kept himself busy on the trail of elands, which are the largest of antelopes. The pursuit was so demanding that Oomph did not have much time for our foremother. At least that's what he told her. What he did not say was that the chase was exciting and the company good. Deciding which of the men was in charge could be awkward, but once that point was settled each of them could be counted on to help his comrades without making complicated demands in return.

One hunt led to another and Oomph covered a lot of territory. He seldom saw Whoopee, his woman (and everybody else's). It was a good arrangement, for Oomph. It was not so good for Whoopee. Her breeding cycle came around only every three or four years, after the last baby stopped nursing. At such times she was a celebrity. At other times the men were somewhere far off, perhaps hunting, perhaps visiting other camps, who knows? Whoopee had to get by on such roots as she could dig up with the rib of an eland. She found enough to eat. In fact (as she reminded Oomph), she often produced more food than him and his damned antelope. But the whining. No sooner was a young anthropoid weaned than she, or especially he, would announce that he hated vegetables. Whoopee would reply that all the children loved vegetables in the good old days. This had no effect. The brats always complained and Whoopee always threatened to toss them to the hyenas, but she didn't. She had a better idea.

Whoopee developed an innovative estrous cycle. Instead of making her attractive to Oomph almost none of the time, it made her appealing almost all of the time. The change scandalized the rest of the mammals and especially sister chimpanzee, who said that, for her, once every few years was more than enough. Whoopee replied that she liked the new arrangement, sort of, and was even thinking of growing breasts. Sis Chimp walked off in a huff and the two have not conversed since.

On Sis Chimp's behalf, it must be said that Whoopee's innovation did open Pandora's box, if you will pardon the metaphor. Some generations later, Freud tried to catch all the odd creatures that had flown out of the box and decided, with Sis Chimp, that sex was to blame for them. What Freud disremembered (or never had a chance to discover) is that sex had been caused by hunting.

Whoopee got some changes made. Oomph started hanging around the camp, going off for just a day or two at a time. He didn't get as many elands but there were bushbucks closer to Home (which was the name of the camp), and if the bushbucks failed, there were always wart hogs or dik-diks or something. Whoopee and Buster (the latest brat) were getting more protein, salt, and fat. On the new diet, Buster's brain grew uncontrollably, leading him to invent prepositions.

By now, however, the deal was better for Whoopee and Buster than for Oomph. He was getting nothing that he had not had before—just getting it more reliably and without hiking so far. He felt tied down. It made him moody. Whoopee thereupon persuaded Oomph that he had exclusive rights to her person. She didn't want to monkey around with the rest of the men, she said. She preferred Oomph even when he got hurt by an eland. (They are not wee timorous beasties, you know.) She bandaged him up with a zebra skin that she had chewed till it was soft. She told him that she liked him as much as she liked the latest baby. Nobody had liked him that much since his mother was eaten by a leopard. He did not admit it, but he liked being liked.

It may be, as Whoopee suspected, that Oomph got frisky when he recovered and visited the distant camps, but he always came home afterward. Later, as the sea shrank, the two of them hiked across the straits of Gibraltar, still together (some of the time). They became the first Portuguese. Oomph learned to hunt mammoths, which were very large but not very bright. When they were gone, he guddled trout in the Mondego River. He found fishing one of the slower varieties of hunting, modern and decadent, but it beat sitting around the cave while Whoopee thought up useful projects for him.

You see, now, why the peculiar human estrous cycle has little to do with making babies. It has to do with persuading Oomph to take on a commitment. But perhaps you find this history, or prehistory, abominably sexist. Be assured that I could do a better job if it had been left to me rather than a couple of primitives. The anthropology here is consistent with behavior of known hunter-gatherers like the Bushmen, consistent too with the paintings in caves not far from the Mondego. Of course there are other versions of prehistory—but the burden of proof is on those who think that progenitors were radically different from their descendants.

Let us take it, then, that hunting and sex are competitive drives. Of the two, the hunting drive is the easiest to sublimate. The hunter can turn into a soldier, scientist, or even a writer without losing his Oomph. What has not changed is the way Oomph and Whoopee are put together. You can dress them in fashions instead of skins but you cannot alter their genes without selective breeding, which is frowned upon for our species. You can take Oomph out of the elands but you can't take the elands out of Oomph. (I shall not venture to guess what the equivalent of elands is for Whoopee.)

One scholar points out that "an accurate account of human

history in 30 minutes would devote 29 minutes and 51 seconds to hunter-gatherers, more than 8 seconds to settled agricultural society and a fraction of the last second to the modern, fossil-fuel-fired industrial world."[1] No wonder that Adriano and I had a useless old urge to hunt for trout.

We climbed the Range of the Star not far from the Alvoco's Nereids, but in a different watershed. We parked for a drink of the Mondego up where it was small enough to spot from a fountain. On impulse I bought a cup from a peddler who was waiting by the spring for live ones. The cup was of tourist pottery, ugly and green, with a shepherd and his Mountain Dog in relief. I baptized it in the fountain, drank from it, and kept it to help me remember the taste.

We stopped at a hotel that Adriano remembered as having been good, once. The ancient couple in the bar seemed surprised that we wanted to spend the night. On my room's wall hung a framed, faded photograph of a British ship—one of the Queens on her maiden voyage. Over the porcelain washbowl was a shelf with a drinking glass and a water flask. I set out to take a sponge bath (useful skill, in Portugal) but stopped when I got a close look at the flask. It was yellowed by a crust inside: mineral deposits from old plumbing. Next door Adriano said O diabo— The devil—which is his strongest language. I looked in and saw him standing at the washbowl, socks wetter than his face. The water had poured onto his feet from its rusted-out drain pipe when he pulled the plug.

Next day at dawn we stopped in Videmonte, but not for long. It was the village closest to the Mondego's gorge. Everything was stone: the walls of the fields, the narrow road that twisted through them, and the houses. The chapel and a few of the other buildings had coats of cement covered by paint. The house of José Sequeira Mendes had no such cosmetics, but it had Adriano's friends. We greeted them—briefly, because there was a long walk ahead, and we would have to hurry to get out of the canyon before dark, even in the long twilight of late May. José loaned his son Manuel to the expedition. Manuel stowed his staff in the car and jumped in with us.

Adriano would fish near the ford across the Mondego, he said.

But first he dropped Manuel and me at the bottom of the gorge. The young man would be my guide. He was lean and strong from a stint in the army, brown fist curled around the staff.

The river was half blue, half foamy-white, and small at the bottom of its canyon. Manuel showed me the goat trail down through the rocks. I rushed to assemble my rod and tie on a team of three Portuguese wet flies. They should have been good before the sun warmed the water, but the trout paid no attention. I cast upstream through the pools, letting the flies drift back past me, deep. Then I fished cross-stream and watched the line swing around in the current. In desperation, I teased the top fly along the surface, the two below it serving to keep my leader straight. It is a good method for eager trout, but these weren't.

(River my love, you are cold. You shove me when you're close. You grumble when you're not. Don't push me away: Give me a fish. I've been faithful to you, in my way, so now be kind.)

I would have to move faster, Manuel said, or we would not get out by sundown. I tried jumping along the rocks like him and suddenly found myself on my back. The water cushioned my fall but I was not grateful. Somehow my whole torso had landed in the river with my legs above, on dry land. It was a position that I had never before achieved despite my acknowledged expertise at falling into rivers. Ego aside, this was not as bad as my conventional tumble because the hip-boots did not fill with water and my trunk would blow dry soon enough. The bright side did not occur to me right away, though.

We came to an eddy that had created a little foothold for alders. A bird was dancing in them but I paid no attention, drifting my fly deep under the brush, troutless. The bird still danced. It was a desperate dance, but then I was getting desperate myself. The flutter came again and I saw that the victim was a *pintasilgo* of sweet song. I waded the stream, boots shipping water. The finch had tried to eat a trout fly that someone had cast across the stream with a spinning rod. The float had caught in the alders, the line had broken, and the fly had dangled, a cruel trap. I unhooked the bird and held it for a moment to calm down, soft black and yellow body quiet in my caress, scarlet face looking at me. When I opened my hand the finch lay for a moment, not realizing that it was free, and then flashed off through green leaves.

Flocks of goldfinches are called charms, with good reason. My damsel in distress did not say thanks but I hoped that it was relieved not to be popped in a cage like most in Portugal.

My own line had been dangling in the current below me during the rescue operation. I waded back to shore, cleaned the flies of some flotsam they had picked up, and cast them to the upstream end of the eddy. My intention was just to get the line straightened out so that I could wind it back evenly onto the reel. Chances of catching anything after that commotion were slim. But the line twitched as it drifted under a limb and I pulled the rod tight. A strong trout flashed gold, hooked on the top fly. I trotted her downstream at once, keeping the angle between me and fish constant till she tired and slid into my net. She was a brown trout, Portuguese native of antecedents older than Adriano's. As I released her, my back began to feel warm and little glints reflected from the current. The sun was out.

I want my Nereids shy and seductive but ardent when I catch them, like those of Camões. In the Latin countries—and even in Germany, of all places—trout are assigned a female gender. You can, of course, find scholars who will tell you that the gender of a noun has nothing to do with sex. I do not fish for scholars. I fish for *a truta, la trucha, la truite, die Forelle.* English speakers may say of a trout "look at 'im jump!" But everybody knows that we're odd. Who else would give trout a gender suitable for making war instead of love? I am grateful to have lived in the Latin world long enough to get these matters straight.

The trout the finch gave me had a secret: mayflies. Her throat contained two of them, caught before they could fly or mate. They are called duns, in that stage, and I recognized them from their sober dress, the color of olives turning ripe. I stowed my wet-fly leader, put on a finer one, and fastened to its tip a single floating fly resembling the real thing. Then I rushed back to the fishing with no time out for contemplation. When Nereids are ready, they must not be kept waiting.

A poem from the mid-fifteenth century addresses the problems of "a man that lovith ffisshyng and ffowling both" and uses them as metaphors for the pursuit of love. It was a "pleasaunce" or "dysporte" with rules,[2] not constant love. There are only so many poetic words, in English, and I suppose that the anonymous author wanted to use the best of them for his strongest passions.

I knew why the trout were feeding: It was because there were mayflies to eat. I did not know why the mayflies and therefore the trout stopped all at once. Minutes after they did, however, the sun disappeared too, and Manuel told me that I must hurry to climb the bad *passagem* before rain made the rocks slick. I looked for excuses. It was climb or swim, though. The river rushed through a cleft between cliffs, too deep to wade.

The passage would have been easy for a rock climber. Even some anglers would have been competent for it. I was not, but I accomplished the thing by scraping my fingertips and taking a minute interest in patterns on the rock before my nose. I did not look at the currents grumbling down below. Having passed the throat of the gorge, I descended sloping granite casually, legs barely trembling. Manuel told me to wait, urgency in his voice. I saw the viper just before his staff hit it. It was small, by comparison to a rattlesnake. I would not have killed it. I am not much afraid of snakes, but still the poisonous kind always stirs some lost emotion.

Above the passage, light-green grass grew from rocks in the Mondego, tall and lush as pampered plants in the office of a banker. I could not remember seeing so much unused forage anywhere in Portugal. Goats can go almost anywhere, but the passage had preserved paradise, or at least stopped the people taking care of the goats. The river felt lonely, my secret. Humans had trickled through it for hundreds of generations, of course. All had been tested by the passage. Ghosts of this quality made such good company that I did not mind a thin, cold rain.

Fishing was slow. Mayflies seem to know that they should not leave the stream bottom till the air temperature is right, though how they can make such judgments is a mystery. Manuel and I moved along, he looking for vipers (which he could see better), I looking for trout (which I could see better). One has to learn to see things, you know. It is not just a matter of visual acuity.

I stood on a rock sloping into the Mondego, looking at a distant side current that had an occasional odd quiver. There was a wink of white under water, then another a minute later. I could not see the rest of the trout, but the white had to be its mouth opening to take something drifting in the current. The something would be nymphs: not the Nereid kind but their namesake, immature mayflies. They had planned to hatch during the burst of sun, perhaps, and been fooled by the change in weather. Hatching is a dangerous passage, for nymphs.

This was a trout worth the full treatment. I clipped off my dry fly, lengthened the leader with a fine strand, and tied on a nymph that I had dressed for the occasion. It had an abdomen wound of two pale fibers from the tail of a late-season pheasant. The thorax was spun of guard hairs from a hare's ear. The thread that held the dressing together was Pearsall's silk and the hook a Partridge, strong for its size. The magic and the science were both studied, you see.

I waded till I was cross-stream from the trout and some 30 feet away. The fly was in my mouth, soaking, and it sank instantly when I cast it. The trout did not move. It did not move on the next two casts, either. On the fourth, there was the little pale wink when the fly had drifted to the right position. The line came tight just long enough for the fish to react and jerk it from my fingers. Small trout cannot do that. This one made a long, wallowing jump and ran upstream—another thing small trout cannot manage—for the shelter of a cliff. The line angled deep and ticked twice on a rock, but the shelter that the trout found was not good enough. It came back into my net, 15 inches long, big-jawed and not pretty. Manuel said that he had not seen a trout quite so big.

When I opined that trout are female, I was referring to those of normal size. This one was hook-jawed, a male characteristic. You admire a trout like that but you do not court it. You fight it.

The rain ended then, the breeze blew in warm gusts, and fish began rising freely, which does not happen often on the upper Mondego. I cast frantically. One small trout made a mistake at last and I derricked it in. Its mouth contained dark specks: black gnats. I tied on an imitation and hooked a better fish, but then the rise was over, almost wasted.

Never mind. We were through the narrowest part of the gorge by then, able to walk along the banks in places, and Manuel wanted to keep moving. We heard bells up above us on the canyon walls. Then we heard high, laughing voices: children trying to drive goats where they did not want to be driven. I would have laughed too but big boys don't just break out giggling with no reason.

Wilderness is a thing in the mind, nobly savage. I want it. It is the last illusion I am allowed, because humans didn't work out, Lord knows, and the animals I tried to ennoble were even more ridiculous. (There was a nature-faking film, one more of a long line, in which father bear reared his offspring. In nature, that cub would have made a couple of good meals.) I want the real thing, beautiful, red in tooth and claw. I enjoy it even in bed, covers over my head. Maybe that is how I enjoy it most.

The Mondego's gorge feels right. It keeps most people out and lets me in. It gives me running water and trout. The trout are the better for having adapted to me over millennia. The laughing and tinkling of bells are also echoes across the ages.

In America, we like to pretend that there is wilderness ruled only by the balance of nature. In fact nature knows no balance, and if she did, we humans would have altered it before now. Calling a place wilderness is nevertheless convenient because it lets us duck decisions on management. If it were not wilderness by law, somebody would find a way to get up the gorge with engines—jet boats or helicopters or something. He would drive an off-road vehicle over the goat trails to the rim. Anyone trying to stop him would be accused of violating democratic freedoms. We are a new, all-or-nothing civilization. It takes an old one to build wilderness from half measures.

I would like to tell you that the gorge of the Mondego is safe. In fact it is known locally as the *sítio da barragem*, place of the dam, because for years the engineers have been wanting to plug it up and flood it. Maybe the European Community will loan them enough money for the job.

The canyon flattened till there were pastures on its right side, and in one of them a bored shepherd sat on a rock. His dog lay beside him, then sat up, glared, and charged us. It was very big, a real Mountain dog (*Cão da Serra*). I waded into the river. Manuel stood his ground, braced his legs, and raised his staff. Only then did the shepherd give a command. He was happy to liven up the day, but not if it meant risking a working-dog's bones. The beast paused, watched us, growled. The shepherd called it back and we heard its name: "*Arombo*." It sounded like the growl. Mountain dogs are bred to attack wolves, which requires dim wits and large size. Portuguese shepherds would not waste food on a big dog with no function. I would have been glad to see this dog's man get a clout with the staff.

(Odd, is it not, that wolves survived in Portugal but died out in the wilder spaces of Montana? I suppose that the European wolves had a chance to adapt to man—hide from him or prey on him—before modern weapons evolved. In America, wolf met man and bullet at the same moment.)

Manuel guided me to Adriano's car by a route that I would never have found, well away from the river. We walked extra miles, but quickly and for the most part downhill. We passed shepherds' cottages far from any road. In one field we greeted a woman who sat on the grass, watching a small herd of cattle, while her young son ran around playing with grasshoppers and rocks. His nose was running but he looked happy. He was not lonely. She was.

Adriano was searching a field near his car, catching crickets for his grandchildren. We climbed in, lazily, and drove off, diesel engine putt-putting in the contented way it always did when we had caught our trout. It did not even frighten a quail calling beside a small field of green wheat.

We stopped near the village of Taberna to buy a wheel of mountain cheese for dinner. It was expensive, in a land where most food was cheap, but Adriano thought it good value for the flavor. We went with the shepherd who made the cheese into a windowless stone hut used for this purpose alone. Real *queijo da serra* could be made only in this region, at this altitude, and in this kind of building, Adriano said; the bacteria or something did not prosper elsewhere. No trace of goat's milk could be allowed to overpower the mild odor of milk from ewes grazed on rockrose shoots. And we paid extra for a cheese made from the shoots before the plant came into bloom. My stomach started to rumble.

It did not stay empty in Videmonte. Mrs. Sequeira Mendes took us upstairs to a kitchen—far from any plumbing—where things were cooking in an open fireplace. After reflection, I am still of the opinion that this was the best-smelling meal ever cooked. There was *medronheiro* wood sputtering under a cast-iron cauldron. There were chestnuts drying in a wooden rack around the fireplace. There were lichens steaming on granite walls. Dinner started with *caldo verde* (a soup of tall cabbage, potatoes, and sausage). Then came rice with kid, more kid in a sauce, two kinds of pastries, and a cheese redolent of rockrose shoots in spring rain. There was red wine in a clay jug covered by a white cloth. There was—well, there was the fragrance of years gone by, because everything in that room would have been the same in the Middle Ages.

We should have taken time to enjoy ourselves, but we were too busy, between sniffs and bites and sips, eulogizing each trout that had brought us here.

CAGES AND BOTTLES

From this land sprang the shepherd Viriato, of whose virile exploits his very name is suggestive. . . . He proved more skilled with his lance than his crook, and lived to strike a heavy blow at the prestige of Rome . . . bequeathing to us the injunction never to be afraid of superior numbers; and since then we have shown a thousand times that we are not.

CAMÕES, *The Lusiads*, Cantos Three and Eight

Viseu is a small city that ripples over green hills and draws its water from tributaries of the Mondego River. Running water led us there, though we had resolved not to fish during this excursion. Adriano and I drove upstream simply because everything is upstream from his old home in Anadia, and he wanted to show me a good piece of Portugal.

We drove not along any river in particular but against the trend of the waters in general, north and west, inland and upward. The road wormed through steep, rounded hills covered by scrubby trees—pines, oaks, chestnuts, and the occasional beech. They were what we would call second growth, in America, but in Portugal had been harvested ever since stone axes could slash and fires could burn. Individually, the trees were seldom impressive, but in this rainy part of the country they protected the watersheds with a mat of dark green.

The hills were everywhere cut by ravines. The streams had carved their own beds during endless hours on the geologic clock, slicing deeper and deeper into bedrock, pulling their tributaries down with them. The canyons were steeper than most in glaciated North America and Britain. Before Portugal I had associated rugged terrain with the ice age, but glaciers are in fact the greatest of bulldozers, moving and leveling. Ice is a blunt instrument; running water is a knife.

Picture the veins on an oak leaf. Imagine the leaf as north-central Portugal. Now pull the leaf away and watch the fanned-out brooks cutting their beds lower with each rain for an epoch or so. This is just my guess, mind you. In Portugal, science has left much of nature to us amateurs. I have counted the layers of seas' beds laminated in volcanoes' forges and been grateful for my ticks of time. I have dizzied myself peering up the walls of those box canyons. They have caged and liberated me, frightened me and turned me loose.

Adriano was tolerant of my amateur geology but felt no need for it. Good waters had been given to him. He had fished them in gratitude and shown the next generation of anglers how to treat them with respect. He was too bright to reject Darwin but content to remain a creationist, trout-wise.

Trout did not intend to found a religion, but they did it. We anglers have a reference from ancient Macedonia that is as tantalizing as the Dead Sea scrolls. We have scripture and psalm by Dame Juliana Berners,[1] who almost certainly did not exist, but then saints are supposed to be evanescent. We have Father Izaak Walton, who did exist but has been dead for a decent number of centuries, and whose book has been through as many editions as any other but the Bible. We have schisms and heresies to keep us busy when we get too ossified for climbing down gorges. We have pundits to lead the arguments. We have relics to collect in museums far from cold water.

But Adriano does not read English, which has most of the theology. His contentment was pure. He knew that where there were trout there was virtue: clear streams flowing from green hills. He could be happy in any such place. Indeed, it was difficult not to be happy when fishing, or recovering from fishing, or being where one might break out of town and go fishing, even though, as I have promised, there will be no trout on this leg of our trip.

For one like me who visited Portugal's offspring before the mother country, it is surprising to see Portuguese people landlocked. When they migrate, they do not disperse like the Irish. The Portuguese settle, for the most part, in Massachusetts, California, Hawaii, Rio de Janeiro, and other places not far beyond the smell of the tides. But in the homeland they prosper in Viseu.

Carlos Pereira's family, in particular, had prospered in the clothing business. Carlos had left the nest to earn a law degree and live in Lisbon, but Viseu was home: always had been, always would be.

He had returned to it now for a visit. In Lisbon, Carlos had been Adriano's apprentice as a law clerk and, informally but not incidentally, as a fly-tyer. Naturally we called on Carlos in Viseu. Adriano felt a duty (I think) to keep an eye on the lad, who was still in his thirties. I am pleased to report that Carlos had not lapsed into, say, fishing flies with a spinning rod and float, as many backsliders do in southern Europe. Not that this was an inspection visit. It wasn't, I repeat, even a fishing trip.

Adriano and I checked into rooms on the fourth floor of a downtown *residencial*. It would have been called a hotel in America, where we have only hotels and motels. In Portugal there is a bewildering variety of categories, with the *residencial* fitting somewhere between hotels and pensions. Our rooms were on the fourth floor, reached either by stairs, if one were in a hurry, or by an elevator that worked fine, after one opened and closed two sliding grates and watched the floors grinding by.

My room was small, as in Portuguese houses, but everything in it was tidied and scrubbed and laundered with the kind of zeal possible only in an underdeveloped economy with developed workers. There were two ironed towels, one for the bidet and one for the rest. There was one small piece of soap made by a local *perfumaria*. The only thing missing was a Gideon Bible for bedtime reading.

I pulled down on the cloth strap beside the window, winching up the slatted shutter that keeps the vapors out of every Portuguese bedroom. From four floors up, the city was not as densely urban as it had looked from the street. There were old courtyards of which I could see just the corners, *quintais* with flowers and tall cabbages, car repair shops, other businesses unidentified, and—right across the street—a modern apartment building. As I watched it, a shutter lifted and a dark-haired young woman walked onto her balcony in a sundress pretty as a trout's speckled skin. She walked to a cage hanging from the wall and spent long minutes watching it, talking to the bird inside. The goldfinch hopped to the far side of the cage and perched. It did not sing.

I worked out the story. The woman had been shopping in the morning, then done the laundry hanging on the balcony. She had dressed up for her husband. In all of these things she had been a success, but with the finch she failed. She went back inside to prepare dinner. On the way, she let her shutters down, as a good Portuguese wife should. In this she disappointed me but not the bird. He began to hop around and, in a minute, to sing. He knew his place, this musician. He had his cage; the young wife had hers; and they got along better when they did not intrude on each other.

Evening had turned into night by then. As I watched, a small, rotten apple whizzed through my window and dropped on the floor—an excellent pitch from boys laughing in the street four stories down. I had the only open cage in the hotel, which made a natural target.

Next morning, Adriano and I walked to Carlos's house, or rather to that of his parents, who were of Adriano's generation. Carlos's mother, bless her, was ready to start feeding us, but we had already breakfasted and wanted to be outside. The weather was as good as weather gets, just on the cool side of warm. It was, I commented, a perfect day for fishing.

Carlos and Adriano vetoed that. No, no: There was more to Portugal than fish.

Well, all right. I do not always notice duty at first glance but am capable of recognizing it when pointed out by two lawyers.

We started in the house's cellar, lined and partitioned with bottles of wine. This in itself was nothing special: Portuguese basements run to wine as American basements run to television sets. But the Pereiras's stock came from a small family winery called *Santos Evos,* in which Adriano and I had a personal interest. It furnished Adriano's table wine and had furnished mine too, during my years in Portugal. Carlos's father showed me my dusty vintages, '78 through '82. They were better than photographs of an odorless two-dimensional man. Wine bottled me roundly, fermented my musts, fined my sediments, oxidized my sulfurous salts. Even so I popped the cork and went outside.

The yard behind the house was cultivated by Carlos's mother and guarded by Official, a small mongrel on a chain. He performed his duties with minimum effort and maximum rewards. No tiresome yapping for Official. He lay quietly till an ankle was within his turf—and he knew the chain's compass precisely—then expressed his indignation. He had a small job but sharp teeth. The neighbor children no longer conducted peach fights with the produce of this *quintal*.

Mrs. Pereira was safe from Official because she was above him on the organizational chart. She had built a wood fire, and over it she was boiling his perquisites in a pot-bellied iron cauldron. They smelled good. I peeked enviously into Official's ragout. There were bones, scraps of meat, rice, and cabbage leaves. The fuel had been pruned from the fruit trees. Total cost would have been too low to count.

The cook, mind you, was a gray-haired woman of means. She had nevertheless shunned Lifestyles (if those are what I think they are). Money coming into the house was for saving, not spending. She was not "too proud or too humble or too soft to bend to the earth and pick up the things we eat."[2]

I do not know how to make you see Carlos without putting him on a trout stream, and we are not going fishing. In my mind he is always hopping from one boulder to another, felt soles gripping the moss just long enough for another hop. Where I shuffle, Carlos leaps. Picture a dark-haired tightrope walker carrying a long fly rod for balance. Dress him neatly, but without tie and coat. For this tour of old Viseu, however, put him in a battered Volkswagen hitting the high spots of the cobblestones, taking blind corners with a downshift and a squeak of tires as the rear end swings out.

Adriano, in the front seat, said "Oh Carlos, you should do something about this car. It does not look good in your profession."

In principle, I liked the car. (This is one of those polite Portuguese expressions meaning that in practice, I was worried.) The car looked as if its owner could afford it, which is the most important feature of any vehicle. The problem was that one rear door had been wedged shut in a minor accident. What if that side were up when the car rolled over with me inside? So I suggested that we walk, and we did, and Viseu looked better from outside the cage.

The old part of town was as rocky as a gorge. From one house's wall, a natural spring poured. The dwellings were more than site-responsive: They *were* the site; had been forever. Only the Grão Vasco Museum looked squarely edificial, having been built in modern times. Make that the sixteenth century.

We went inside. You have to do that, commonly, to see art. The old landscapes in the museum looked like the Portuguese countryside today, which is good. (American period landscapes are inclined to look quaint because they were painted before the business of the countryside was to take care of refugees from the cities.) There were drawings made by the Portuguese discoverers, too, and in their clumsiness was a vision that will not return to Western man. Call it true faith. Like all empire builders from the Olmecs to the Soviets, the Portuguese propagated their religion. It justified all suffering, theirs and that of the subjugated peoples. The natives did not look quite human. How could they, being pagans?

Carlos would not let me skip the religious art. We entered a reproduction of a wealthy family's private chapel, low ceiling and all. It was a dark little theater specializing in agony. People enjoyed terrifying themselves, it seems, long before horror films were invented. There were reliquaries with (I guessed) bits of bones and wood, the latter being fragments of the true cross or reasonable facsimiles thereof. If you are to believe Eça de Queiroz, Portugal's greatest nineteenth-century novelist, the commerce in such relics used to be brisk.

The Grão Vasco came as a relief. *Grão* means great, in ambition, reputation, and scale. I welcomed the high ceilings that his paintings demanded. He peaked in the early sixteenth century, time of the discoveries, when each of the million Portuguese seemed to be doing something well and Vasco Fernandes was doing the best of the art. His Saint Sebastian was a comely young male. Men with bestial faces were puncturing the martyr with arrows, but his face had conquered pain. Explorers would have needed that lesson in preparation for similar fates.

By all accounts, however, what actually came about was different. The beautiful saint, bound and penetrated, attracted more devotion from the women back home.

* * *

The Saint Sebastian of the painting was tied to a *pelourinho*. The word is, I surmise, a false cognate of pillory. The latter merely held offenders by their neck and wrists, exposing them to ridicule. The *pelourinho*'s victims were hung (if they were lucky) from cross pieces at the top of a tall pillar. The unlucky were tortured like Saint Sebastian. Many *pelourinhos* were ornate, and still are, for you will see them all over Portugal in towns large and small, preserved as tourist attractions. They would have been centers of entertainment back when their purpose was pious. Sometimes they stand next to a church and sometimes elsewhere. They always try not to look like a cross.

Saint Sebastian, unlike the *pelourinho,* has a uniquely Portuguese resonance. You can't know the country without knowing *sebastianismo.*

A prince was born on the twentieth day of January 1544. It was St. Sebastian's birthday too, so the heir to the throne was named for the saint. The prince grew up blond and handsome as the martyr, with an odd but appealing personality. His subjects looked to him for redemption of a society that had been spoiled by the success of the discoveries. "Luxury and pleasure" had made the people "corrupt and lazy."[3] Saint Sebastian's namesake would, they hoped, make Portugal like Portugal again. No wonder that he thought he had been born for great deeds. The logical one was conquest of the ancient enemy: the Moors across the Mediterranean in Morocco.

Sebastian was thoughtful, methodical, and determined. He was also young, spoiled, and inexperienced at war. His expeditionary force was enormous for a small country—some 18,000 men in 1,018 ships—but it was a confusing mixture of foreigners, mercenaries, and Portuguese too poor to buy off. Even so it came close to winning at Alcácer Quibir (Portuguese spelling) on August 4, 1578. Defeat was caused by a failure of what would today be called command, control, and communication. Opponents superior in numbers then slaughtered most of the invaders, including Sebastian. By some poignant accounts, the Moroccan battlefield was littered with guitars as well as bodies. It had been a romantic expedition, while it lasted.

The loss was too great to be borne. Recall the impact of Custer's last stand in America—and remember that its victims were a few good soldiers and one foolhardy general. Suppose that something like it had occurred in the 1960s. Wipe out the whole American army. Make its dead leader a handsome young chief of state—John F. Kennedy. Suppose that American independence was compromised as a consequence, like Portugal's.

The loss led to collective delusion. Sebastian was not really dead but preparing to return in the mists of dawn, saving his homeland. (Wouldn't you like to resurrect JFK?) *Sebastianismo* became odd only when it lasted beyond its hero's conceivable life span. There was a wave of it during the Napoleonic invasions of the nineteenth century, and Portuguese scholars still mention *sebastianismo* to explain the public's hope for a hero who will save the nation without demanding individual effort or responsibility. It may be a harsh judgment. Bodies politic naturally look to deliverers when deprived of choice for so long. The tendency to do so is marked in those three great religions of the desert: Judaism, Christianity, and Islam.

The puzzling part is that few cars stop at the battlefield where Nuno Álvares won national independence against the odds. Portuguese tourists prefer to visit Alcácer Quibir, where heroism died with Sebastian the Fool.

We smelled Carlos's house before we got back to it. His mother must have been fixing dinner for two days, soaking a whole salt cod, shelling the broad beans and nuts, making the dough, baking the sweet things. We did not let her down. The American contingent in particular got a firm grip on his fork and charged. I had a two-knight serving of the *bacalhau* encased in *broa,* a sourdough cornbread. I defeated at least one portion each of: mountain cheese, *marmelada* made at home of quinces, the semi-dry cakes called *palitos,* and the yeast-risen "bread of God," studded with dried fruit. The cook who commanded our table must have known that she was appreciated.

I am pleased to report, also, that the glass did not break. It did not even have much wine left inside when I knocked it over. And no one at the table blinked as the glass teetered and fell. I watched. Your average person knocking over a glass might try to catch it, but I know from experience that the thing to do, in my case, is to keep hands off. I'd just make the accident worse. So I lean back and observe the audience. None outside Portugal has ever shown such self-control. When a glass teeters, teeters, and falls, it is exceedingly hard not to twitch.

It is possible that this group, having known me for some time, knew also what to expect. It was not that I had drunk much. I was just oversized and enthusiastic. My hands started demonstrating the length of trout in Montana and the inevitable happened.

Europeans, as you know, consider Americans young and innocent. After much research, I have figured out why this is so. We *are* young and innocent. Every object made by man more than fifty years ago impresses us. We question strangers on the sidewalk. We open our windows at night. We drink sugar water with our hamburgers, serve our salads in little pieces, mash our boiled potatoes, and cut our meat into bites before we start on it. We hold our forks in our right hands or, in my case, switch them back and forth. No wonder the glasses tumble. (I will say, though, that I get my peas from plate to mouth with less fuss than the average Englishman.)

You can learn much of the nation you are visiting by observing the reactions of the nationals as you perform these stunts. The French enjoy a thrill of horror. "I was forever in their eyes the product of a naive, underdeveloped, and indeed infantile civilization," writes M. F. K. Fisher (who probably knocked over fewer glasses than me), "and therefore I was incapable of appreciating all the things that had shaped them into the complicated and deeply aware supermen of European culture that they firmly felt themselves to be."[4] It says something about the Portuguese that I do not know quite how they feel. They do not dislike me. I think they see both sides of America, the *gaucheries* and the triumphs.

*   *   *

In a quiet side conversation during dinner, I asked Carlos's bright thirteen-year-old son what his favorite foods were. "Sheeseburgers and pizza," he said. I did not dare ask what he liked to drink.

Do you want to know why Europeans really worry about Americans? It is because they look at us and see the future.

The wine was all from *Santos Evos,* in vintages from the latest back to 1974. My own years were good, if I do say so, ripe and experienced. What puzzled me was that the wine of the year was just as good in a prepubescent way. Its flavor was so light that one expected it to be fizzy, but it wasn't.

Don't worry about the adjectives; mine mean neither more nor less than the conventional viniferous folderol. I like wines and babies but am relieved that someone else has the responsibility for producing both. Flavors cannot be described, anyhow. You can evoke them (good for a giggle, if you are not careful), taste them (safer), or describe their components. Even that is risky: The oenophiles get higher than their grapes. Reading about wine is too much like reading about trout fishing. You look for information and get rosé pornography. You rebel, fish a worm, and wash your catch down with spring water. It's fun. It does not hold your interest like catching trout on a fly and serving them with wine. Both fly and wine capture nature in ways that make the alternatives seem like Concord grape juice.

For what it is worth, the lighter red wines from *Santos Evos* taste good with trout in cool weather. In the heat, though, you want a wine that can be chilled. That means a *vinho verde.* The literal translation is "green wine," not because of its color but because it is made from unripened grapes. It began as a product of straitened circumstances, as you would guess. Much of northern Portugal is so cool that vines have to be grown on trellises, catching what little sun is available, and even then the grapes do not mature. They are made into wine anyhow. It is low in alcoholic content, which for any solid European peasant means that the product is second-class. It just happens to taste good. When the world's wine drinkers became more interested in flavor than in supporting a habit, *vinho verde* caught on.

In Portugal, wine has been made since perhaps the fourth millennium B.C. and the process is reasonably down-to-earth. I asked Carlos about it. He said that, with a few exceptions, wine was made from several *castas* (grape varieties) blended for flavor, color, and sugar content. Winegrowers had learned the right grapes for granitic local soils, taking into account sunshine, moisture, molds, and probably other conditions that I did not grasp. The main varieties at Santos Evos were Tourigo, Penamacor, Muscatel (two varieties), and Cão. (As far as I know, none is widely grown in America, with the possible exception of the Muscatels.) Grapes used in neighboring Portuguese regions might be very different, but all were varieties of *Vitis vinifera*. The "American grape," *Vitis labrusca*, was rigorously avoided. It produced abundantly and cheaply even in cold weather, but the quality was unacceptable.

The Pereiras must have been doing something right to produce wine that was good both young and after aging sixteen years. For the most part they drank it young. Big old wines go with the big-flavored meals that a person does not want all the time. The old ones have to be expensive, too. *Santos Evos* of the year cost less than gasoline, which struck me as a snapshot of the difference between Portuguese and American cultures.

Not all Portuguese consumers are moderate. Manuel, a worker at Santos Evos, drank a jug (*garrafão*) each day. That's 4 liters. It was *aguapé*, light young stuff containing 7 to 9 percent alcohol. Even so the feat amazed me, but not Manuel. He worked hard from "sun to sun"—dawn to dusk.

Manuel became a living fable, which is more than most of us can claim. There was the time he gashed his leg with an axe and was given raw brandy to sterilize the wound. He drank the antiseptic and felt better. Like all good fables, this one has a moral: Systemic curatives are the best.

As you may imagine, Manuel had no use for physicians. He was taken, protesting, to see his first when he was seventy-six years of age. He died the next day. Maybe he wanted to prove his point.

*   *   *

I had been through Viseu many times without stopping at Viriato's fort, but those were fishing trips. This one wasn't. Adriano and Carlos convinced me to see an approved sight. Forts are fun anyhow—not that much was to be expected of this one. Viriato popped up at the beginning of Iberian history, taking command of the Lusitanian tribe in 147 B.C. Two millennia are enough to erode mountains, let alone battlements.

The myth is sparser than that of Odysseus but recorded in more accurate detail. Viriato whipped Roman legions, humiliated their generals, blocked the advance of civilization. He did it with inferior forces. He must have been a military genius like Nuno Álvares or Afonso d'Albuquerque—the kind that bends history out of line if something can't be done about them. The Romans found something. They bribed Viriato's own ambassadors to assassinate him.

The rest is speculative. Even the Lusitanian language left no traces, unless they are to be found in the speech of today's Portuguese. Viriato's tribe may have been Celtic, or an older people Celticized. He was a shepherd, so his people must have been pastoral. You know (if you read your Gideon Bibles) that pastoral tribes, unlike hunter-gatherers, have often organized themselves as formidable warriors.

It can be no accident, moreover, that the Spanish word *guerrilla* (*guerrilha* in Portuguese) originated in this accidented geology. It is the perfect place to be independent and poor. Guerrilla means "little war," and small forces could have run around forever in the box canyons, administering humility lessons with stones and arrows. One man's cage would have been another's opportunity.

I must report, however, that the myth did not fit Viriato's fort. It was still there, an enormous circular earthwork. Judging from the decisive angles of its high rim, a stone skeleton may lie underneath. This was no hideout of a guerrilla band: It would have been a good bulwark against any army without air support. But it would have required hundreds of disciplined defenders, who in turn would have needed support from a structured society.

It is the kind of thing you run up against in Portugal, time and again: The science has not been done. Portugal cannot afford it. For foreign archaeologists, I suppose, the country is less tempting than

Greece, Rome, or the Middle East. So the history and prehistory sit there, stratum on stratum, unscraped by glaciers but reworked by people. Flat land is too scarce to sit idle. Viriato's fort—if that's what it really is—has been breached not by Romans but by Lusitanians of the modern period. They have built trellises inside and used the ground fertilized by blood for producing green wine.

When we had finished our serious business, we rushed to the Vouga River and jumped to every rock in it after uncivilized, cold-blooded invertebrates that treated us as Viriato treated Roman generals. Serves me right for promising that there would be no trout on this leg of the trip. They kept me to my pledge.

SINGING TO THE CUCKOO

Now fishing requires so much attention, and so pleasant is its delectation, that the fisherman in his time thinks neither of offending God nor harming his neighbor; nor even of eating, because hunger does not tire him; nor of sleeping even if he has not slept; nor of his loves, even if he be in love.

Fernando Basurto, 1539[1]

If I had a baby daughter, I would call her Zêzere, if my wife would let me. Zêzere is a brook that sounds as good as it looks: ZEH-zeh-reh, ZEH-zeh-reh. What other stream rocks you to sleep when you murmur its name? The word must have meant something once, in a language that died when the Romans poisoned Viriato. Suppose the whole world was mapped then by song lines, as Bruce Chatwin suggests.[2] The first Europeans would have slept by this stream running over these rocks and called it Zêzere, Zêzere, because that is what it calls itself.

Manteigas is the Zêzere's town. It lies in what we would call a hole, in the Rockies: a valley crowded by mountains, with one rift where the water leaks out. If there were a dam instead of a town, it would hold the stream in a dungeon and we—Adriano and I—would have to settle for a glutted lake instead of a thrifty brook. As it is, the town divides headwater music from the lower, slower roll of a river. The inn has shady rooms that look east over a watercourse lit by evening sun. Insects rise from the stream and make little points of light in the low rays. Swallows circle and dart. We swing open the windows and hear Zêzere, Zêzere floating up to our beds.

We got there in late afternoon, twisting down from a pass 2,500 feet higher. We saw the town, and beyond it the upper Zêzere valley, at every hairpin turn. We took our bags to the *Paragem Serradalto* (meaning, roughly, the High-Mountain Inn), found out that the dinner would be worth waiting for, and walked around town long enough to be sure where we were.

Among Portuguese towns, the *Vila* of Manteigas has one novelty: It was founded rather than just evolving forever. The date was

1188. Before then the site was a last refuge of Viriatro's warrior tribe—according to one of those traditions that everyone knows and no one can substantiate. It makes sense, anyhow. A shepherd on these rough slopes would not have had to be civilized till he got good and ready.

The town that Adriano and I explored was almost a geological feature: granite houses fronted by granite roads that passed over granite bridges above the Zêzere's granite tributaries. I could have taken photographs that would convince you of the residents' sense of beauty. These old houses looked better than the best in Beverly Hills—unless I focused on the ravines below, flecked with empty bottles and cans and chickens picking at refuse. It was hard to understand. Were these people unable to cope with the flux of civilization? Or, as Adriano seemed to suggest, did they not define filth as I did? (John Steinbeck went out of his way to avoid driving through American cities because they were "like badger holes, ringed with trash—all of them—by piles of rusting automobiles, and almost smothered with rubbish."[3] But we like our yards neat.)

I was overtaken by an afflatus, or possibly just a message from an empty stomach. Here it is: Manteigas's beauty is a testament to impeccable thrift, not impeccable taste.

These people had ignored problems that time would cure. (Zêzere's floods cleanse filth.) They had built the simplest structures that would do the job. (Zêzere flows down the easiest channel.) They had made no statements (Zêzere has no ego), but they had not flaunted austerity, either. (Zêzere is no minimalist.) And they had built for the ages. (Zêzere's shape is economy prolonged.)

The effect is that the old houses seem as much a part of nature as their river.

Manteigas being a respectable town (*vila*) instead of a casual village (*aldeia*), there were no sandy streets with children romping in them, and Adriano seemed subdued. He could not play Pied Piper where there was no one to be piped. I wondered if Viriato's hideout was really hidden in the mountains nearby. I asked what hepatic insufficiencies and neurasthenia were, and whether the local mineral water could cure them as claimed. Adriano showed no interest in my diversions. He approved of two blackbirds singing on, respectively, a branch and a television antenna, but he was not moved to poetry. He was a family man with no one to father but an American full of questions that had no answers.

Enter Diphthong. We concluded that he was a dog after ruling out the alternatives. He was not big enough to be a bull and lacked the mane of an ass. A hyena would hardly have found its way to the Range of the Star. No, Diphthong had to be a canine built by a committee. Sometimes mongrels turn out right like Pirolito, back at the Alvoco, and sometimes they turn out like Diphthong, who was trying to be several things in the same syllable. His head was too big for his forequarters. His back curved to one side. His hind legs marched to a different drummer, perhaps because they were thrown out of time by an enormous, wagging tail. Adriano made an instant conquest and Diphthong trotted along with us rather than waiting for whomever else he had in mind.

Diphthong cleared the way. The few people on the sidewalks at dinnertime flattened against the walls with a nice-doggie-don't-bite look on their faces. Diphthong had no interest in biting but his tail must have bruised a couple of shins. We noticed also that his testicles hung low between his hocks, swinging with the ponderous grace of Foucault's pendulum. It seemed a fair guess that Manteigas's puppies were going to resemble Diphthong in coming years.

Adriano asked if I had bred my dog Huckleberry, back in Montana.

I had not and tried to explain why.

"Egoism," Adriano said. "You should think of your dog, not yourself. He will never be happy if you do not breed him."

Diphthong was happy, anyhow, and so was Adriano.

The evening turned cool and Adriano changed into his tweeds for dinner. I stayed with jeans and a flannel shirt but put them on over skin washed of travel. The bathroom down the hall had prewar faucets polished down to bare brass, cracked floor tiles smelling of bleach, and a fresh coat of white paint on the walls. The stairs down to the ground floor had worn the bristles off generations of scrubbing brushes. The dining room's shortage of dust seemed miraculous, given that the walls held one stuffed head of boar, one of ram, two of goats with dry grins, some quart-sized cowbells, several old hand-held scales, and a vast, gleaming copper cauldron.

There was also one modern decoration: a frame containing large-denomination Angolan banknotes fanned out in artistic display. I guessed the story and was probably not far wrong. A young couple had gone to Angola when Salazar called it part of Portugal, worked hard, made some money, lost their business in the revolution, returned to the mother country, and found that even their currency was worthless. They had turned it into a wall display and spent the rest of their youth turning the inn from a wreck into an opportunity.

The scrubbed thrift was consoling. So was the smell from the kitchen: faint wood smoke and powerful *dobrada.* (You wouldn't get tripe in a modern place. It has to be made by people willing to scrub the wrinkles of a calf's stomach.) Dona Manuela brought us the steaming bowls. The strips of tripe were bubbling in white beans, slices of *chouriço,* and chunks of black blood-sausage. The trimmings included a bottle of *Dão* red, not too subtle for the tomato sauce. Afterward there were pieces of chocolate cake, solid and not too sweet. It would be incorrect to say that we ate more to please Dona Manuela. I had been smelling *dobrada* all the way from Montana, where my wife, though in other respects perfect, will not cook it.

Dona Manuela talked to us after dinner. Her son had come home from school for the weekend, she said. He was a good boy and handsome too. If she were ever to forget that he was coming home—though of course she wouldn't—she would have only to look out the door to be reminded. The girls always started strolling around in front of the inn on Friday evening.

We had noticed, Adriano said. Even Diphthong had not frightened them off.

Mother Manuela was not displeased that her son was worth the girls' attention. She did not understand their behavior, however. In her day, young ladies had been modest.

Adriano agreed. Decency had been forgotten.

I joined the chorus. The girls had not loitered at my door, damn it.

But if it's food you must settle for instead of girls, never pass up the contents of a bubbling pot brewed by a good mother to keep her eighteen-year-old son off the sidewalk.

"Make yourself at home," hosts say. It is the kind of decision that no one can make for you. You are home or you're not. If the place is old and scrubbed, if the pretty little trout are flirting their tails in the Zêzere just outside, and if mother Manuela is simmering *dobrada,* you are home.

Adriano and I (as I have already confessed) are no travelers. We are not even pastoral wanderers. We are foragers, hunter-gatherers. We must have both field and home—the one for the catch and the other for the cooking. Travelers cannot bear home.

Travel is extensive, hunting intensive. Travelers escape; hunters arrive. Travelers look for *divertissement,* like Pascal. Hunters don't want to be distracted. Travelers think hunters are primitives. Hunters think travelers are lost. Chatwin the traveler wrote that "If you walk hard enough, you probably don't need any other God."[4] It must have been a hunter-gatherer who wrote that "The kingdom of the father is spread upon the earth and men do not see it."[5]

This is meant to be honest, not smug. The world looked right to Adriano and me because it was a big, old, ramshackle inn with nooks in which we happened to fit, that's all. No amount of searching would have made us happy otherwise. Bruce Chatwin would have looked for the ghosts in the attic.

I asked Dona Manuela about the great copper cauldron on the wall of the dining room. You don't find kettles like that in the gourmet cookware departments these days. It belonged on a moor at midnight, with cronies to help it double, double, toil, and trouble.

It was used three times a year, Dona Manuela said. Had been for generations. Its only purpose was the *matança do porco,* killing of the pig, or rather the scalding of the pig after it had been killed and drained of blood for the sausages. And then the kettle was hung back on the wall. (She did not mention that it always had to be polished first. If you have polished a copper saucepan, imagine the labor in shining up a vessel big enough for your bath.)

I asked, then, how much of the inn's food was made from scratch. But that is an idiom, and I probably did not translate it well. She did not mention the plucked chickens, anyhow, or the vegetable garden or fruit trees. She did say that she gathered most of her own herbs. She mentioned bay leaf, oregano, savory, coriander leaves, thyme, cumin, and anise; plus lavender for the moths.

Dona Manuela rushed off to the kitchen, then, and Adriano listed the food that he got at its sources in the villages. There were the chickens and eggs, he said, and the ducks, turkeys, kid, and occasionally beef. There were apples, oranges, figs, and pears, if they were extra good. Of processed products, there was bread, *chouriço*, cheese, olive oil, vinegar, and wine. With these he was cautious. He would wait till something was served to him at a meal and then, if it were of superior quality, buy more to take along.

Adriano did not purchase food for its associations. I'll buy a jug of wine if it is grown on the banks of a trout stream, but it seldom tastes as good at home. Adriano was beyond souvenir shopping. Dangerous man, Adriano. His ideas would destroy the American economy if they got around. He bought for (1) flavor and (2) thrift, though the two concepts seemed inseparable in his mind.

Some moderns would see goodness and cost as different, even opposed. And the Australian aborigines might see even Portuguese habits as mindless materialism. But then I might be less eager for a tripe dinner among the aborigines.

At breakfast, Zé Francisco stopped by the *paragem* to meet us. He was the best fisherman in Manteigas. He was curious about dry flies (the kind that float, though they are not literally dry). Adriano reported his experiments, which were favorable, but said that I had tied the flies. Zé Francisco believed what he heard but did not quite understand. Why, he wondered, would a fish rise to the surface of the water, exposing itself to predators, when it could eat in comfort down below?

The Zêzere, I guessed, offered hard choices. It had a stony bed, low in alkalinity and nutrients. It could not produce much food. Vegetation on the banks, however, held abundant insects that would be blown to the water, where surface tension whould hold them prisoner at the metaphysical boundary between trout's world and ours. Such casualties were easy prey. Brown trout had evolved to exploit them.

Zé Francisco said that he had in fact found trout stomachs full of grasshoppers and other land-based aircraft. (Fishermen check trout stomachs as the Romans consulted entrails of sheep.) But he told us that there were few decent trout left in the Zêzere. The local men killed too many before they reached legal size.

Adriano and I were not dissuaded from trying. We said what anglers always say and sometimes feel: Well, if there aren't any trout, at least we'll spend our day in a good place.

We had looked down on the upper Zêzere from the mountains on the far side of Manteigas, as we drove into town. From that distance, the valley appeared so perfectly straight as to be a curiosity. Clearly the brook did not just erode itself lower and lower along the path of least resistance. There was an act of creation— sudden, as geology goes. The last of the Pleistocene glaciers must have run like a scoop along the surface of ice cream, scraping deeper and deeper, unwavering. Not much soil was left. The sides of the valley, where they support vegetation at all, are steep moors for the sheep.

When you get close, however, everything changes. Zêzere is a self-made brook, embarrassed by her straight background. Ice-age boulders still stand firmly opposed to nonsense but Zêzere laughs at them, twists her way through, and gives the old granite a tickle on the way.

An angler's route is harder. Stone forms impassable waterfalls and protects banks from the uninvited. There are even pools so defended by rock forts that you cannot fish in them, but they are few, because you try, you try. (By our wives ye shall know us, and our wives say that we lose our senses on the stream. In fact our senses are sharper while fishing than at any other time but not devoted to our wives, and they know it. Fernando Basurto[6] pled guilty five hundred years ago. It was probably not an original excuse even then.)

You cast over a cobweb stretched between two boulders, hoping that it will hold your leader off the water. The cobweb breaks. You retrieve your fly stealthily and clean the wadded web from it. You try again, casting side-armed to get under overhanging rock. Pale brown line makes S-shapes in the sun. After three failures your little fly lands in deep shadows. You wait while it eddies as if free. The black water shivers. The fly disappears. There is another shiver in your spine. You tighten the line and ease the trout out, splashing, straining to get back where boulder gapes like clamshell. She does not succeed. You hold her at the surface in unaccustomed sunlight and run your hand under her, deciding whether to put her back or take her home. She is old enough, but keeping is commitment.

This is the only place where you are allowed to fondle Venus. If you tried it in a museum where she is made of marble, you would be arrested. Some museum keepers want to ban fishing too, having guessed that nothing which feels so good ought to be legal.

Zêzere gives no cheap thrills, though. The trout in open water are all too small, flickers of sun and shadow as they flee. When they do so, you move on, because if there is a bigger one in hiding, the little ones' alarm will have frightened her too. Otherwise you try every shaded side of boulder, every still refuge near deep current, and especially every nook that might have foiled other anglers. You try to maintain concentration. You pretend that the fly is the only object worth watching in a cold universe. You cannot do it. When attention wavers your fly is sucked down. You tighten into a deep weight that surges and is gone, leaving a mercurial hump on the water, and your hopes vanish in its ripples. Despair is an ache in your chest.

At least your effort to ignore your surroundings has made you enjoy them more. The best way to appreciate anything is to tell yourself that you must not look at it. You will recall, for example, that Vasco da Gama tried not to watch Venus's slipping gown on the Isle of Love, and what happened next got him bowdlerized.

Zêzere is your private museum from Manteigas to the cirque. The exhibits are constantly changed and highlighted by a sound-

and-light show. There are no rules against feeling or sniffing. Alluvial soils bear sweet dark cherries that you can squeeze between tongue and palate. The boulders are warm in the sun, cool in the shadow. They are rubbed perfect by a supple artist, buffed to gentle curves. You step on one with felt-soled boot, leaving a wet track. You mount the next by reaching to the top with both hands and pulling yourself up its flank. Shadow lines move along the granite. Reflections from running water flutter back over the stony surfaces it has polished, light fingers checking their work. Your fingers follow. They find every line but straight, every angle but square.

By some alchemy that no one has been able to explain to me, the rocks in Zêzere's bed are all golden. Above water they are gray, from a distance, but speckled rust and white up close. Moss grows bright green at the water line and dark above it. Olive lichens wind through patches of blossoms red as hothouse flowers, but so tiny that you do not see them till a slippery climb presses your nose against them. Up close you also see little shiny flakes of quartz and depressions where the current has carved softer minerals out of the matrix. In one of the hollows are three pearl-sized pebbles of different colors, just where high water dropped them. Another contains a stone as big as your fist. Some hollows have picked up enough sediment to nourish grass—not the wispy, struggling stuff you would expect but broad green blades shooting from the rock like fireworks.

The biggest of the hollows carved by Zêzere lies atop a boulder on a flat surface the size of a bed. The inverse sculpture holds water from the last rain. It has no algae, and though it is shallow, water gives the curves depth. The hollow is the size of a woman and about the depth of her body, with waist and compliant curves. You remember this place because it is where you want to stop fishing now, and come back after lunch.

The brook sings you back to your car, ZEH-zeh-reh, ZEH-zeh-reh. A cuckoo sings too. It sounds like a Bavarian clock, though distant and elusive. You echo the call instantly, with a slight change in the consonants. Be ready, now.

Challenge: "Cuckoo! Cuckoo!"

Reply: "You too! You too!"

*   *   *

Marcel Proust thought that "we never fully experience anything except retrospectively. . . . The presence of the beloved person or object or landscape activates the senses; the imagination functions only in their absence."[7] This is a child's way of relating to things. By that I do not mean that it is good or bad, only childish.

I had no idea that I was experiencing anything when I was a child running around in the Minnesota woods. I was simply doing what I had been shown by two wiry old hunter-gatherers named Grandma and Aunt Mary, who knew where to find wild blueberries for the pies and pine knots for the fire. We lived near the town of Pine River, then, on the shore of Woman Lake. I liked all the things that nature had created for my amusement. For the old woman I was, no doubt, a beloved nuisance. But I can go back in a moment, just by tossing a knot in the flames or tasting a wild berry.

It is different when you grow up. Unlike Proust or Camões, you do not settle for long-range passions. You'd rather make scratchy love to the Venus of the rock. You live in the present, not the past, and your experiences fade with time rather than becoming more intense. The loss of a 9-inch trout turns from ache to smile. You are no longer sure, after all, that you were in the best of all possible places doing the only thing in the world worth doing. Zêzere runs somewhere inside you—a smell or sight or sound can jerk you back on a dizzy trip—but the memory is just an echo, like your song to the cuckoo.

Adriano took me to a *tasca* called *As Trutas* for lunch. It means *The Trout* (plural), and we liked that, our goals for the afternoon being to catch more than the trout (singular) that we already possessed. Trout shrink fast. When you slide one from the water, it is fat and shiny and full of flapping energy, but when you carry it around for a while, even wrapped in ferns, it sheds its calories. It becomes wrinkled and scrawny, a thing that you are embarrassed to take back to your inn. If you catch no fish at all, you can at least pretend that you had better things to do. If you return with a half dinner of trout, however, you must confess that you wanted the other half but were not good enough to get it.

The *tasca* was for snacks, but we were too hungry for snacks. We declined the puffy yellow chicken feet, skinned and stewed. We did not want the *escabeches* of chicken gizzards or ide (a tiny relative of the carp). The woman in charge found some vegetable soup for us and then fried some strips of beef. Surprise: They were good. The marinade of wine and olive oil must have helped them. We finished off what the woman had planned for her family's dinner.

The radio was playing American music onto the sidewalk. "West Virginia," it sang, "Mountain Mama, take me home, take me home." Three half-drunk men were standing there, swaying. Adriano sat upright at the table but I may have swayed a little too. It was a good song.

Water music is never nostalgic or erotic, strictly speaking, though a fisherman in Zêzere's embrace can be both. Her song is more soothing than the best of imitations, can be just as stirring when thunder keeps time, and is more frightening when the flood scours soft rock from granite and drops pebbles into the cavities. But part of the emotional range is missing.

Art is an improvement on nature, say we humans. There is no humanity without art. We can judge when a hominid became sapient man by his paintings, which have the power to make us shiver twenty or thirty centuries later. The Grão Vasco's vision of Sebastian at least makes us shudder. The pictures we buy in the mall are at the other extreme—possessions small enough to fit in our decor. They spare us the inconvenience of going outside to look at nature.

Art that falls between the extremes is the real thing, for its creator, an original vision. Other adults may see it too but it is invisible to children, every one of whom would trade a Renoir for a madeleine. Do you know why there are no windows in art galleries? Curators will mention lighting problems, but the truth is that windows make paintings disappear. Where there is a window, children run to it and poof! Art is gone, preempted by nature.

I don't know. If art must be original, then another person's vision cannot be *my* art. I am obliged to create that for myself. Zêzere helps. As compared to the exhibits in museums, she is usually more beautiful and always more interesting, because she changes. She is new with every cloud, every trout. I tire even of Beethoven faster than Zêzere. Her music is part of a multimedia presentation and the conductor is me. I have been in training for a couple of million years and what I have learned comes flooding back on the flow that sings Zêzere, Zêzere.

My last trout of the day was too pretty to dress right away, so I laid her in the creel on fronds of fern. She was still moist and glistening when I got back to the car. Adriano had three fish, one a little too small that he had kept because it swallowed the hook. We dressed them all for dinner by a spring that ran under the road. Adriano was so happy that he waved his hands (a thing no Portuguese does often) as he told me about the time at the edge of dusk. A sparse flight of mayfly spinners had come back to the river, laid their eggs, and died on the water. The trout had sipped them down. Adriano had been ready with his fly.

Each of us told his story not so much to help the other understand (though perhaps he did) but so that the actor could remember his own performance. We created ourselves no less in the telling than the doing. This is not to say that we lied. We would have thought poorly of our lives if they had been too small to keep. What we created in the telling was not the event but its structure and memory. We made each trout happen twice—once in the stream and once in the hand, once in death and once in love—before we were sure that it would last.

· 15 ·

NOBLE SAVAGES

Cupid observed, in short, that no one loved what he ought to be loving but only the objects of unworthy desire. . . .

CAMÕES, *The Lusiads*, Canto Nine

All Adriano is divided into three parts: the upstairs of his Lisbon house, which is family; the downstairs *casa da pesca,* or fishing store, which is tackle and old hip-boots that might be patched some day; and the cellar properly speaking, which smells better. The first thing you notice in it is the half-dozen cheeses ripening on shelves near the door. Then you scent the apples in baskets and the potatoes in crates. Your eyes adapt to the dark and you see the dusty bottoms of wine bottles protruding from shelves. Finally, from the back of the cellar comes its best fragrance: an oaken cask of Port wine. Adriano must not mind losing the vapors that leak out, because otherwise he would bottle the contents and slow the aging process. To me the rejected smell seems big enough to keep.

This is not a hobby room, much less a tourist attraction. It is a hunter-gatherer's cave. I was admitted as one of the clan. Adriano told me that he had started gathering old Port decades back, on his fishing trips to the north; or perhaps hunting for fish on his gathering trips. This was before the oil sheiks and geisha houses became willing to pay any price for wine that someone told them was the world's best. Adriano bought bottles from old men who had taken care of what their fathers left them and wanted to be sure that it fell into good hands. Port was not given away, even then, but the price was a bargain if one remembered that it included a hundred years of compound interest.

Adriano lifted from its rack a bottle painted 1887 in simple white letters. He climbed the stairs carefully, without disturbing the sediment inside or the dust on the outside of the bottle. After dinner we had big sniffs and small sips from wide-bottomed glasses. There was a special cake for the purpose, a sort of dense bread yellow with egg yolks, not too sweet.

I could not describe the taste of the Port. Doing so would require experience with other flavors equally old and intense—and there are none. Big red table wines are just within the realm of experience, like roast woodcock. Port is more complex than the rest of nature. You can't claim to taste things like blackberries or hazelnuts. You just have to say that the flavor is better than any of us deserve.

Mind you, this is an old man's game (and perhaps an old woman's, though I don't recall old women making a fuss over it). Not even old Port is as intense as love's labor won or trout's labor lost. But you appreciate Port more after the other flavors; maybe it reminds you of them. It captures what I most admire about Adriano's version of Portugal: a view of what is good and a stubborn willingness to stay with it, for generations. Most of us admire individuals who defer gratification. How about a people who keep wine in the bottle for a century?

The Port wine region lies in the Douro province—northernmost but one for travelers following the coastline, like Adriano and me. I had never been there and will not rush back. It is all hillsides, steep because they are of slow-eroding schist. The brown-gray rock soil would be of little commercial value except for the flavor that it gives to wine. Port is worth so much now that international corporations have bought in. They have clawed or blasted terraces for the vines out of slopes that amount almost to cliffs. The upper Douro valley is not like wine country elsewhere—more like a town with excavations done and houses missing. Below the terraces, the Douro River has been imprisoned, allowed to run free only in short stretches downstream from dams. As a whole, there can be few other rural areas so altered. It is a constructed landscape.

Short horizons are all right when you can walk beyond them—in big whispering woods, for example, with trees receding, succeeding, changing. In tight little valleys the horizon is fixed. Those of the Douro are all vines. You cannot even climb out of your car and hike to the top of the ridges for a view.

A boy in one of the villages here would surely want to run away and look for a living, or at least for a lark. If he saw the same girl three times in his own village, people would begin to talk. They would say that it was about time to do the right thing by the young lady. He would want to do the wrong thing and not get caught at it, and know that it was hopeless, and wake up sweating. And soon he would be trapped anyhow, squeezed by walls of schist forever. He would spend the rest of his life swinging a hoe, protecting a few sheep, cutting tiny fields of rye with a sickle, and working the vineyards in season.

Most of Portugal would have been subject once to this grinding social confinement. No wonder young men volunteered to sail down the coast of Africa: The thirst and heat and dying of the discoveries would have seemed like a release, by comparison to staying home. After seeing the Douro, one wonders not why Iberia is split but how even Portugal ever managed to build a community and language. If social horizons were tight everywhere, however, most of the people would at least have been able to *look* into the distance, and in the Douro they cannot.

We had thought of spending a night near the vineyards but decided, by acclamation, to drive on through the Douro to the Minho province. Perhaps, Adriano said, we could make Castro Laboreiro not long after dark. From the way he said the name, I gathered that it was a place where he would feel more comfortable. Not that either of us had anything bad to say about the Douro. Adriano wouldn't. I didn't, out of courtesy. But I thought: Poor little Portugal, saved by poverty from the mistakes the rest of us made, but determined to make them as quickly as possible now that it can afford them.

I offered to spell Adriano at the wheel. This may be small country when seen from a flat map, but it is big when you climb its contours and wind around its branches. Adriano declined my offer: didn't think I could get the honking right, perhaps. He beeped at every bullock cart and pedestrian, and a few even waved in reply. The horn was courtesy rather than aggression. Adriano honked at every blind curve, too, and there was one about every thirty seconds. Even the trains chugging beside us had short cars for negotiating the twists of that topography. The road was roughly one-and-a-quarter lanes wide, by American standards, and had no shoulders. Where there was 10 feet of space between pavement and drop-off, someone had squeezed in either vines or a linear house.

A bus coming toward us had pulled up at one such house to discharge a passenger. We might have squeezed by but did not, and Adriano was rewarded for his courtesy. A woman with a shopping bag tried to step down from the bus and failed. The wall of her house was too close. She turned around and tried to step out backward. Most of her might have made it. Her bottom, however, took up more space than that available between bus and wall. She became flustered and tried again, repeatedly: in-out-bump, in-out-bump. It was a scene from one of those silent films, round bottom emerging, banging on wall, retreating, trying again. It might have worked, in time, like a Winnie-the-Pooh stoutness exercise, but Adriano was turning pink from the effort of keeping a straight face. He backed up and let the bus driver pull ahead for more clearance. The plump woman scuttled into the skinny house. We chuckled our way north.

The countryside of the Minho province was a jumble. An active-duty baronial mansion overlooked a junkyard. Small industrial plants mingled with houses. Motorcycles whined around trucks, trucks bellowed around motorcycles, and the engines all smelled as if they were pulling too much cargo. In every spot where the soil was not paved, crops grew in stories: turnips or carrots on the ground floor, beans on the mezzanine, tall cabbage one floor up, and *vinho verde* vines in the penthouse.

In America today, we do not grow our food where we work, and we increasingly move from the old industrial cities to the suburbs or the sunbelt. Portuguese practice could hardly be more different. The sunny, beautiful Alentejo is still empty and the drizzly, polluted north still thriving. An economist might note that the country is organized for efficiency, not comfort. An ecologist would argue that people have clustered in the areas with good precipitation. I seem to be an ecologist. If modern man has lasted here for twice as long as native Americans have been in the western hemisphere, it must be because there has been enough water every year to make things grow.

Adriano was neither economist nor ecologist. For him, this part of the world had been put on the map by Afonso Henriques, first king of independent Portugal. His great sword was still in a museum somewhere, Adriano said. Few men could lift it with one hand. I did not see the sword but was glad to hear that it had been treated like old Port. (King Arthur's influence might have lasted longer if Excalibur had not been chucked into a lake.)

As we got nearer to Castro Laboreiro, the countryside changed from urban to rural. Bullock carts crept in front of us. Columns of hay dried on ropes hung from the limbs of chestnuts. Big sea-pines found space to grow. A man led a cow on a cord.

It was a short cord. Rural Portugal is entering the Age of Information and the Industrial Revolution at the same time. More and more citizens will wander the hypermarket that is the European community. They will buy sportswear in its shops. They will use interactive software to explore the virtual reality of simulated worlds. They will dine on bread that moves from electric ovens to plastic wrappers by conveyor belt, untouched by human hands. Evolution can no more be stopped in the world of technology than in the natural world, but the extinction of a way of life is frightening. One writer "wonders if the type of society in which one believes—the modern liberal, industrialized and democratic society—is able to provide less or more happiness in individual terms. . . . I wonder if there is in fact more or less happiness in the developed world, and I don't have an answer. I am terrified to get an answer to this. . . . In the United States, in France, in Germany, the amount of unhappiness is really enormous."[1]

Castro Laboreiro is remote from it all. The town had no road to the rest of the world, Adriano said, till a few years back. Outsiders arrived only on horseback or afoot, after sleeping in shelters along the trail. Few residents could leave, but then why should they wish to do so? They had given up the wandering life 4,500 years ago. That would have been in the Iron Age. Before then, they were nomads. They had settled down, more or less, to agriculture and cattle raising. To defend the new way of life, they had built a *castro*—a fortified village atop a hill. They had fought Rome until the advantages of civilization became clear. The village (*aldeia*) had grown into a town (*vila*). It lies at what is today the northernmost tip of Portugal, up against Spain.

I added history to geography and failed to produce a sum. I knew towns only as places where roads met. On the other hand, I was not sure that I should think of Castro Laboreiro as rural. Can a place be rustic when it has been a center of civilization forever?

Adriano was tired but talkative as the sun set, revived by the twisting, lonely road atop wild ridges. I was concerned. All expeditions have responsibilities to be divided and I had taken over the worrying because Adriano was not good at it. I had wanted to telephone ahead for a reservation at Castro Laboreiro's only inn. If it had no room for us, we would not have time to return to the main highway before all the other inns and restaurants were closed for the night.

Adriano was confident that something would turn up. He remembered the lady who ran the inn and was sure that she would not turn us out cold and hungry. And she wouldn't have, either. Unfortunately, we found when we got there that the place was being rebuilt with a grant from the European Community. There was not a single room with beds, plumbing, or glass in the windows.

I worried. Adriano didn't. The lady at the inn tried the telephone, which did not work, and then put her coat on and ran around town looking. She found another woman who had just finished putting in a room for tourists. We rushed to it. There was a fireplace in the corner and some big, gnarled roots of broom for fuel. They made a crackling fire. The tank in the bathroom had enough warmish water to wash all of an average Portuguese or 80 percent of a large American before turning cold. I fooled it: got the suds out of my hair and eyes first, saving the last cold dribbles for my nether regions, which were used to mountain streams anyhow.

The food was worth it. I am not at all sure, in fact, that such a dinner would have been as good without a little torment for the appetizer. (The feud between angel of happiness and imp of unhappiness takes place along a borderline as wiggly as that between Portugal and Spain.) There was homemade bread, anyhow; a red wine from 1984; a soup of carrots, turnips, onions, and beans; poached heads of whiting with drizzles of olive oil; and mountain potatoes so good that we ate them like chestnuts. This was back at the inn. Its kitchen at least was working, and from the size of the portions, it was clear that the hostess did remember Adriano.

Next morning we went looking for Secundino Domingues and found everything else. On Adriano's last trip, a few years back, Secundino had been good company. Adriano remembered where he lived—a cluster of stone houses on a dirt road just outside Castro Laboreiro. When we got there, however, they were empty, every one. Even the dogs and chickens were gone. The only sound was of a trickle running down a granite trough into a granite pool—source of water for all the houses. To call the place medieval might have been an exaggeration. It had been there, perhaps, four thousand years before the Middle Ages, stone walls occasionally rebuilt or fitted to new wooden doors after the old rotted away.

"They've gone to the *brandas,*" Adriano opined. I had not heard of *brandas.* They are houses higher in the mountains, Adriano said, and even simpler. The herders move to them on March 15 and return on September 15. Everybody goes, old and young—even Secundino, apparently, though Adriano had not remembered him as a herder. I would have liked to visit the *brandas.* They might have been the right way to manage an ageless human urge to move with the seasons. But we did not know where to find the herders so we drove on, at little more than walking speed.

The countryside was all edges. A high ridge to our north bristled like a hedgehog with granite prickles. From the side of the cliff, rocks stuck out and down like hawks' beaks. Down by our dirt track, boulders were piled upon boulders, sometimes five deep. Adriano told me that he had tried to take a shortcut back from the river, once, and spent the night lost among these dark leering presences. That was when he decided that he needed Secundino Domingues to show him around.

At first glance, the boulders looked like glacial deposits, but then you noticed that one fit into another like pieces of a puzzle. They must have formed and eroded where they were. This place had not been bulldozed by obstreperous glaciers a mere ten thousand years ago. This was the bedrock of a nation, weathering with its people and language. It was also a national park, but I could not see that anyone paid much attention to that. If the region still looked as it had for the last several millennia, it was just because it was too cold and hard to be violated.

We jounced past the village of *Ribeiro de Cima*—Upper Brook. Adriano looked at it, down in its hollow, and decided that Secundino did not live there, so we gave up and drove on to *Ribeiro de Baixo,* which of course meant Lower Brook. We parked at the foot of a stone cross by the Chapel of Our Lady of the Olive Tree. I called her three times, under my breath. She was soft with esses and els, *Nossa Senhora da Oliveira,* and her chapel grew from a gentle green lawn in that hard landscape. She would have made a good title for a poem if I'd had a poem handy.

The houses stood around us with blank eyes, and I wondered if this place were deserted too, and then we started putting our fishing rods together. It must have been a sign that we were harmless. A door opened and Célia came running down. (I do not suggest that she was sent; even *Nossa Senhora da Oliveira* would find it difficult to tell a nine-year-old girl what she wanted to do.) Célia was better than Secundino Domingues, anyhow. She achieved an instant conquest of Adriano, and vice versa. His face bloomed with benevolence. She told us that her father had gone to France in a train, returned for Christmas, and would be back again for the month of August. He would do some building on the house then, she explained. We took time out from assembling tackle and waders and lunches. Célia's mother came out of the house, a young woman in a black dress, and told Célia not to be a pest. Adriano gave fervent assurances that Célia was no trouble at all. When we were ready to go, he told Célia that she had a pretty face. She gave him a kiss.

I would have liked a kiss on my cheek too, but did not know how to manage it. Kisses are the best thing for fisherman's luck. My incompetence with them is genetic, I think. One of the sharper Angles among my ancestors passed his clumsiness down the generations, so that when I need a kiss now, I make all the wrong moves.

We walked down a steep slope to the Castro Laboreiro River then, leaving Célia and Our Lady of the Olive Tree behind.

We entered nature without leaving civilization: dropped down the wall of the valley through a commingling of trees and houses, stones and fields, streams and ditches. The brook that gave *Ribeiro de Baixo* its name split and ran through the ditches toward the roots of the crops. We followed a path under oaks and found ourselves in the yard of an old man who was caulking beehives made of cork with cowdung, to keep the mice out. We wound up next under the chestnuts and found ourselves in a pasture with goats who were tending a little boy. We were lost. We knew where the river was—heard it always and saw it sometimes, shining below us—but every twisting of our trail took us instead to somebody's door. Adriano had a laugh with each of the residents. He got new directions, followed them a few yards, and got lost again. "I feel like a child here," he said, and grew taller and straighter with every bend in the path.

I stared at a donkey chewing straw in a stone yard. If the animal had talked, I'd have known where I was. It did not, so I kept disbelief half suspended. At bedtime I had read books about this place to little boys, one after the other, and learned as much about Narnia as they did.

Like the vineyards of the Douro valley, this was a constructed landscape, but there the similarities ended. *Ribeiro de Baixo* had been built for subsistence, not cash, and therefore included houses and a diversity of crops. It had been built by hand labor, not bulldozers. Cars would never be able to reach most of the dwellings. Above all, *Ribeiro de Baixo* had evolved as if it were part of nature, pieced together over the millennia by people who did the best they could in this unlikely place because they had no other.

We got to the river eventually—couldn't miss it by trending always down—and then crossed, sat on a boulder, and looked back. Adriano answered questions. He knew that I had to catch *Ribeiro de Baixo* right away, as a big trout has to be netted before it tires and drifts downstream.

This new side of the river was in Spain and mostly rough pasture, but we could look back and see the steeper Portuguese side clearly. Its dominant features were not in fact houses and paths and irrigation ditches, as we had thought close-up, but a series of terraces that had turned wild slopes into cultivated lands. The lowest terrace was held up by a massive wall of rocks. Behind it grew maize, rye, potatoes, and tall cabbage. Around the edges, *vinho verde* vines reached for whatever heat there was. There were far more hewn stones in the walls of this one terrace than in all the houses. I supposed that the wall had been raised gradually as soil accumulated, consuming hundreds of man-years of labor. The dirt must have been constructed too, by tillage and compost.

An agriculture that builds topsoil? That too would be almost a non sequitur in America. With us, the question is the speed of depletion. We wonder how many generations can be fed before we hit bottom. Such farming is akin to mining.

Above the lower terrace, the features of *Ribeiro de Baixo* were scattered as nature scatters acorns. Smaller terraces and pastures fit into the hillside around stone houses. In a few cases, migrant workers returning with cash had carried cement, paint, and roof tiles down the paths. Underneath the red roofs and white walls, however, the old granite was there. If in the course of history or prehistory a single house in Lower Brook had ever been torn down or abandoned, I saw no evidence of it. The place had evolved like any other biological community. It looked better than the original nature.

There is a word for it: picturesque. It describes "places and images which contain the clues of historic continuity, domestication of nature, and evidence of the presence of man in the landscape."[2] We are not good at the picturesque in America. We have few landscapes in which man and nature have been getting along well enough for long enough. In western America we have much of the sublime: landscapes that inspire fear, almost, by "vastness, power . . . and overwhelming solitude." And in some of North America, we have more natural beauty than Europe. We were the first to create natural parks and wilderness areas, and we had more space for them. Where we have failed is in mixing man and nature. It can be done, though. It had been done right across the Castro Laboreiro River from Adriano and me.

We saw less refuse than in Manteigas—the residents of *Ribeiro de Baixo* were poorer—but what trash there was lay around on the rocks till rains washed it down to the river and the sea. The community had not learned what to do with containers other than wine bottles, which were recycled. Human and animal wastes must all have been turned into the topsoil. There was no sign of them in the river. We looked down the sides of its boulders through water clear as air and saw schools of fingerlings flying over pale sand.

We walked upstream, then for a mile or so. Adriano fished little. He was content with the smaller sensations of May: wagtail busy on rocks, nightingale practicing chords behind a shimmer of birches, stream harmonizing, rugs of grass so velvety that one's mind rolled on them. But in between there was torment enough if we had given it a chance. There were waist-high barriers of *silvas*—the brambles that caught the Portuguese noncombatants at Aljubarrota and held them to be speared. Adriano was ready. He pulled small pruning shears from his fishing jacket and opened the way for us a snip at a time. It had not been necessary to do this a few years ago, he said. The men used to cut the thorns back. Now they had gone to France, Spain, Germany, and even the Middle East, finding work that paid. The villages had been left to the women. They kept the crops growing but did not wander in the wild places.

I fished, sometimes. In the deeps where alder limbs brushed the water there were little rise bubbles, and shadowy shapes under them got my lust up. There were sunny riffles too, interrupted by rocks that had to shelter a trout, and a man of my age cannot scorn a fish that wants to be caught. There were two or three keeping-size trout that I returned to the water and smaller ones in which I did not set the hook. But more often I walked with Adriano. He showed me the *poldras*, stepping stones across shallow reaches. He pointed out old broken pieces of *mó*—millstones from the time when this stream ground grain. I was surprised by two words so much more frugal than their English equivalents. Perhaps Adriano's ancestors had spent even more time working the streams than mine.

For lunch, Adriano found a tablecloth of moss spreading near granite stools. I guessed that he had remembered the place from years back. We ate our *chouriço* and bread with the smell of trout faint on our fingers. We let our twisted orange peels fall on the green moss. I drained spring water from a backpacker's flask that had traveled the world with me, and still does. Adriano pulled a plastic bottle from his creel, drank the mineral water in it, and discarded the bottle on the moss. He said that he liked the disposable bottles because he did not have to carry them back to the car. It was the most innocent of remarks, and habits. It gave me a problem of conscience. Adriano's Nereids do not object to plastic rubbish. Mine do, but I chose to offend them instead of my friend. The bottle stayed there for the next high water.

Adriano stayed there for a rest, too, while I pushed farther upstream. The day was blue and gold above my head, green beneath my feet. A trout rose silver in a black pool.

And then I hiked away from the stream, looking for an easier route back to Adriano. The valley had widened here, forming a natural route for walkers between points upstream and down. I looked down and found my feet on cobblestones—the kind laid when men were giants. The cobbles were not overgrown pebbles but great rocks hauled from the river and pounded down to make a *via* wide and straight, good for the centuries. I walked till it angled uphill and ended, just like that. It had been torn up and used to make walls for a field that had been abandoned in its turn. I turned around and looked back along the Roman road. It had been surveyed, not improvised, built to regulations long forgotten. The soft felt soles of my boots had followed granite worn shiny by the leather sandals of people who were strangers here before me.

I have always been a stranger. It is part of the American condition. We transplant ourselves to places where no one knows us. We are cottonwoods, not oaks. We spread our roots wide and shallow. We grow fast but would not make good backlogs for a fire.

I am innocent because I lack experience. I grow from rich prairie soil, so why should I worry? The people of Lower Brook, on the contrary, have reached innocence via experience. They have always had to grope for nutrients in the crannies of bedrock, pushing their roots down through the strata, accumulating topsoil little by little. If they live simply now, it is because they have learned to be content.

Being a stranger means that I am not required to be anything else. I don't need to be put in my place because I have none. It is easier than being a local boy, of whom certain things would be expected. The Portuguese accept me not because I am one of them but because I am foreign.

But if I am an *estrangeiro,* and innocent, I am at least not a tourist. Tourists are interlopers. My fishing rod naturalizes me. In the Alentejo, a shotgun does as well. "It is my experience," Steinbeck said, "that if a man is going hunting or fishing his purpose is understood or even applauded." The men, rich or poor, want to go along. The women relax because, of all the ingenious ways men find to waste time, this is the one least likely to make trouble for the community.

The fishing part of our trip ended abruptly. We were walking along the edge of an abandoned, overgrown terrace. The top of its retaining wall was our path. There was an old field to our left and a drop of some 30 feet to our right. Adriano the Fearless stepped over the pitfall without stumbling. Datus the Concerned dropped off the wall. The good news, sort of, was that a bed of brambles caught me before I hit the rocks at the bottom. Adriano's pruning shears got me out bloody but unbowed. Well, I was bowed a little, but the damage to my fishing rod was worse. It had landed underneath me.

This obliged me to refine my thesis. A fishing rod is an instrument of serendipity—no doubt about that—but the things you stumble into when carrying one are not always what you had in mind.

On our drive back, we stopped at Upper Brook, where Secundino Dominigues was not supposed to reside, which meant that we did not look for him, and so naturally we found him, if you see what I mean, as by now you probably do.

It all happened because of the smell. We were innocently fording the brook when it—the smell, I mean—reached through our open car windows and grabbed us. Somebody was baking bread. Adriano parked on dry ground and went looking for the cook. I hobbled behind. Our noses led us to the right cottage. Its occupant was in the field at its side, wielding her *sachola* (a kind of hoe used for weeding rather than tilling, but still of heavy cast iron). We waited till she finished her row of potatoes and came to see us. She was white-haired but sturdy in her black dress. We would be welcome to some bread, she said. We could come back in an hour and watch her break the seals on the oven. And then she told us where to find Secundino Domingues.

The finding was not as good as the looking. Secundino lived in one of the biggest houses in *Ribeiro de Cima*. His wife had died and he was camping in his own kitchen with a cold stove. He admitted that, with no woman to cook for him, he was not eating as well as he should. He would not have had the strength to chase trout, he said, even if we had come to him in time. We declined his offer of brandy. I wondered if the *aguardente* had anything to do with the liverish color of his skin. And then we left. Said our farewells and walked off. I thought that there ought to be something more, some way to put flesh on our ghost, but we had found what was meant to stay lost. Adriano knew and I followed him.

Adriano and I took up residence on a comfortable pair of stones at what seemed to be the confluence of the village. The brook ran nearby for the children with buckets. By our fork in the path there was a soul-chapel—a block of stone roughly a meter to the side, hollow and painted inside, with a cross and pictures of the saints. Passers-by could say prayers there for their dead. Food for the living was wandering loose: a cock with his flock of hens, a young male goat, three sheep looking for scraps of grass, and a *Barrosã* steer. It would be delicious from its diet of herbs, Adriano said. It was small and brown with a face that seemed intelligent, and you don't see many bright cattle these days.

We met the whole village, or at least its female half, which was the one in residence. Upper Brook was a Garden of Eden with Adam gone off somewhere, leaving Eve to wait for him in a black dress. I asked Adriano about the color. He said simply that it was the custom. I surmised that black was also a no-trespassing sign for widows temporary or permanent. A teenaged girl passed us wearing jeans with a swing in them as good as any in the soap operas. We saw only one middle-aged man—an emigrant back on vacation from Germany. But we saw young children, so Adam still visits Eden now and again.

Mind you, this Eden did not feed the fantasies that we Westerners like to project on Noble Savages. Sexual liberation? Not with half the town in hands-off dresses. Freedom from materialism? Not with the other half making money in foreign lands. Freedom from sex roles? I would wager that the men, wherever they were, did not advertise virtue by black raiment. Freedom from social stress? Secundino was dying of loneliness in the middle of his village. Freedom from exploitation of man by man? These men would still have been in Africa, if their side had not lost the war. Freedom from repressive religion? Not if you find the Catholicism of the *almas* repressive.

Harmony with nature, then? Well, yes, but not the kind of harmony that we nature fakers yearn for. If I had confessed to releasing good-sized trout, the Upper Brookers would have thought me frivolous. They eat nature. They are nature.

The bread was smelling good to me, too.

I eat; therefore I am.

Our benefactress took us to the oven in the corner of her *quintal*. We could have found it by scent anyhow. It had been built by her grandfather seventy years ago of granite blocks hewn to make a cubical cavity about the size of a soul-chapel. The door was a square of stone lifted into place. She had heated the oven with grapevine trimmings, she said, and then put five loaves inside— enough for the week.

We stood (not at attention, but respectfully) while she lifted her baker's peel of black old iron. With it she broke the seals of cowdung. Daubed on while moist, they had dried hard, keeping heat from leaking out of the oven. Our hostess removed the door and slid the spade-shaped peel under each of the loaves in turn, moving them to paper fertilizer bags spread on the ground. The loaves were round, a foot in height and almost twice that in diameter. We would have to let them cool for a time, she said, before they could be moved without cracking.

She did not mind sharing the recipe: one part rye flour to two of maize. To hold the loaves together, she sometimes added a kilo or two of pale wheat flour from America. The total might have been 15 or 20 kilos. Sourdough provided the leavening. There were no other ingredients but salt, and water from the brook. She did not brag but was satisfied, clearly, that the loaves were good. Adriano complimented her quietly but firmly, Adriano-style. I seconded the motion. I remember her reply: *"Aqui vivemos mais à portuguesa."* "Here we live more like Portuguese."

She asked, then, how much bread we needed, and Adriano invited me to choose, and I thought that he looked disappointed when I wanted only half a loaf. (It would have fed both of us for a day with nothing on the side.) He offered her no money and told me, later, that she would have been offended if he had.

As we departed, we asked whether she ever left the village. She preferred not to do so, she said. Her children kept urging her to visit, but she liked to wait for them back here, at home. We learned then that she had a son who was a lawyer and a daughter attending the University of Braga. She would not have told us if we had not asked. That kind of reticence also impressed me as *à portuguesa.*

The bread stuck to my ribs and the last thing its baker said stuck in my mind. "Don't wrap it in plastic," she insisted as we left for the car. "Plastic makes bread go soft."

When I asked Adriano for an opinion, he paused for thought, as usual, and then told me that yes, the children would return for the holidays, and probably one or both would move to the old house in time. They would rather die in Upper Brook than anywhere else. It was home.

I hoped that he was right. We bounced back down the road to the world talking, Adriano sure and me wondering, each taking big bites of bread that had not been wrapped in plastic.

NOTES

CHAPTER 1

1. Camões, Luís Vaz de. *The Lusiads*. First edition 1572. For the epigraphs, I have used William C. Atkinson's translation (London: Penguin, 1952), altering it in some chapters, including this one. Camões' original was rousing poetry in the Spenserian stanza. No prose translation captures the feeling, and no poetic translation can be accurate. (Camões is often rendered in English as Camoens, which seems to me no more pronounceable. The tilde in the Portuguese spelling accents the last syllable and gives it a nasal sound.)
2. Gould, Stephen Jay, in *Natural History*, March 1991, p. 9.

CHAPTER 2

1. From a letter by President Franklin D. Roosevelt authorizing the Nisei combat unit in World War II.
2. Faria, Francisco Leite de, in *Portugal/Brazil: The Age of Atlantic Discoveries*. Edited by Guedes, Max Justo, and Gerald Lombardi. Lisbon: Bertrand, 1990, p. 249.

CHAPTER 3

1. This piece of the Portuguese myth probably has little to do with the minutiae of history.
2. Scully, Vincent. *Architecture: The Natural and the Manmade*. New York: St. Martin's Press, 1991. I got the phrase from Brendan Gill's review in the *New Yorker*, Dec. 30, 1991.
3. "I have realized as I grow older that history, in the end, has more imagination than oneself." Gabriel García Márquez quoted by Roger Cohen. *New York Times*, August 22, 1991.

CHAPTER 4

1. Morris, Jan. *Spain*. NY: Oxford, 1979. p. 85.
2. These thoughts on the Information Explosion and Industrial Revolution borrow from Michael Rothschild's *Bionomics* (New York: Holt, 1990).
3. According to Marques, A. H. de Oliveira. *História de Portugal*. Lisbon: Palas Editores, 1985 (first edition, 1972), p. 255.
4. Boxer, C. R., in *Portugal/Brazil: The Age of Atlantic Discoveries*.

(Guedes, Max Justo, and Gerald Lombardi, editors). Lisbon: Bertrand, 1990, p. 264.

5. Zurara, Gomes Eanes de (1410–1474?). *Crónica do descobrimento e conquista da Guiné*. From the frontispiece in *Portugal/Brazil: The Age of Atlantic Discoveries* (see previous note).

6. Bradford, Ernle. *Southward the Caravels*. London: Hutchinson, 1961, p. 64. This is not a reliable biography of Prince Henry, but the passage quoted captures the fears of the time.

7. My main source of facts is A. H. de Oliveira Marques's *História de Portugal*, which is rigorously researched. (There is an English-language edition that I have not seen.) Some details in this chapter also come from *Os Descobrimentos Portugueses* by Luís de Albuquerque. In English, Daniel J. Boorstin's *The Discovers* has a brief but useful summary.

8. Holland, Barbara. "Vespucci Could Have Been Wrong, Right?" in *Smithsonian* magazine, March 1990, p. 164.

9. Keefe, Eugene K., et al. *Area Handbook for Portugal*. Washington: Government Printing Office, 1977 (written by a team of scholars at American University), p. 33.

10. Campbell, Joseph. *Historical Atlas of World Mythology*. New York: Harper, 1988. Volume I, Part 2 (*Mythologies of the Great Hunt*), p. viii.

Chapter 5

1. Keefe, p. 22.

2. Campbell, Joseph. *Historical Atlas of World Mythology*. New York: Harper, 1988. Volume II, Part 3, p. 295.

3. Volume I, Part 2, p. xx. Campbell is drawing here on Eugen Herrigel's *Zen in the Art of Archery*.

4. Steinbeck, John. *Travels with Charley*. New York: Viking. p. 19.

Chapter 6

1. The myth of The Battler is probably based on historical facts, but I have seen no scholarly research on them.

2. Twain, Mark. *Innocents Abroad*. New York: Library Classics, 1984 (reprint). He visited the Azores, not continental Portugal.

3. My translation from Saraiva, José Hernano. *História de Portugal*. Lisbon: Alfa, 1983.

4. This again is myth based on history.

Chapter 7

1. The scientists do not agree on all of the details, but this paragraph summarizes what I take to be the best current knowledge. See also Oliveira Marques, pp. 14–22.

2. The information on falconry is drawn from José Mattoso's contribution to Saraiva's *História de Portugal.*
3. Oliveira Marques, p. 230.
4. Hardin, Garrett. "The Tragedy of the Commons," in *Science*, Volume 162, pp. 1243–1248, December 13, 1968.
5. Information on the American process is drawn from "The Thoroughly Modern Olive" by Raymond Sokolov in *Natural History*, April 1989, pp. 102–104.
6. "The bounty that spilled from the basket was of venison, gift of the universal Hunter, the Sun, while the rain of maize which that night fell was of the proven goddess Moon, herself." Campbell, Joseph. *Historical Atlas of World Mythology*, Volume II (*The Way of the Seeded Earth*), Part 2 (*Mythologies of the Primitive Planters*). New York: Harper & Row, 1988, p. 155.
7. An American scrub woodland would typically have greater diversity in both plants and animals. In Britain, however, the diversity would be less for (I think) three reasons: greater impact by civilization, greater destruction by the glaciers, and greater difficulty in colonizing an island.
8. The quotation is from Raymond Sokolov's "Eating like a Noble Savage" in *Natural History*, June 1991, p. 74.
9. Campbell, Joseph. *Historical Atlas of World Mythology*, Volume II (*The Way of the Seeded Earth*), Part 1 (*The Sacrifice*). New York: Harper & Row, 1988, pp. 72–87. All quotations in this section are from Campbell's work.
10. Maurice Goudeket on truffles, as quoted by Raymond Sokolov in *Natural History*, January 1991, p. 81.

CHAPTER 8

1. McDonald, John *Quill Gordon*. New York: Knopf, 1972, p. 153. The quotation is from *The Treatyse of Fishing with an Angle*, the first versions of which appeared early in the fifteenth century. Dame Juliana Berners was almost certainly not the author but she has become part of the myth.
2. Sokolov, Raymond, in *Natural History* magazine, November 1990, p. 95.
3. In *Travels with Charley*, p. 128.

CHAPTER 9

1. Attributed to Oliveira Martins by Simões, Viriato. *A Serra da Estrela.* Lisbon: Self-published, 1979, p. 44. I have altered the nonstop punctuation.
2. In *Travels with Charley*, p. 102.

Chapter 10

1. Oliveira, Frederico Alcide de. *Aljubarrota Dissecada*. Lisbon: Serviço Histórico-Militar, 1988. This is a scholarly work drawn from the most recent field research. I have used it for the battle details that follow unless another source is cited.
2. Attributed to Vaclev Havel, poet-president of Czechoslovakia.
3. This is my recollection of a televised interview with Bill Moyers.
4. My translation from an old Portuguese text cited by Alcide de Oliveira.
5. In the Narnia books for children and their parents.
6. I have not confirmed the history.

Chapter 11

1. In this section I have used the figures published by Bill Bryson in *The Mother Tongue* (New York: Morrow, 1990). They are all too low, by now. The latest figure I have seen for native speakers of Portuguese is 180 million.
2. Barreiros, Antonio José. *História da Literatura Portuguesa*. Lisbon: Pax, undated, p. 120.
3. Gilmore, David D. "Manhood," in *Natural History* magazine, June 1990, p. 64. The article is "Adapted from *Manhood in the Making: Cultural Concepts of Masculinity* . . . Published by Yale University Press," 1990.
4. Gilmore's findings are consistent with those of Joseph Campbell. See chapter 7, note 8.
5. From an article by Alan Riding in the *The New York Times*, February 15, 1991. The quotation is attributed to Norma Couri, Lisbon correspondent for *Jornal do Brasil*.
6. Goleman, Daniel, in *The New York Times*, December 25, 1990. The article summarizes recent work by several researchers on individualism versus collectivism.

Chapter 12

1. The thought is attributed to Clive Pointing, a "British environmental historian." The source is an article by Jessica Matthews in the *Washington Post*, January 4, 1991.
2. Hoffman, Richard C., in *Speculum*, Volume 60, Issue 4 (1985), pp. 898–899.

Chapter 13

1. See chapter 8, note 1.
2. John Steinbeck in *Travels with Charley*, p. 58.

3. Loureiro, Francisco de Sales. In *História de Portugal*, edited by José Hermano Saraiva. Lisbon: Alfa, 1983. The quotations are from p. 529 and some of this account is from succeeding pages.
4. Fisher, M. F. K. *Two Towns in Provence*. New York: Vintage, 1983, p. 63.

CHAPTER 14

1. My translation, faithful but not quite liberal, of an old Spanish text published by Richard C. Hoffman. ("Fishing for Sport in Medieval Europe: New Evidence," in *Speculum*, Volume 60, Issue 4 (1985), p. 898.) Fernando Basurto was Spanish, despite the spelling of his first name in the modern Portuguese style. His *Diálogo* is of high quality. It captures sport fishing— including fly fishing—independently of the English literature, though the latter had more important consequences.
2. Chatwin, Bruce. *The Songlines*. New York: Penguin, 1987, pp. 281– 283.
3. In *Travels with Charley*, p. 25.
4. Chatwin, Bruce. *In Patagonia*. New York: Penguin, 1977, p. 33.
5. Campbell, Joseph. *Historical Atlas of World Mythology*. New York: Harper & Row, 1988. Volume I, Part 2, p. xvii. Campbell's source is *The Gospel According to Thomas*, Coptic text, as published by Harper Brothers in 1959.
6. See epigraph.
7. From *Proust*, a biography by Ronald Hayman. (Edward Burlingame Books/HarperCollins). Quoted by Michiko Kakutani in *The New York Times*, November 13, 1990.

CHAPTER 15

1. From an interview with Peruvian writer Vargas Llosa in *The New York Times*, October 22, 1990.
2. Meyers, Steven J. *On Seeing Nature*. Golden, Colorado: Fulcrum, 1987. Quotations in this paragraph are from pp. 35–37. The author defines the beautiful, the sublime, and the picturesque and points out that our notions of them emerged in the eighteenth century as part of a system of classification in the visual arts.

INDEX